Kashmir Under 370

Praise for the Book

'*Kashmir Under 370* by Shri Mahendra Sabharwal is a first-hand account of some interesting twists and turns that Jammu and Kashmir witnessed during its tumultuous history. Written in a lucid anecdotal style, it touches upon the interplay of internal political forces, Pakistan's multi-faceted offensive, international intrigues, and the vagaries of changing public mood and temper. Most importantly, it brings into sharp focus the compulsive hostility of Pakistan, which subverts the loyalties of the Kashmiri people – by exploiting the religious card and unleashing a virulent form of terrorism. J&K Police has had to bear the brunt of this offensive and Shri Sabharwal has dealt with it at various levels. The abrogation of Article 370 had become a necessity to save Kashmir from the agony caused, by the inimical forces, both within and outside. The book provides a new perspective to some events of the Kashmir story that will help both scholars and practitioners to understand Kashmir better.' – **Ajit Doval, national security advisor**

'An important and reflective account from the corridors of power of a crucial slice of Jammu and Kashmir's recent history – in its most turbulent and violent decades' – **Srinath Raghavan, author of *The Most Dangerous Place: A History of the United States in South Asia***

'Mahendra Sabharwal, the first IPS officer allotted to Jammu and Kashmir in 1964, is a senior police officer with multiple ties to Jammu and Kashmir. In this book he has given us an interesting overview of the politics and the problems of terrorism that have afflicted the state. A refreshing analysis of the Article 370 situation makes this a readable book of contemporary interest.' – **Karan Singh, former Sadr-i-Riyasat and first governor of J&K**

Kashmir Under 370

A Personal History by J&K's Former Director General of Police

Mahendra Sabharwal
with
Manish Sabharwal

JUGGERNAUT BOOKS
C-I-128, First Floor, Sangam Vihar, Near Holi Chowk,
New Delhi 110080, India

First published by Juggernaut Books 2024

10 9 8 7 6 5 4 3 2 1

P-ISBN: 9789353454265
E-ISBN: 9789353459123

The international boundaries on the maps of India are neither purported to be correct nor authentic by Survey of India directives.

The views and opinions expressed in this book are the authors' own. The facts contained herein were reported to be true as on the date of publication by the authors to the publishers of the book, and the publishers are not in any way liable for their accuracy or veracity.

Typeset in Adobe Caslon Pro by R. Ajith Kumar, Noida
Maps created by Mohammad Hassan

Printed at Thomson Press India Ltd

Dedicated to

My late wife Vina – I would have retired as a junior police officer without her optimism, wisdom and balance,

and

the police, civil servants, CRPF and Indian Army in J&K, whose strength and sacrifices have upheld India's constitutional sovereignty despite the dangerous designs of Pakistan and its terrorists

Contents

Preface

Poetim mashravv, bronh kun nazzar thaav
(Forget the past, look to the future)
– Kashmiri proverb

The abrogation of Article 370 is what triggered the writing of this book. In 1964, destiny decided I would be the first Indian Police Service (IPS) probationer directly assigned to Jammu and Kashmir (J&K). But unlike my batchmates from the civil services who mostly retired in their cadre states, my retirement years since 2001 haven't been spent there because Article 370 designated my wife Vina and me 'outsiders' and prohibited us from buying a house in our adopted madre watan (motherland). We both related to Bahadur Shah Zafar's lament 'Kitnā hain bad-nasīb zafar dafn ke liye do gaz zamīn bhī na milī kū-e-yār meñ.' (How wretched is your fate that for your final resting place, you couldn't get two yards of earth in your beloved land.)

This book's thesis is simple: there would be no terrorism in J&K without Pakistan's terror factory. Despite this, I am optimistic about its future because the game has changed in five important ways. One, the abrogation of Article 370 ends the use of soft separatism as a profitable local political strategy. Two, cross-border military strikes have created conventional military consequences for Pakistan's terror factory, and continue to do so. Three, India's rising economic strengths constantly improve our geopolitical position.

Four, Pakistan's growing weaknesses undermine its garrison state. And five, radical Islamic terrorism sponsored by Pakistan is now accepted as a global problem. But I get ahead of myself.

Kashmir became the vessel for Pakistan's anger at itself because its founding idea – the two-nation theory that Hindus and Muslims can't live together – died at birth, with a majority of Muslims staying back in India during Partition. This anger was fuelled by Maharaja Hari Singh's dithering. Had he signed the merger agreement with India a hundred days before he did, Pakistan wouldn't exist. Since 1947, the state hasn't just created the pain, tears and blood in J&K; it has harnessed radical Islam, Cold War geopolitics, fraught federalism and separatist politics in which it is the protagonist.

During my time as J&K police chief, all five Indian forces came together during two sieges at the Hazratbal Shrine. My first day on the job in 1993 was interrupted by a wireless message about terrorists entering Hazratbal. This siege ended in thirty-three days, with thirty-two militants surrendering with arms. The second siege in 1996 ended in five days, with twenty-two militants killed by the Special Operations Group (SOG) of the J&K Police. Both sieges had common roots: planning in Pakistan, orders from Pakistan and terrorists trained in Pakistan. While security forces can shorten the lives of terrorists, ending terrorism requires changing the game rather than playing the old one better. This has now happened.

Cynics suggest my new J&K domicile certificate is merely a piece of paper. But so is our constitution, and both are sacred and invaluable to me. Due to Article 370, which granted J&K special status in India, J&K wasn't fully integrated into the national structure. This lack of integration soon became clear, and personal, as my allocation to the state cadre triggered academy batchmates to joke about my transfer to the Indian Police 'Foreign' Service. In fact, on my first day in the state, I had Rajput and Muslim policemen asking me when I was returning to India. My first day as a district police chief involved the infuriating insanity of

Article 370 legitimizing a tehsildar's refusal to register a telephone exchange property that had been bought in the name of a 'non-state subject', the president of India (all central government property is held in that name). The state home minister Ali Mohammed Sagar not only described the Rajatarangini Cooperative Society legally set up to buy houses locally for All India Service (IAS and IPS) officers like me as 'the East India Company', but he forced it to be liquidated and proposed punishment for officers involved.

It seems to me that people read about Kashmir with hope and curiosity. Hope to understand the present, interpret the pain and anchor our dreams for peace. Curiosity about what happened, why it happened and who did what. I hope this bifocal lens of history – if the *past as past* and the *past as present* – comes through in the pages ahead because peace in J&K was undermined by five interconnected forces:

Troubled Pakistan: No prime minister in Pakistan has completed a full term because Pakistan's 'garrison state' uses the false threat of India to establish its supremacy over both state and society. But the military's incompetence – losing every war it has fought and destroying its economy – is now empowered by its partnership with religion. The military peddled propaganda about a conspiracy to destroy the Pakistani quam (nation) by Hanud-Yahud-Nasara (Hindus, Jews and Christians) is military self-interest masquerading as national interest. The narrative of 'Pakistan Islam ka qila hain' (Pakistan is the fortress of Islam) justified the financing of their 'Islamic' nuclear bomb terror factory for Kashmir. Pakistan's military believed that nuclear capability deterred India from conventional warfare and sensed the short-term advantages in Cold War partnerships and exporting radical Islamic terrorism. In 1995, we had received direct intelligence from captured terrorists that Western countries were likely to be the next target of radical Islam sponsored by Pakistan. I wish the FBI officer deputed to

Kashmir to help with negotiations with the kidnappers of two Americans had acted on it instead of dismissing me as trying to 'internationalize a Hindu–Muslim and India–Pakistan conflict'. And so, it was no surprise to me when the US killed Osama bin Laden in Abbottabad in May 2011, fifty-four kilometres from the J&K Police post in Teetwal.

Cold War geopolitics: Kashmir became a pawn in the Cold War chessboard after India asked for intervention on 1 January 1948, with thirteen UN resolutions being passed over the next decade in favour of Pakistan. Nehru regretted his mistake within a month. Unlike India, which refused to compromise its sovereignty and provide military bases, Pakistan embraced the US. The U-2 spy aircraft shot down by Russia in 1960 took off from Rawalpindi, and Henry Kissinger used a Pakistan Air Force plane for the secret meeting for rapprochement with China arranged by Yahya Khan in 1971. Americans believe radical Islamic terrorism began in 2001. However, the J&K Police recovered a Kalashnikov for the first time in 1988 after Pakistan had generated resources for Kashmir by over-invoicing Americans for their proxy war in Afghanistan; after the US had abandoned Afghan Mujahideen, once arming them with weapons and jihad; and General Zia-ul-Haq had Islamized his military.

Radical Islam: India is home to more Muslims than Pakistan; many non-Muslims live in J&K. In addition, the practically Sufi Ahle-et-Quad Islam sect of Kashmir, the sect most Kashmiris belonged to, has nothing in common with the Wahhabis. Kashmiri Islam practices of the veneration of ziarats (shrines) and relics are considered budh parasti (idol worship) by the Wahhabis. Sheikh Abdullah, whose grandfather was Hindu, suggested that the Kashmiri Muslims' religion was a mixture of rishi worship, Buddhism, Shaivism and Sufism with a veneer of orthodox Islam.

Yet, Pakistan's claims on Kashmir have religious roots, arising from the eternal conflict between dar-ul-Islam (the house of Islam) and dar-ul-Harb (the house of the infidels). Kashmiri syncretism has its origins in literary works like *Rajatarangini* and historical figures like Shah Hamdan, Nooruddin Noorani, Lal Ded and Habba Khatun. I was sad that Kashmiriyat, a term hard to define but which reflected a very real mix of culture, religion and tolerance, didn't prevent the ethnic cleansing of the Valley's Hindus, but Kashmiriyat is authentic, and radical Islam's tools of terror, guns and religious conservatism are alien.

Fraught federalism: Many Delhi pillars of power – prime ministers, governors, the home ministry, defence ministry, foreign ministry, finance ministry, etc. – keep a watchful, engaged eye on J&K because of Pakistan's attack on Kashmir in 1947, our mistaken United Nations (UN) reference in 1948, the implementation of Article 370 in 1950, three wars with Pakistan and three Delhi Accords (1952, 1975 and 1987). Most other state governments only deal with Delhi obliquely, remotely and infrequently, but J&K has found it more challenging to find the madhyam marg (middle path) between centrifugal and centripetal power. Every Indian prime minister has been a constant political and administrative presence in J&K. Unfortunately, most chose incrementalism or firefighting when lasting peace required two decisions only Delhi could make: abrogating Article 370 and cross-border military strikes.

Separatist politics: B. R. Ambedkar refused to give inputs for Article 370 because he believed it would create sovereignty within sovereign India. Syama Prasad Mookerjee wrote to Sheikh Abdullah, saying, 'There cannot be a republic within a republic. India has been torn into two by the two-nation theory. You are now developing a three-nation theory . . . this cannot be good for your state or India.' History suggests both leaders were right. Article

370 made soft separatism a profitable local political strategy, and Kashmiris use the phrase 'nazer tchott assin' (short-sightedness) to describe their politicians who reaped a harvest of fear, wealth and dynastic politics. The Gupkar People's Alliance delusion of representing Kashmiri people echoes the maharani of Jaipur Gayatri Devi's quip three decades after we adopted our constitution: 'We [the princely states] are the real India.' India has created the world's largest democracy on the infertile soil of the world's most hierarchical society because our competitive politics breed ideas, realism and compromise. Politicians in the rest of India were not less corrupt, self-centred or myopic. But first-generation regional politicians like Lalu Prasad Yadav in Bihar, M. Karunanidhi in Tamil Nadu, Sharad Pawar in Maharashtra and Jyoti Basu in West Bengal changed the status quo of power, caste and class. In contrast, J&K suffered 'elite capture' and became a closed society, economy and polity.

Pakistan had a two-instalment strategy for Kashmir: independence followed by annexation. This started with acts of assassination in the 1980s: Inspector Saiddullah in Maisuma (who was the police officer known for arresting Pakistan-returned militants), Tika Lal Taploo in Habbakadal (who as the head of the Rashtriya Swayamsevak Sangh [RSS] in the Valley was vocally against Pakistan), Neelkanth Ganjoo in Hari Singh High Street (who as sessions judge had delivered the death sentence to the Jammu Kashmir Liberation Front [JKLF] leader Maqbool Bhat) and Mohammed Din in Tangmarg (who received the Padma Shri for alerting the Indian army to Pakistan's invasion of Rajouri in 1965). In the 1990s, Pakistan began diverting their support from the pro-independence JKLF to the pro-Pakistan groups like Hizbul Mujahideen.

The ideologies of Pakistan-supported terrorists like the Jaish-e-Mohammad's Masood Azhar and Lashkar-e-Taiba's Hafiz Sayeed later found a mirror in Osama bin Laden's beliefs. Yet, until 9/11, the US refused to believe the radical Islam targeting India would turn its attention to them. Terrorists everywhere are similar – they ignore the laws of war by removing the distinction between combatants and non-combatants, peddling falsehoods about their religion, legitimizing mass murder. Those who kidnap, assassinate, bomb and maim children, women and men in the name of Islam do not represent Islam or all Muslims and find it hard to thrive in real dcmocracies.

Every eighty-five-year-old knows it is impossible to tell whether luck, skill or choices matter more in determining professional outcomes. My own career path was very exciting: as Jammu police chief, I administered Pakistani territory after 1971 and met Asian sprint champion (and now surrendered soldier) Abdul Khaliq. When I was chief of police in the Anantnag district, a mob convinced that India was behind Zulfikar Bhutto's hanging in Pakistan once came to burn down my house. As Kashmir police chief, I broke my baton on separatists trying to dig up the pitch in a cricket match between India and West Indies. As the state intelligence chief, I once split a single work day between meetings with an elected chief minister and the governor selected to dismiss him. A year before becoming police chief, our success in dispersing a mob carrying four terrorist dead bodies meant the only arrest was one of the 'dead' bodies that tried to run away. Five months before becoming police chief, I was held hostage in the Control Room by police officers angry with the army. My years as the J&K police chief also involved getting the force back in the fight against terrorism by forming special operations groups, an unscheduled helicopter trip that rescued a kidnapped American and a bomb technician telling me not to worry about a grenade that bounced off me but didn't explode because it was Chinese-made. My subsequent stints in Delhi as special director of the Intelligence Bureau, Central Reserve Police Forcc (CRPF) chief and secretary (Security) gave me a deeper insight into Pakistan's terror factory.

I pray that the Kashmiris now see Pakistan's activities in their phrase 'lookan hoondh khoon lookini muth' (smearing the blood of the people on their faces). After Operation Searchlight – the genocide conducted by the Pakistani army in Bangladesh – the terrorist Maqbool Bhat thoughtfully wrote to his niece, 'Rulers who declare war against their people cannot offer anything to anyone else but injustice.' Pakistan inspired its terrorist proxies with tales of Russia's defeat in Afghanistan, the US's defeat in Vietnam and the fall of the Berlin Wall. But those comparisons are flawed – those superpowers ventured far from home while India fights terrorism on its territory with our institutions intact. I am optimistic about peace and prosperity in my adopted motherland because the world has changed for murderous Pakistani actors, calculations and proxies. I paraphrase medieval warrior Saladin to remind them: you have the watches, we have the time.

During my decades of service in J&K, thousands of Kashmiris bade me farewell saying, 'Ghaste kormukh Khodayes havele.' (Go, I have handed you over to God.) I offer this precious blessing to the next generation of politicians, civil servants and police officers in J&K. Better days lie ahead, and always remember, khidmat chheh azmat (service is honour).

Mahendra Sabharwal
Kanpur, June 2024

Introduction

Jaki rahi bhavna jaisi, prabhu moorat dekhi tin taisi.
(You see who you are and what you believe in.)
– *Ramacharitmanas*, Tulsidas

The impossibility of immaculate perception
– *Thus Spake Zarathustra*, Friedrich Nietzsche

Age has given me a deeper appreciation of the concept of anekantavada, the multiple versions of truth. Where you stand on an issue depends on where you sit. People may be central to historical narratives but understanding them requires accounting for the totality of their influences because any recounting is inevitably distorted by family, experiences, ambitions and memory. Thus, this chapter attempts to give you a sense of who I am.

It is every police officer's dream to become police chief in their state, and my dream came true in October 1993. However, the seeds of public service were planted in my mind in my birthplace Kanpur – an important centre during the independence movement – which infected me with the idealism of a newly born democratic nation. I remember looking at and detesting the British police officers on horseback enforcing curfew, unaware that God's sense of humour would ensure I would repeatedly use this tool in Kashmir. My National Cadet Corps (NCC) 'C' certificate and attending half-a-dozen NCC camps stoked my attraction to uniform. My father,

Hridaya Narain Sabharwal, was a professor of political science at the universities of Agra and Kanpur and had written five books on statecraft. Finally, my law degree from Allahabad University and preparation for the civil services exams at Muir Hostel (now A.N. Jha Hostel) expanded my political and historical horizons. I lived in a joint family headed by my dadi (paternal grandmother) and was homeschooled until the fifth standard – the streets and grounds of my neighbourhood were my sports curriculum. A prized possession was the Hercules bicycle my father gifted me for being the only person to achieve a first division in my matriculation exams.

My early love of sports – representing my college in football, hockey and cricket, and captaining the Allahabad University hockey team – set the stage for my first encounter with J&K in 1959. I travelled to play football for Agra University at S.P. College, Srinagar. The journey from Kanpur to Pathankot via Delhi, followed by a two-day bus journey with a night halt en route (the Banihal Tunnel was under construction at the time), was exhausting. However, the challenges of crossing the Pir Panjal mountain range were more than amply compensated for by the spectacularly scenic last hundred kilometres' drive to Srinagar. We stayed at the Tourist Reception Centre, and little did I know that I would later spend years living in houses a few kilometres away. Football was, and is, a popular game in Kashmir, and our matches attracted large crowds, but we lost in the quarter-finals. When people in Kanpur asked about my visit, I described the beauty while wistfully reflecting that I would never go back to this distant place. Clearly, humans plan, and God laughs!

Sports helped my career; my appointment as the district police chief in Jammu was hastened by playing for their hockey and football teams and by my tenure as the co-chairperson of the university's youth welfare and sports board. In later years, politician Prem Nath Dogra nominated me to succeed him as the head of the Jammu Olympic Association, and the Abdullahs co-opted me for the state cricket, football and hockey associations. After Sheikh Abdullah passed away, it was my honour to be part of the organizing committee for a fortnight-long football tournament in his memory in the autumn of 1983. Sports, a universal language, created valuable local connections, deepened my understanding of the community and helped me be accepted quickly.

At the time, I didn't realize our lengthy and loud debates in the university hostel about my friend K.K. Mishra's PhD thesis titled 'Kashmir and India's Foreign Policy' were excellent prep for my career. Mishra soon joined the university's political science department and maintained until his death that any solution would involve legitimizing the 1949 ceasefire line. These debates prepared me for my UPSC exams and interviews. The most torturous time for aspiring civil servants is waiting for the results; I found solace in a temporary appointment as a lecturer for English literature at my college, where I brushed up on Browning, Shaw and Shelley. My joy at passing the UPSC successfully in May 1964 was blunted with the news of the passing of Prime Minister Jawaharlal Nehru, who was an icon for our generation. In 1962, I had cycled many hours with hostel mates to an election rally in his Phulpur constituency. However, he didn't show up, and we realized then that he won elections with almost no campaigning. I must confess the four hours of cycling were also motivated by the rumour that many Kashmiri girls were part of his campaign team!

Many who join the civil services are inspired by a desire to undertake public service and the ideal of yogah karmasu kausalam (yoga is perfection in action) enshrined in the Bhagavad Gita. However, we are not really ready when we start our jobs. The joint foundation course for IPS, IAS and IFS officers at the National Academy of Administration, Mussoorie (later renamed after Lal Bahadur Shastri) marks the beginning of their careers. I shared a room in Happy Valley Hut with M.K. Kaw, a Kashmiri Pandit in the IAS, and C.R. Bala Chandra from Karnataka in the IFS, showcasing India's rich cultural diversity. Our neighbours included Naresh Dayal from the IFS and Kevi Chausa from Nagaland in the IPS. This period fostered enduring cross-service friendships, expanded our knowledge and built essential social capital. Weekly mess nights introduced us to formal dining, where, despite an introduction to liquor, I chose to remain a teetotaller. After a rewarding six months, we received ten days of home leave before progressing to specialized training at the Central Police Training College in Mount Abu. The memories of these formative times were rekindled during our golden jubilee reunion in 2014, where my wife Vina finally met my batchmates and saw the campus. An academy plaque now reads 'Sheelam param bhushanam' from *Bhartrhari Nitisatakam*, which means 'Character is the supreme embellishment'. I couldn't agree more: all my batchmates who had illustrious careers distinguished themselves not only with their intelligence but also their character.

The next phase of training at Mount Abu was different from Mussoorie, with increased discipline, physical demands and rigour. Our instructors, T. B. Spedigum, M. K. Menon and Rajinder Singh, were hardly popular for their harsh commands, such as 'Don't walk like a pregnant duck!' Looking back, however, their strictness was instrumental in preparing us for the challenges of a police career. Despite my high rank in the batch, I was initially dismayed to find myself assigned to J&K, a result of my oversight in submitting my preferences. My initial reaction was to consider retaking the exam, and I even voiced my discontent with the director. However, fate had its way, and the realities of the 1965 Indo-Pak War – night patrolling, air raid drills and blackout protocols – quickly overshadowed my concerns about J&K's special constitutional status and its distance from home. Missing a week of training for my sister's wedding adversely affected my standing with the instructors, but I doubled my efforts, compensated for the lost time, and graduated near the top of my class. Unlike my batchmates, who enjoyed four weeks of leave after our passing-out parade, the impact of the war required me to report immediately for duty. This, however, wasn't my last encounter with shortened leave. My leave for my wedding was approved so late that I arrived in Kanpur just a day before the ceremony, only to be called back early for the state's first parliamentary elections.

Arriving in Pathankot by train, I found my way to the Jammu police headquarters at Kacchi Chawni, taking a cycle rickshaw, bus and auto rickshaw. As an IPS probationer – a new species since I was the first officer allocated to the state from the civil services academy – I didn't have a house, office or clear posting. My presence puzzled senior officers, who often inquired when I planned to 'return to India'. A storeroom with no bathroom and containing condemned office files was cleared for me to sleep in at the police headquarters. But things soon stabilized, and I dropped my plans to retake the civil services exam.

In 1967, my parents arranged for me to marry Vina (Khanna), whose family lived not far from us in Kanpur. I was surprised she came from a business family and a different world from ours. I guess her educationist grandfather, who had hidden Chandra Shekhar Azad from the British in his house, and parents, who funded charitable schools, gave my parents comfort. Vina finished her final exams for her masters in English Literature, before making her way to Jammu a few months later with a dramatic entry. With no official transport, I drove to Pathankot station on the Rajdoot motorcycle I had brought from Kanpur to pick her and my mother up. My mother took a public transport bus, while Vina and I headed off on the Rajdoot. We had barely entered J&K state lines when a herd of running cows crashed into our motorcycle. Vina was thrown off the bike, landed on her head and began to bleed profusely. I landed on the opposite side, and the bike caught fire. Providence kindly ensured that an ambulance equipped with a doctor was returning to Pathankot from Jammu, and it took us to a nearby medical centre where Vina was treated. After receiving stitches, we were driven to our official residence, beginning our life together with Vina's head bandaged but spirits undeterred.

My probation was an early indication of how my career would differ from my that of batchmates. My compulsory military attachment and three-month deputation to the regional police training college at Phillaur were waived. My learning-by-doing training involved two months at the police headquarters, two months at the district police lines, one month at the armed police battalion, two months at the prosecution branch in Purani Mandi and three months each at the Sadar and Jammu city police stations. My tenure as Jammu district police chief began in 1968, and it was where I learnt the nitty-gritty details of my profession: people management, civilian relations and military liaising. The job was intimidating – I'd had five predecessors in three years, including two who had been suspended from service!

Of these, I felt sad about the professional fate of T.R. Kalra. He was technically my senior in the state IPS cadre, but he had joined directly under the refugee quota and was not a direct recruit. His Urdu was immaculate, his sense of humour delightful, but age-old vices undermined his career. Great first bosses are crucial to learning, and I received invaluable training and knowledge from M.M. Wazir, Surendra Nath, Bakshi Vishwamitra, P.R. Khurana and Sheikh Ghulam Qadir Ganderbali. During this time, Vina's ventures into police welfare work demonstrated her organizational and people-management skills. She continued this work throughout my career and never expressed any regret in walking away from the admission she had obtained to Carnegie Mellon University in the US (in my defence, though, this was much before our wedding).

In 1972, my career took an exciting turn when I was selected as first secretary to the Indian embassy in Washington. Horizontal mobility across the central services like IFS, IAS and IPS is rare because these services guard their posts, cadres and turf diligently. But this mobility shouldn't be so scarce given how much both sides

– the embassy and I – benefited. The few months of training in Delhi in their fabulous South Block building that also housed the prime minister's office was an excellent induction to the rules and expectations of foreign service while exposing me to an informal work culture that I hadn't seen in J&K. The ambassador T.N. Kaul was a chance Kashmir connection, and I learnt a lot from A.P. Venkateswaran, J.N. Dixit, E. Gonsalves, G.V. Ramakrishna and Satish Chandra. I witnessed Venkateswaran's professional integrity when he refused to do Ambassador Kaul's bidding with the retort, 'I am a public servant and not anybody's private servant.' We entertained widely, and my children still remember tennis players Vijay Amritraj and Arthur Ashe, and musician Ravi Shankar visiting our home. I remember being on a cruise organized by the US State Department the evening President Nixon resigned. Our host US foreign service officers were ecstatic, and some even drove us by the White House after the cruise to celebrate their vibrant democracy together. Our family made new friends, we met diplomats from many countries and our children broadened their horizons. These friendships endured over time, and a few years ago, Colonel Cook of the US Army and his lovely wife Nell hosted a delightful lunch for us with all our North Glebe Road neighbours in Arlington. This posting upgraded all our future houses since we brought everything back from our Washington home. I still watch TV on the reclining sofa we bought for $9 in 1976!

I returned to J&K in 1977, entering a rocky patch. Sheikh Abdullah had stopped appointing new IPS officers in the state cadre. The state government gave me a tent to work out of, but I made the most of the downtime by meeting people to get reacquainted with the state and volunteering as assistant secretary of the state unit and preparing a note for the National Police Commission (a role nobody else wanted). Things soon changed as they always do. Over the next few decades, with a few interludes in Delhi, I served as district police chief in Anantnag and Srinagar, Kashmir division police chief, state intelligence chief, police headquarters chief, state vigilance chief and, finally, state police chief. My last few years in service were at the Intelligence Bureau, CRPF and Cabinet Secretariat in Delhi, and I lived in a nice house on Humayun Road.

A lifetime of serving my country in a police uniform didn't leave me rich or famous but it did make me happy and proud. My early angst at being allocated to the J&K cadre was misplaced because knives are sharpened on rough surfaces, and I doubt my career would have been as exciting or fulfilling had I been granted my wish for my home-state cadre of Uttar Pradesh. At the end of my career (and now as well), I have one piece of advice for young people. Be wary of wishing for familiarity. Instead, seek out risk and trust the Almighty has a plan.

After retirement, since Article 370 prohibited us from buying our own house in J&K, Vina and I moved to Kanpur in 2001. Vina energized her school education trust, reaching more than 8,000 students when she left us, and I ran a small farm that sold wholesome grains, fruits and vegetables. My son Manish lives in Bengaluru with his wife, Kavita, an educator. My daughter, Miti, lives in Delhi with her husband, Gaurav, a golf champion. My three grandchildren – Dhruv, Raghav and Noor – are endless sources of joy, affection and learning. I am confident the next generation of my family, Kashmiris and Indians, will find solutions to the problems our generation didn't.

I had three fears while writing this book. The first came from self-awareness: I am not a good writer. I don't think many civil servants are, despite our confidence in our ability to do everything. I overcame this fear by getting Manish to help. My second fear was that any book hung on memories would dance close to the poisons of ego and narcissism. I searched the text multiple times to purge the word 'I', and I still don't believe it conveys that everything was teamwork. Finally, as a practitioner not an academic, I intuitively grasp the medical wisdom that a post-mortem has a certainty that a prescription never can. Hopefully, being physically away from J&K for two decades gives me the honesty and detachment that accompanies the long eye of time.

I overcame these fears because of Vina. Sadly, during the last stages of writing, Vina passed away and broke her promise to leave this world after me. Our children often introduced her as the reason I reached the peak of my profession, and I agree. We were married for fifty-eight years despite different interests, instincts and inclinations – or perhaps it was because of these differences. I miss her and wait to join her.

Anybody who loses a spouse knows that the motivation to do anything is torture to find. But this book was Vina's wish, so I got over my feelings and finished it. So, let us then dive into the mysteries of J&K.

Timeline

Five Forces Through the Years

(See overleaf)

Year	Radical Islam	Fraught Federalism	Separatist Politics	Troubled Pakistan	Geopolitics
1930s	• Two-nation theory • Muslim Brotherhood in Egypt	• Council of Princes • Glancy Commission recommends legislative assembly	• Muslim Conference • National Conference split • Kashmir Martyr's Day		
1940s	• Partition • JUI formed	• Sheikh arrested • Maharaja Hari Singh's accession to India	• Naya Kashmir	• 1947 tribal invasion • M.A. Jinnah dies	• World War II
1950s	• Muslim Brotherhood expands to Sudan • Iraqi monarchy overthrown; Sunni domination intensified	• Article 370; separate constitution for J&K approved • Syama Prasad Mookerjee's death • 14 UN references	• Sheikh arrested • Plebiscite Front formed	• First Army Coup; President I.A. Mina exiled	• Dalai Lama seeks refuge in India • China attacks Aksai Chin in Ladakh • Cold War Alliances

Year	Radical Islam	Fraught Federalism	Separatist Politics	Troubled Pakistan	Geopolitics
1960s	• Muslim World League founded in South Africa	• India's atomic reactor project set-up; ISRO established • Goa brought under India; Maharashtra and Punjab split into smaller states	• Hazratbal Moi-e-Muqaddas stolen and recovered	• Radio Kumarkund • Police officer Amarchand killed • Bank robbery • Operation Gibraltar–Mujahids invasion	• Sino-Indian conflict • US fighter jets arrive • Arab–Israel War
1970s	• Iran revolution • Al Fatah formed • JKLF formed • Shia reform movement launched in Saudi Arabia	• Delhi Accord • Simla Agreement • Nuclear power	• Sheikh Abdullah back as CM • First Governor's Rule imposed	• 1971 War: Birth of Bangladesh • Military coup; Zia • Bhutto hanging	• US partnership for Afghanistan • US loses Vietnam War

Year	Radical Islam	Fraught Federalism	Separatist Politics	Troubled Pakistan	Geopolitics
1980s	• Islamist military coup in Sudan • Al-Qaeda founded by Osama Bin Laden • Muslim Brotherhood contests elections in Egypt • Lashkar-e-Taiba founded by Hafiz Sayeed	• Income tax raid conducted on Sheikh Abdullah in Srinagar • Punjab terrorism	• Sheikh Abdullah dies; Farooq takes charge as CM • Rajlv–Farooq Accord • 1987 state election; G.M. Shah coup • National Opposition Accord	• Operation Topac: Two instalments plan • Zia islamizes the army • Amanullah Khan exiled to Pakistan • Mhatre murder • Two blasts in Srinagar • First Klashnikov's recovered	• USSR breakup • Germany reunification • Afghan victory in the Soviet War
1990s	• Targeted attacks on religious shrines in J&K • Shift from JKLF to Hizbul Mujahideen	• Frequent leadership changes in Delhi; seven PMs in ten years	• Kashmiri Pandit exodus	• Shift from JKLF to pro-Pak terrorists • Kargil War	• Taliban establishes control over Afghanistan

1

Hazratbal: A Tale of Two Sieges

The siege of 1993: Thirty-two terrorists surrendered after thirty-three days

The two most powerful warriors are Time and Patience.

– *War and Peace*, Leo Tolstoy

The siege of 1996: Twenty-two terrorists killed after five days

Khud ko bulund kar itna, ki khuda bande se khud puche, bata teri raza kya hain.
(Rise to such heights that before your destiny is written, God asks you what your desire is.)

– Allama Iqbal

As I raced to Hazratbal in my bulletproof Ambassador on 15 October 1993, an inner voice told me this was likely the biggest challenge of my career. It was my first day as J&K police chief and I had hastily left my predecessor's farewell function after receiving a wireless message from the police control room. Ghulam Mohammed Chisti of the Muslim Auqaf Trust was trying to reach me; heavily armed terrorists had entered the Hazratbal Shrine, broken the outer locks of the room containing the shrine's holy relic and taken civilians hostage. Thirty-three days later, this siege ended, and I had the honour of waking Governor General K.V. Krishna Rao at 4 a.m. to inform him of the militants' surrender. My last year as police chief in 1996 also involved a siege with terrorists, and this ended in five days with twenty-two militants being killed by the Special Operations Group (SOG) of the J&K Police.

Both situations sound similar but were handled differently by the same team because, as the ancient Greek historian Heraclitus said, you can never step in the same river twice because both you and the river have changed. In 1996, the terrorists gave us another opportunity, we were ready to take bigger risks, and the J&K Police was more powerful.

Our strategy in both sieges was constrained and informed by context and memory. Years after Operation Blue Star, where the army entered the Golden Temple in Amritsar to flush out terrorists, the deep scars Punjab had sustained had yet to heal. The Hazratbal Shrine has a unique place in Kashmiri imagination, society and politics. During the first siege, the recent memory of the demolition of Babri Masjid meant India's Muslim community was still in shock, and the second was only a few months after Charar-e-Sharief had been burnt down.

Located by the Dal Lake and surrounded by the Zabarwan Mountains, the Hazratbal Mosque houses the Moi-e-Muqaddas, a hair from Prophet Mohammad's beard. The relic's journey, as recounted in Sheikh Abdullah's biography, began in 1635 when a Kashmiri trader bought it from one of the keepers of the holy Kaaba, but it was confiscated by Emperor Aurangzeb and placed in the dargah of Khwaja Moinuddin Chisti in Ajmer. The emperor soon had a dream in which the prophet asked him why he wanted to stop his journey to Kashmir, and the relic reached Kashmir in 1699 along with Khwaja Nur-ud-Din Ashawari. The Dargah-e-Naqshbandi in Khanyar housed the relic before it moved near the Dal Lake to a wooden prayer house. The khwaja's daughter, Inayat Begum, then became the custodian of the relic. She had married into the Banday family, and her descendants have been the custodians of the Moi-e-Muqaddas ever since. The existing mosque structure was completed in 1979 with marble from Makrana in Rajasthan, which is also the source of marble used to build the Taj Mahal.

Terrorists targeted Hazratbal twice for different reasons. The obvious reason was the constraint on interventions, tactics and weaponry imposed on security forces to ensure nothing would endanger the holy relic or shrine structure. The previous crisis of December 1963, when some miscreants had stolen the holy relic, had created chaos in the Valley when agitating workers for the Plebiscite Front (supporters of Sheikh Abdullah) had set aside their differences and allied with his arch-rival Mirwaiz Moulvi Farooq to whip up anti-India sentiments through the Tehreek-e-Bazyabi Moi-Muqaddas (the agitation for the recovery of the Moi-e-Muqaddas). The police recovered the relic after nine days, but the agitation had questions about the authenticity of the recovered relic. Sceptics were silenced by the rasook (influence) of the well-known spiritual leaders Syed Mirak Shah and Maulana Syed Masoodi, who had it verified by Muslim scholars and imams. The bedridden eighty-seven-year-old Masoodi was shot dead by Pakistani militants in 1990.

Second, Hazratbal symbolized political power, housing the headquarters of the affluent J&K Muslim Auqaf Trust, with Sheikh Abdullah as its lifetime chairman and trustee. After Sheikh's death, Farooq took on the lifetime position. Even Amanullah Khan of the Jammu and Kashmir Liberation Front (JKLF) said, 'Whoever controls Hazratbal controls Kashmir.' Sheikh's supporters were initially assigned to the Pathar Masjid near the National Conference headquarters at Mujahid Manzil for prayers but they later moved to Hazratbal. Every Friday, everybody offering namaz heard the Sheikh give a pre-khutba (sermon). His fondness for the shrine was deep enough for him to want a final resting place a few hundred metres away. During both sieges, I remember being grateful that Sheikh

Sahib was not around to witness armed terrorists threatening to kill innocents in his favourite house of God.

Finally, Kashmiris value their shrines as a significant cultural and religious inheritance, but fundamental Islamists like the Wahhabis, Salafis and Deobandis, along with their masters in Pakistan and Saudi Arabia, regarded Hazratbal as but parast (idol worship). Security forces had already foiled multiple attacks on the Mazar-e-Shoda shrine in Khanyar and Makhdoom Sahib in the Hari Parbat area, and terrorists would soon target shrines like Baba Reshi and Aishmaquam. They would sadly, however, succeed at Charar-e-Sharief on my watch.

Constant rumours about militant plans for Hazratbal meant that a strong contingent of paramilitary and army troops was permanently stationed there. The shrine had also become vulnerable because a JKLF breakaway group had abandoned its 'independence' demands, adopted a fully Islamic agenda and established operational headquarters nearby. A small contingent of the J&K Police had been guarding the outer perimeter of the shrine in uniform while providing a plain clothes inner security cover in the sanctum sanctorum. In 1993, this outer cordon shamefully collapsed without a fight but the brave plainclothes officers in the inner cordon successfully bought us time by scaring the terrorists about Khuda ka keher (the wrath of God) falling upon them if they handled the holy relic. In 1996, our outer cordon fought back, and we lost two brave policemen after they killed seven terrorists.

The Siege of 1993

In 1993, the siege of Hazratbal began around noon on a cold October day when heavily armed terrorists entered the dargah to evade pursuit by paramilitary and army troops. These terrorists included JKLF intelligence chief Mohammed Idrees, divisional commander Basharat Raza and publicity chief Shabir Siddiqui.

Despite the stereotype that most Indian soldiers lose their heads in the heat of battle, these jawans made us proud by exercising commendable restraint and not entering the shrine. They created a circular cordon, blocking the outer periphery, and escalated the issue while waiting for further instructions. Our objectives were clear – ending the standoff with minimum bloodshed, without heavy arms entering the mosque and avoiding any solution that could undermine the morale of the security forces. These were vital for personal, professional and national reasons.

Hostage situations are always tricky, but concerns about the relic complicated our siege. The chairman of the Auqaf Trust, Ghulam Qadar Draboo, was unavailable, so Secretary Abdul Chishti briefed us about the multiple locks on multiple doors including the fact that the keys to the innermost lock did not fit. We could see terrorists had taken offensive and defensive positions at various points in the shrine, including on the minarets, and were wiring the dome with explosives. We decided that any direct exchange of fire between the security forces and militants at this stage would be unwise and evacuated over 5,000 people from nearby mohallas to a nearby regional engineering college complex. The army soon took over the cordon with the competent Brigadier S.P.S. Kanwar in charge on the ground, supported by Chinar Corps Commander General Padmanabhan, who was also known as Paddy. I was not surprised to learn that Paddy had later become army chief. His unique leadership abilities were an unbeatable combination of decisiveness and openness.

On the first night, a fire broke out in a building in the complex called Noor Khan, which was used for offering namaz by women. It wasn't clear whether this fire was arson or an accident, but in retrospect, it was helpful in later negotiations and reminded people how the terrorists could damage their beloved dargah. Predictably, the All Parties Hurriyat Conference's (APHC) S.A.S. Geelani suggested the police had set Noor Khan on fire to defame the terrorists. This was a patently hilarious idea as cowardly terrorists hiding behind God and civilians surely don't have a reputation to protect!

On the second day, my colleague A.K. Suri contacted the militants inside the shrine. Their demands included getting the authenticity of the Moi-e-Muqqadas verified, opening the shrine to the public, removing the curfew and exiting with their weapons. We rejected these demands, so the militants asked to speak to Divisional Commissioner Wajahat Habibullah or Chief Secretary Sheikh Ghulam Rasool. Later in the day, Suri, now accompanied by Habibullah, was given the same demands. At this point, we were only willing to offer an unconditional surrender with a fair trial.

The militants were now barricaded inside without access to food and water. We let them walk around and collect rice bags already in the shrine complex. But our plan to cut off the food, water and electricity supply into the shrine was cut short by Chief Justice Aziz Mushabber Ahmadi of the Supreme Court when, on a petition by Hurriyat leaders, he ordered calorie-measured food packets to be distributed to everybody inside the shrine. Frustrated by the clearly flawed order, General Padmanabhan and I made public statements against it as it was needlessly prolonging a tense standoff with armed terrorists, some of whom were from Pakistan and Afghanistan. These food packets, however, played a key role during later negotiations as they gave us entry into the shrine and face-to-face interaction with the militants. Of course, this gave the Bharatiya Janata Party (BJP) in the Opposition the chance to coin a cheeky slogan: 'Biryani for the terrorists, bullets for the innocent.'

The siege provided a lot of publicity to the APHC, a coalition of thirty political, religious and underground organizations who 'would not replace the gun'. Militant groups were initially hesitant about supporting the APHC. However, a week before the Hazratbal surrender, seven groups – the JKLF, Hizb-ul-Mujahideen, Al Jehad, Al Umar Mujahideen, Ikhwan-ul-Muslameen, Al Burq and

Operation Balakote – issued a joint statement asking the public to cooperate with the Hurriyat. But early in the siege, it had become clear that the Hurriyat and terrorists were working together and were planning protests in the Valley to improve their negotiating position.

On 18 October, the Hurriyat issued a warning stating that unless armed security forces withdrew from around the shrine, they would go to the UN Military Observer Group headquarters to submit a memorandum before marching to Hazratbal. Their spokesperson, Abdul Ghani Lone, said the 'siege of the shrine is a direct interference in the religious affairs of Muslims'. S.A.S Gilani said, 'The militants were within their rights to use places of worship because we believe in the unification of religion and politics,' and 'Mosques had been used as sanctuaries since the inception of Islam.' The next call by the Hurriyat to defy curfew was issued on 22 October, and this received some response across the state since it was Friday, but we were able to control the crowds. Disappointed, the Hurriyat threatened that 'the government must remove all security forces and bunkers around the Hazratbal shrine within six days or face serious consequences'. And again, we ignored the deadline.

The public's trust was fragile due to a tragic incident that had recently taken place in Sopore, where forty-three civilians lost their lives after the Border Security Force (BSF) responded to a mob with gunfire. I'm unsure if it was easier or more difficult to handle misinformation in the era before social media and WhatsApp, but the rumours of security forces harshly suppressing crowds worried me. I urged my police colleagues across the Valley to communicate more, increase surveillance, control mobs early and improve community outreach. However, our efforts were undermined by an incident in Bijbehara, where a clash between a mob and the BSF resulted in thirty-one deaths. The BSF claimed they were targeting terrorists blocking the national highway, but I believed they used disproportionate force and authorized the local police to file a first information report (FIR) against the BSF. This led to a reprimand from Union Home Secretary N.N. Vohra, but I stood firm. Fortunately, the governor supported my decision.

A siege is not a media-friendly event; it takes its own time and typically, no news is good news, which makes journalists impatient. I remember feeling saddened by the *India Today* article published halfway through the siege, titled 'Operation Blunder', suggesting we had goofed up by not storming the mosque. From our perspective, the scars to the Sikh psyche expressed in Khushwant Singh's remark post-Operation Bluestar, 'To kill a rat, you don't have to bring down the house', had still to heal. The international perspective was also crucial, especially with Robin Raphael, the American assistant secretary of state and known Pakistan sympathizer, casting doubts on Kashmir's accession to India and peddling falsehoods.

The local press, calling the situation a 'crisis', often exaggerated or reported unsubstantiated incidents, worsening the already tense and emotional atmosphere. As the official spokesperson, my daily briefings at the Tourist Reception Centre, following visits to Hazratbal, aimed to temper local emotions, communicate our intentions to the terrorists and reiterate our stance to their overseers in Pakistan. My colleague, Mehmood-ur Rehman, joined us during the later stages to report on the progress of the negotiations. Mehmood, who later became the vice chancellor of Aligarh Muslim University, humorously remarked that university negotiations were marginally simpler than those at Hazratbal.

To appease the growing public demand for information, we began organizing media visits to Hazratbal during non-negotiation times, a rare practice before the era of 24-hour news coverage. Our deliberately slow pace of negotiations was strategic. We not only wanted to sow confusion among the terrorists whose orders from Pakistan were becoming increasingly contradictory but also convince the local population of our commitment to a peaceful resolution. Despite straining the media's patience, with some even suggesting the situation was being deliberately prolonged, the Kashmiri ethos of 'taabus scho laabh' (patience pays) remained a guiding principle.

Soon, negotiations passed through several phases with several faces. The demands of the militant group remained similar – they wanted safe passage with their weapons, the curfew lifted in the Valley and the authenticity of the Moi-e-Muqqadas confirmed. We insisted on not giving them safe passage and demanded they surrender in full view of the media. We knew that video images of terrorists coming out of the shrine with their hands over their heads would be a powerful weapon in our ongoing psychological operations arsenal. By the second week, the militants accepted a visit by four doctors appointed as Red Cross commissioners, who found the living conditions subpar and some hostages suffering from minor illnesses.

Four militants led by the JKLF operational chief Idrees would come out clad in pherans with their faces covered to negotiate with various political and religious leaders (including co-opted members of the Hurriyat Conference). We allowed this to present the liberal human face of the administration and to engage the militants. These negotiations continued patiently for weeks as our priority was peaceful surrender. My colleagues, General M.A. Zaki and Wajahat Habibullah, handled the negotiations for the state despite direct taunts from the militants about being 'paid' Muslims and accusations of them acting as agents of the Hindu government.

Midway into the siege, General Zaki and Wajahat had an accident when their bullet-proof car collided head-on with a fast-moving military truck in convoy. Mehmood-ur Rehman and I rushed to the accident site and took them to the Soura Medical Institute. Both had severe injuries and were airlifted to the All India Institute of Medical Sciences (AIIMS) in New Delhi. Providence mandated their survival, and the good news of their health progress in the next few weeks warmed us that cold winter. However, on cue, rumours began spreading in the Valley about Delhi having engineered the accident to kill two Muslim officers, Delhi arresting Habibullah , and much else.

Following this tragedy, Rehman and I now assumed responsibility for the day-to-day situation at Hazratbal. Sheikh Ghulam Rasool, the chief secretary, had already failed to contribute to the situation because of local pressures. He had even avoided appealing to the militants for peaceful surrender despite being advised to do so by the governor. Later on, he suggested he could arrange for the terrorists to surrender on the terms of safe passage with weapons as proposed by some Hurriyat members known to him. But we did not yield to his suggestions, and he even travelled to New Delhi to convince the highest political circles that we should accept the Hurriyat solution. However, he failed in these attempts.

By 7 November, the negotiations had hit an impasse. The demands on either side remained the same with minor tweaks. The militants wanted to surrender with their arms and ammunition and without the humiliation of a televised surrender, but this was non-negotiable for us. A successful resolution required a complicated balancing act between many security forces, central agencies and political sensibilities. My earlier postings as police chief in Srinagar and Kashmir helped me prepare for this siege; we knew the topography, understood the inner workings of the shrine, and had even attended trustee meetings of the Muslim Auqaf Trust at its office in the outer structures of the shrine. The governor was at the centre of the coordination effort with detailed strategy and negotiation terms, and the complex trade-offs between precedents, perception and safety were always run past him.

We sensed the end of the standoff was near because of a number of factors: the shifting public opinion, the dwindling processions in support of the militants across the Valley, the continuous defiling of the mosque after the bathrooms were clogged, the contradictory instructions the terrorists received from Pakistan, and our own competence in enforcing the siege. The terrorists were getting tired. We also had help from the Pakistani prime minister Benazir Bhutto, who, during the siege, said the Independence Act of 1947 had no provision for independence, implying Kashmir would have to merge with Pakistan. Bhutto allowing the purdah to fall from 'azadi' and revealing their true intentions of annexation was useful. Our intuition was accurate and over the next few days, we negotiated an agreement of surrender.

At 10 p.m. on 16 November, Mr Mehmood-ur Rehman and I travelled to Hazratbal for the surrender. Lt. General Padmanabhan, then commander of XV Corps, also joined us to ensure all security forces worked together. The army had quietly installed hidden night-vision cameras at the place of surrender to film the process. At around 1.30 a.m., the militants began walking out with their arms held up high. The process continued for two hours, and we took them into custody and transported them to the nearby Zakura Camp for interrogation.

Our recoveries included AK-47 and AK-56 rifles, a Dragunov sniper rifle, a heavy machine gun, two light machine guns, a rocket launcher, IEDs, wireless sets, binoculars, grenades and bullets. It was then that we also found the four Second World War-era .303 rifles that had been used by the J&K Police armed guards posted at the outer cordon; their contrast with the militants' weaponry was no excuse for the men's poor performance, but I made a mental note about a police weapons upgrade. There were a total of thirty-six armed militants in the shrine, of whom thirteen belonged to the JKLF, six – including two Pakistani nationals – to Al Umar, three to Operation Balakot, six to Ikhwan-ul Muslmoon, five to Al Jihad and three were members of other groups.

We had complete control of the militants and their weaponry by 4 a.m. on that cold winter morning. The governor's security adviser General Saklani, Mehmood-ur Rehman and I decided they would stay at the spot to further liaise with the army while I would go home to inform Governor General Rao at Raj Bhawan through my RAX (secret) telephone. The governor had told me he would await through the night the official confirmation of surrender. I reached home at 5 a.m. after the night-long surrender process to the anxiously waiting Vina, who was aware that something significant was happening that night at Hazratbal. Governor General Rao picked up the telephone on the first ring, and I greeted him with the details of the successful surrender. He immediately shared the news on his hotline with Prime Minister P.V. Narasimha Rao. Knowing that Governor General Rao did not have a personal equation with Home Minister S.B. Chavan, I called Union Home Secretary N.N. Vohra to tell the home minister.

Announcing this significant development to the nation was a privilege and joy. I roused Ajit Singh, the Srinagar correspondent for All India Radio (AIR) and Doordarshan with a lively 'Jaago Mohan pyaare, jago'. My fondness for AIR dates back to when I first learnt of being selected for the IPS through their broadcast from Lucknow. Despite our personal acquaintance, Ajit took no risks, requesting a pause until he could activate his recorder. The news went public in the 8 a.m. broadcast and was echoed throughout the day by Doordarshan and AIR, highlighting the surrender as a triumph for the J&K Police, although many other security forces played crucial roles in this victory. Today, in an era where Doordarshan's viewership has waned, my loyalty remains – perhaps the feeling is a nod to Ajit Singh or because I find Doordarshan's reporting to be less sensational, emotional and hysterical compared to others.

Following the surrender, our immediate focus shifted to ensuring the safety of the area, tasking our bomb squad units with meticulously searching and defusing any explosives the terrorists had left behind. To facilitate the transition to normalcy, we appointed Mr Bandey, a police officer whose family had been associated with religious administration of the Hazratbal Shrine Board for generations, as the person in charge. The militants had desecrated the shrine's main building, connected outhouses and toilets to the main building and defiled the sanctity of the place. Besides cleaning the place up, the Auqaf shrine management removed the prominent notice the militants had installed barring the entry of non-Muslims.

Following the resolution of the siege, Home Minister S.B. Chavan and Finance Minister Manmohan Singh travelled by special aircraft from Delhi to pay their respects at the shrine and start the healing process. Meanwhile, Prime Minister Rao convened a meeting in Delhi to assess the aftermath of the situation. A slight shadow was cast over this meeting by intelligence reports that indicated that the Inter-Services Intelligence (ISI) was furious about the militants' surrender and were ordering new chaos, but otherwise, the mood was celebratory. Parliament also passed a unanimous resolution reaffirming J&K as an integral part of India, declaring India's resolve to repel any attempts to meddle in its internal matters and demanding Pakistan vacate areas of J&K under its illegal occupation. Pakistan's National Assembly has passed many resolutions on Kashmir, but this was only the second resolution passed by the Indian Parliament concerning J&K, with the first occurring during the 1962 China war.

The Hurriyat tried to salvage their defeat by calling people to defy the security cordon on 7 December. They called for people to march to Hazratbal in white shrouds, symbolizing readiness for martyrdom, for deedar (viewing) of the holy relic. We enforced a strict curfew, rendering their efforts unsuccessful. We collaborated with the J&K Muslim Auqaf Trust to dismantle the bunkers within the shrine complex and reintroduce police checkpoints to prevent the re-entry of the terrorists, but the Hurriyat maintained that 'nobody can stop a Muslim from entering any place of worship'. Despite our keenness to resume prayers at the mosque immediately, the Hurriyat's stubbornness delayed this process for eight months.

Most Muslims in Kashmir were relieved by how this situation was resolved. They credited the Prophet with having blessed and ensured such a peaceful solution to the detriment of the militant's causes and efforts, and I agree with them. We were blessed; many things could have gone wrong in an armed standoff at the religious shrine, but they didn't. The siege taught us many lessons we thought we would never need again. But we were wrong.

The Siege of 1996

The surrender of the militants in 1993 punctured the early bluster of the Hurriyat spokesperson Abdul Ghani Lone, who said, 'If armed forces storm the shrine, we will win. If they withdraw, we win.' He admitted later that 'the end of the episode was not according to the wishes of the Hurriyat conference'. We knew that televising the militants' surrender would create dissent, and predictably, the bickering soon began. The Jamait-ul-Mujahideen told local newspapers that the Hurriyat's 'coffin sellers' had let the people of Kashmir down, and the Hizbul Mujahideen said, 'We gave them guns to use rather than surrender.' I observed many personal jeers and sneers in local circles about the militants' cowardice in surrender, their inability to live up to their lofty talk, and for coming out at night with their hands above their heads. As my friend Sati Sahni wrote, 'Hazratbal was a god-sent opportunity for the Hurriyat leadership, but the lack of imagination, factional rivalry, inept reflexes and incorrect appreciation of the situation meant they failed to capitalise on it.' Pakistan clearly agreed, as their proxies soon killed Hurriyat leader Abdul Ghani Lone.

The 1993 surrender marked a pivotal moment, with the ISI accelerating resources towards pro-Pakistan and pro-Islamic organizations with directions to assassinate JKLF leaders like Idrees Khan and Farooq Ahmad Wani. It also created discord between Amanullah Khan in Pakistan and Yasin Malik in Kashmir, which simmered for nearly two years. Events reached a tipping point on 21 September 1995 when Amanullah Khan ousted Yasin Malik as the president of the JKLF because he had 'damaged the Azadi Movement at the behest of the Indian government and had not complied with directives from the high command . . . he is only interested in the chief ministership.' The UK wing of the JKLF responded by ousting Amanullah because 'he has been indulging in an opportunist, undemocratic, and dictatorial style of functioning. He has been making financial gains in the name of Kashmir and compromising the position of the JKLF at the behest of his masters.' Yasin Malik rejoined the Hurriyat and Abdul Ghani Lone welcomed him, saying, 'The emergence of Malik as the JKLF supremo under the aegis of Hurriyat has restored the independence movement to a sound footing.'

Amanullah Khan responded by appointing Shabir Siddiqui as the JKLF president in Kashmir, 'General' Basharat Raza Khan as chief military commander, and Salman Yavar 'Nikka Bhai' as deputy chief commander. The presence of Shabir's family's schools in Budgam led to friction with the Jamaat-e-Islami over their demands for him to close his educational ventures. Choosing defiance, Shabir aligned himself with the JKLF. In February 1996, Shabir called a press conference suggesting that 95 per cent of ordinary Kashmiris wanted independence and said, 'I call upon people to strengthen their militant activities . . . only an armed struggle can deliver freedom to the people of Kashmir. We won't ever lay down our weapons. We are soldiers of Allah and will fight to the last drop of our blood. Our quam will bleed security forces till they surrender to our demand of Azadi. We will not rest, nor will we allow them to rest.' He soon held another press conference to rant against Malik and Hurriyat for their 'failure to represent the aspirations of the people of Jammu and Kashmir'. He also promised that 'We are soldiers of Allah and will bleed Indian security forces till they surrender to our demands.'

We would have let this slide, but our intelligence team had intercepted communications between Shabir, Basharat and Amanullah Khan discussing Hazratbal, and this felt like a bad omen. I met with my colleagues A.K. Suri and P.S. Gill to bolster security around both the shrine and the new JKLF office established across the shrine in a building that was previously the shrine's library. The leadership duo had complementary skills; Shabir was articulate and cautious while Basharat was aggressive and violent. Basharat's tactics – kidnapping faculty members from the Regional Engineering College, extorting local merchants and harassing women – created ill will that proved valuable during our siege.

After the morning namaz on 24 March 1996, Basharat and Shabir led a JKLF group to the main gate of Hazratbal. Shabir had told his men he did not expect much resistance from the J&K Police but told them to shoot to kill if they resisted. When they tried to enter the mosque armed, a J&K Police officer barred their entry. In response, Basharat fatally shot the officer at close range, and charged into the mosque with his henchmen. In the ensuing two-hour confrontation, our courageous policemen eliminated nine militants, including Basharat, his deputy Nikka Bhai, Srinagar district commander Dilawar, Baramulla commander Tipu, Budgam commander Waseem, and four others. We lost two valiant police officers that day.

The siege of 1996 triggered a different response from J&K Police from 1993. We immediately threw a cordon around the shrine and met with Governor General Rao to decide strategy. Unlike in the previous siege, we took the primary responsibility for resolving the standoff. The priorities were the same as they were in 1993 – no damage to the shrine, free the hostages unhurt and ensure the sanctum sanctorum was safe. The recent memory of Mast Gul burning the Charar-e-Sharief shrine worried us, but we found comfort in Shabir's dislike for Pakistan and Wahhabism.

Inside the mosque, Shabir was recovering from the shock of

police resistance that had left nine of his best men dead, but soon he began carrying out Amanullah Khan's instructions to use saws, hammers and fire to break open the safe. They tried all night but failed. We sent Moulvi Bashir-ud-din to Hazratbal to speak to Shabir, and their demands echoed what JKLF had asked for three years earlier: the removal of security forces from Kashmir, tripartite talks between the JKLF, India and Pakistan, and safe passage for the group with their arms.

The next day, A.K. Suri began negotiations with the militants at the shrine's entrance. The police offered safe passage without arms and let Shabir know that arranging tripartite talks required the central government's permission, which would take time. Shabir soon held a press conference saying there would be no prayers at the shrine until the government met his demands. As in any hostage situation, we tried to prolong the negotiations while developing alternative solutions. The J&K Police now had a trained SOG, vital intelligence and local support.

So, we modified our negotiations to get the terrorists out of the shrine by offering them a security-free corridor to move back to their office. We sweetened this offer with vague inducements of prioritizing the JKLF over other organizations in future political and peace talks. Shabir's team members were hesitant to vacate the dargah, but Shabir prevailed. On the fourth day of the siege (27 March), the JKLF terrorists, a few women and children made their way from the main building (where the sanctum sanctorum was) and moved right across the street to an abandoned library, which was also a part of the dargah complex. A team, which included Suri and members of the shrine trust, entered the dargah and confirmed the vault was damaged but unopened.

This change of location felt like an opportunity. We asked Farooq Khan (the head of the SOG) to present some options for an assault. This attack reminded me of one of my favourite lines in George Bernard Shaw's *Arms and the Man*, which reads, 'Soldiering is the art of attacking mercilessly whenever you are strong. Take the enemy at a disadvantage and never fight him on equal terms.' Farooq deserves credit for the immaculate planning and execution of the operation; he was the right man at the right time with the right strategy and team. The SOG was already familiar with the layout of the shrine complex and the area around it; they soon surveyed the bylanes and sent some team members in civilian clothes inside the shrine to conduct a recce.

On 31 March, my colleagues from the intelligence team intercepted a late-night wireless message from Pakistani agents asking Shabir and his team to 'go back to Allah's protection'. We interpreted this as an order to return to the dargah building as we had convinced Shabir to stay out of the shrine, but not his bosses. We kept negotiating but gave the go-ahead for the SOG operation. Farooq handpicked a small team equipped with AK-47s and personal sidearms, requisitioning light machine guns, sniper rifles, bulletproof jackets, grenades and tear gas. We also decided Farooq's team of thirty officers would take mortars into an operation for the first time, and the inner and outer cordons would be provided by the CRPF and BSF. The SOG planned to move in at night and be out by dawn, and all roads leading to the shrine from the Dhobi Mohalla and the Kashmir University campus would be closed. SOG spotters would be positioned on all sides of the building with powerful night-vision binoculars to report on movement inside the building every few minutes.

Soon, Farooq came to me, asking for a final go-ahead and his final briefing also included what could go wrong because of the narrow lanes and high civilian density. But his confidence, team and track record gave me the courage to give the approval after consulting with the governor. At 2.30 a.m. on 31 March, the SOG used handheld loudspeakers to give the terrorists one last chance to surrender.

The terrorists had hunkered down in the building, but a little while later, the building doors opened, and a group of women and children walked out. I have never asked Farooq about it, but I later heard that some SOG officers were hesitant to storm the dargah premises carrying weapons. Farooq assured them they were not entering the mosque and reminded them of their duties. The SOG continued its announcements for two hours, and it felt like the militants were going to surrender. But soon, the militants began firing from the second floor of the building and threw some hand grenades at our bunkers. A few shots rang out from the corridors of the main dargah, but the SOG quickly shot two militants stationed there. An hour later, the SOG had killed twenty-two militants and wiped out a large part of JKLF leadership.

Conclusion

In the dark years before the Hazratbal siege in 1993, slogans like 'Hum kya chahte hain? Azadi! Azadi ka matlab la ilaha illala!' (What do we want? Freedom! What does freedom mean? Allah!); 'Yahan kya chalega? Nizam-e-Mustafa!' (What will rule here? Islamic law!); and 'Asi gasyi kasheer, batav warai, batnyav saan!' (We want Kashmir without Kashmiri Hindu men but with Kashmiri Hindu women!) were common. These slogans faded with the two sieges puncturing the notions of the invincibility of the terrorist, the invulnerability of Pakistan and the inevitability of azadi.

Valley Muslims mostly practise a moderate Islam and were horrified by the guns and bombs in the house of God. They were surprised by terrorists threatening to blow up the structure, making shrill threats to kill innocent hostages, and using women and children as human shields. The notion of jihad was alien to Kashmiris, and the two sieges made the contrast between radical Islam and Ahle-et-quad (Muslims who believe in saints and shrines) obvious. Though conducting elections required many other inputs, the result of the two sieges which increased confidence amongst locals created conditions for elections to be held after almost a decade.

One positive outcome of these sieges was the confidence boost that the J&K Police rank and file received. The daily press briefings, favourable coverage about our firm but restrained response and the opportunity to learn from cutting-edge Indian army formations really helped. In addition, the partnership such as the one between the state and central governments, J&K Police, army and other central forces working together in the first siege hadn't been seen for some time. It sent a strong message across the border and brought international attention to Pakistan's support of terrorism.

In my life, few things have hurt me as much as the subsequent release of some of the terrorists who surrendered at Hazratbal in 1993, because they soon crossed the border into Pakistan and returned to cause chaos with their murderous ways. But the J&K Police's SOG ensured that karma caught up with most of these terrorists in the second siege.

2

J&K Is Not the Valley

Mosaics are made of broken pieces.

– Persian proverb

Yeh waqt bhi dekha hain tareekh ke safahon ne,
Lamhon ne khata ki thi sadiyon ne saza payee.
(The annals of history have witnessed many tragedies.
When mistakes made in mere moments bring punishment and suffering for centuries.)

– Muzzaffar Razmi

The Kashmir Valley, a compact area, eighty-four miles in length and twenty-five miles in width, is strategically positioned along historic Silk Road routes. To the north, it connects Central Asia with China through Tibet; to the east, a route stretches from Leh to Sinkiang in China, crossing the Karakoram Pass; and to the west, a path runs from Gilgit to Sinkiang via Huaza and the Khunjerab Pass. Despite being encircled by mountains – the Great Himalayan Range to the east, the North Kashmir Range to the north, and the Pir Panjal Range to the south – the Valley has twenty accessible passes. Three of these are particularly significant: the one linking Srinagar with Punjab via the Shopian and Pir Panjal Pass; another connecting the Kashmir Valley with Jammu over the Banihal Pass; and a third, now not in use, connecting Balakot in Pakistan's North West Frontier

Province (now Khyber Pakhtunkhwa), Rawalpindi in Pakistani Punjab, and Muzaffarabad in Pakistan Occupied Kashmir with Baramulla, Uri and Srinagar.

J&K is not limited to the Kashmir Valley, nor is it exclusively Muslim, Kashmiri-speaking, or represented by the Urdu script. It never has been. The debate about whether India is a constitutional state born in 1947 or a civilizational state for thousands of years as Bharat Varsha is also nonsensical because India is both. So is J&K. Constitutional states are always shaped by their civilizational inheritance. Constitutional J&K is a child of the instrument of accession signed in 1947, the adoption of India's constitution in 1950, the adoption of J&K's constitution in 1956, the acceptance of All India Civil Servants in 1959, the extension of India's Supreme Court jurisdiction in 1959 and the abolition of Article 370 in 2019. The three strands of civilizational inheritance that make up the state – Kashmir, Jammu and Ladakh – have histories that greatly influence its politics, economics and governance.

People say geography is destiny, but I disagree; people make their own destiny. Besides a small number of violent Islamists, the people of J&K are warm, cultured, smiling, kind, resilient and moderate. Fortunate people like me have two families: the one we are born into and the one that adopts us. Over decades, our family in J&K blossomed to include Razia and Khurshid Fazili, Sushum and Joginder Kuthiala, Kiran and Vijay Dhar, Aman and Poochoo Wazir, Kishen and Usha Amla, H.L. and Shashi Maini, Farooq and Khalida Ahmad, Farooq and Nasreen Khan, Shamas and Rukhsana Khan, Surendra and Indira Wazir, Mumtaz and Azhar Nomani, Madhu and M.M. Khajooria, Dr A.S. and Mala Anand, Hamidullah Khan, Omar Jan, Niaz Mir, Sushma Choudhary, Hafeez Akhtar, Peer Ghulam Hassan Shah, Allahbaksh, Captain Dewan Singh and family, and so many others. Unlike some locals who reminded us of our outsider status – and it is important to remember that a crowd of this kind confronts every migrant in India, including my son in Maharashtra and Karnataka – the people in J&K accepted us warmly.

My IAS colleague Mehmood Rehman came from Uttar Pradesh, but his wife Nuzhat was the daughter of a retired local IAS officer Jenab S.A.S Qadri (my children called him Abbaji, and so did, I think all of the Rajbagh area, where he lived). Qadri Sahib and Ammaji (his wife) had a home in Rajbagh, full of warmth and wonderful food. My kids spent every Eid with them and even stayed there in times of need. I vividly remember that Vina left them there for weeks while I was being treated in Jammu for a cardiac complication in 1980. Nuzhat was among Vina's closest friends and sadly passed away early. Life is short, but its length is measured by the relationships of the journey. The enforcing of Article 370 deprived me of spending my retirement years with my family in J&K, but some joy has been restored during the reunions organized by my kids in Srinagar in the last few years.

In 1932, British missionary and educator Tyndale Biscoe wrote, 'To write about the character of Kashmiris is not easy . . . it is large, and people differ considerably in features, manner, customs, language, character, and religion.' The Kashmir Valley is about a fourth the size of Delhi's National Capital Region, is mainly Muslim and 25 per cent of the population depends on pampered government employment. Ladakh is predominantly Buddhist and has the population of Chandni Chowk in a land area bigger than France. Jammu combines the plains with the mountains, and the city is only thirty-three kilometres from the Pakistan border. Reconciling these regions in terms of governance has always been challenging. In 1872, Maharaja Ranbir Singh felt moving the darbar (government offices) every six months between Jammu and Srinagar would connect the three parts of the state (though cynics say this was the normal instinct of Indian royalty to imitate the Raj, which moved every summer to Shimla). In 1987, Chief Minister Farooq Abdullah unsuccessfully tried to counter his growing political weakness in the Valley by ending the moving of the darbar.

According to local folk etymology, Kashmir means 'land desiccated from water' (from 'Ka' meaning 'water' and 'shimeera' meaning 'to desiccate'), and is believed to have been originally a lake drained by the sage Kashyap. By 250 BCE, it became part of Ashoka's empire, who established Srinagar and introduced Buddhism to the area. It was later governed by Hindu dynasties until 1003 CE, when Islamic conversion began to take place. In 1819, Ranjit Singh incorporated it into the Sikh empire, with Gulab Singh and his general, Zorawar Singh, annexing Ladakh and Baltistan in the 1830s. Zorawar's death in 1841 during an expedition into Tibet marked a significant 'What if' in history because a victory in Tibet might have integrated it into India.

After Ranjit Singh's death, the British secured cession of Kashmir from the Punjab kingdom to Dogra General Gulab Singh in 1846 through the Treaty of Amritsar for Rs 75 lakh. This treaty also acknowledged British supremacy, with Gulab Singh agreeing to pay an annual tribute that included a horse, twelve shawl goats, and three pairs of Kashmiri shawls. The British were rewarding Gulab Singh for facilitating their passage to Afghanistan, ensuring the Dogra army's neutrality during the Anglo–Sikh War and promising loyalty amidst the Central Asian 'Great Game' with Russia. In J&K and Punjab, there's still debate over whether Gulab Singh's actions constituted treason. His biographer K.M. Pannikar, in *The Founding of The Kashmir State: A Biography of Maharajah Gulab Singh 1792–1858*, suggests, 'Where his interests required, he did not hesitate to resort to tricks and stratagems which would in ordinary life be considered dishonourable.' Gulab Singh's successors – Ranbir Singh (1857–85), Pratap Singh (1885–1925) and Hari Singh (1925–50) – transformed Kashmir into what Nobel laureate Douglass North described as a 'limited access' society, where power was divided among the elite.

Unlike most princely states, Maharaja Hari Singh did not sign the instrument of accession by 15 August 1947. Karan Singh, his son and a former union minister and J&K governor, writes, 'Indecisive by nature, he [Hari Singh] played for time. A typical feudal reaction to a difficult situation is to avoid facing it. My father was particularly prone to this.' This indecisiveness has cost India, Kashmir and Pakistan heavily. People say Hari Singh had three wishes before he died: the downfall of both Nehru and Sheikh Abdullah, and for Karan Singh to have children. He lived to see only two of these come true.

Kashmir

Dominated by the Sunni-majority Ahle-ait-quad sect, religious life in Kashmir revolves around pirzadas – ranging from Sufi mystics to religious mendicants, petty ulema and local clergy – anchored in both rural and urban areas. Islam spread in the Valley in the fourteenth century and owes significantly to Persian Sufi mystic Mir Sayyid Ali Hamdani (Shah Hamdan), remembered and honoured by the construction of the Khanqah-e-Moula Mosque in Srinagar. However, the locally born Sufi saint, Sheikh Nooruddin Noorani (Alamdar-e-Kashmir or Nund Rishi), commands a deeper reverence for his spiritual contributions, encapsulated in his *Noor Nama*. His mausoleum in Charar-e-Sharief was tragically destroyed in 1995 by the terrorist Mast Gul, a shameful memory for me as this occurred when I was J&K police chief. Lalleshwari, a woman Shaivite Hindu mystic, profoundly influenced Noorani. Known as Lal Ded, her sayings (Vakyas) live on, celebrated through the naming of Srinagar's leading women's hospital in her honour.

The ancient text Nilamata Purana marks Kashmir as a hub of Shaivism. This tradition was notably carried forward in the fifteenth century by Badshah Zain-ul-Abidin – who is commemorated in Badshah Chowk – through his sponsorship of the Persian translation of *Rajatarangini* (*The River of Kings*), a detailed chronicle by the poet Kalhana. Marc Aurel Stein's English translation of *Rajatarangini* in

1900 highlights Kashmir's virtues as 'learning, lofty houses, saffron and ice water'. This legacy of syncretism is evident at Aishmuqam Dargah, which still receives a portion of the offerings from the Hindu Amarnath Shrine. However, the 1990s saw some of this tolerance eroded by the targeted violence against Kashmiri Pandits.

Sunni Muslims are the majority, but intense rivalry and scarce intermarriage existed in the community, especially between the sher (lion) supporters of Sheikh Abdullah and bakra (goat) supporters of his rival Mirwaiz. I have received dozens of stitches on my face and hands over the course of my career in incidents of stone throwing between these two groups. Their rivalry peaked in the 1977 elections, and there was a reconciliation in the double Farooq Accord of 1982. Shias make up only 10–15 per cent of the Muslim population, but they balance out sociopolitical dynamics. Historically subjected to oppression and violence since Mughal times, Shia politics have oscillated between calls for independence, alignment with militants and partnering with Delhi to counter the Sunni majority's dynamics. Militancy led to a ban on the traditional Muharram procession but in 2023, a procession from Gurubazar to Dalgate in Srinagar was finally allowed to take place after thirty-four years. I hope it continues forever.

Kashmiri society has many quirks. The saying 'Asav na, ta lasav kith paeth?' (If we don't laugh, how can we live?) is reflected in their nicknames for their leaders: Kakar Khan for Jagmohan, Gul Curfew for G.M. Shah, Mufti Whiskey for Mufti Mohammad Sayeed and Farooq Disco for Farooq Abdullah. This extends to militants like Bitta Karate, Latrum and Javed Nalka. In this close-knit society, rumours spread fast from Qazikund to Kupwara. This rapid dissemination of news was often referred to as the Lal Chowk Gazette and it became the hub for disinformation. They are a highly politically conscious society and voracious consumers of news. (The BBC was a favourite source in the 1990s with its clear anti-India bias.) Their food is delicious but often unhealthy

– I think the generous usage of red meat and refined flour must ensure that the Valley is among India's largest per-capita markets for allopathic medicine.

Kashmir is a land where the divine and nature's bounty seamlessly merge. It is blessed with soil and a climate so fertile that even a planted chicken leg might sprout. The region effortlessly yields cherries, apricots, apples, walnuts and almonds. Kashmiri saffron is more valuable than gold by weight. Tourism flourishes in Pahalgam, known as the 'First Village', Gulmarg, the 'Flower Meadow', and Sonamarg, the 'Golden Meadow'. The pristine Dal, Nagin, Wular and Manasbal lakes and various rivers are fed by springs like Kokernag and Verinag. Kashmir is also a haven of sacred Hindu sites such as the Amarnath Temple, Kheer Bhawani Temple, Shankaracharya Temple and the ancient ruins of Martand.

The elaborate wazwan feast embodies Kashmir's deep social, political and cultural connections. These primarily meat dishes, requiring two to three days to be prepared by master chefs known as 'wouste wazas' or simply 'wazas', use sheep sourced from Rajasthan. In Srinagar, wazwan has distinct identities and flavours depending on political influences, with Mirwaiz Maulvi Farooq's followers preferring chefs known as 'mam waza', unlike their counterparts from Sheikh Abdullah's followers who favour 'ahad waza'. Traditionally, four people share a wazwan on a trambi (copper plate) laid on a dastarkhan (white sheet). The meal begins with rice followed by various meat dishes served from large copper pots. This practice reflects the egalitarian nature of Kashmiri society, with ministers and their drivers often dining from the same plate. Initially a vegetarian, I found myself only eating haak saag and chaman (paneer) in twenty-one-course wazwan meals and missing out on the information, bonding and gossip that came from eating in a trambi together. Duty and curiosity won, and I gave up and ate the full wazwan for the rest of my time in the state. I have now switched back to being vegetarian for an inescapable reason: old age.

Kashmir's economy, grounded in agriculture, horticulture, handicraft and tourism, faces challenges in realizing the full potential of these industries due to slow design innovation, weak market access and lack of investment. The horticulture sector, heavily dependent on apple production, which is 80 per cent of the output, suffers from limited profitability due to the fruit's short shelf life and the tendency to sell unprocessed or in bulk. The security situation has also hindered organized industry and led to significant financial reliance on the central government. In 2023, local taxes contributed only 17 per cent of the total state government expenditure. This state's weak financial position explains the central government's crucial, often dominant, role in its politics.

The bitter winter cold in Kashmir, locally called chillai kalan for forty days starting 21 December, followed by chillai khurd (twenty days) and chillai bacha (ten days), has spurred local innovations like the pheran, kangdi, and bukhari. The pheran, a woollen garment, allows for the hands to be kept inside the garment while carrying a kangdi, a clay pot containing live coals, cradled in a cane frame. Sadly, pherans could also easily conceal Kalashnikovs and pistols. The bukhari, a coal- or wood-fired steel room heater with a smoke pipe, provided warmth but had drawbacks, including drying out the air, the risk of poisoning from gases like carbon monoxide and potential fire hazards from improper lighting. My colleague Ghulam Nabi in Anantnag burnt his eyelashes so frequently that we had to relieve him from bukhari duty.

The annual winter cold presented significant challenges for me as the police chief of the Kashmir division and Anantnag district, including law-and-order issues stemming from acute power shortages – largely due to hydroelectric power deficits from freezing conditions – and essential supply shortages caused by frequent closures of the national highway from Jammu to Srinagar. Although logistics have improved since the days when Srinagar was a two-day bus journey from the last train stop at Pathankot, I await the implementation of resilient supply chains. But these can only arise from all-weather rail connectivity between Delhi and Srinagar. I hope to be among the first to buy the train ticket for this journey, which signifies integration more than travel.

The closure of cinemas in the Valley for decades due to militant threats and bombings contrasts sharply with Kashmir's iconic status in Indian cinema, especially in my personal favourites *Junglee*, *Kashmir Ki Kali*, *Jab Jab Phool Khile*, *Silsila* and *Bobby*. Sheikh Abdullah adjusted Friday screening times after seeing larger crowds at theatres as compared to mosques, but he never banned or prohibited anything. The militant-enforced prohibition on liquor shops is easing now, but it must be entirely rejected if tourism is to reclaim its role as the primary engine of prosperity.

Jammu

The history of Jammu, as documented in texts like the Mahabharata and Timur's memoirs, traces back to the twelfth century when Rajput rulers founded independent realms like Jammu, Kishtwar and Basohli. The city itself was established in the fourteenth century by Raja Jamboo Lochan, who built a city at the spot on the Tawi River where he observed a goat and a lion peacefully sharing water during a hunting expedition. Over time, 'Jamboo' evolved into 'Jammu'. From 1723 to 1783, Ranjit Deo, a ruler of Rajput lineage, unified twenty-two Dogra chieftains, elevating the kingdom of Jammu to a preeminent position among neighbouring principalities.

Jammu has a special place in my heart since it is where Vina and I began our lives together, and my children Manish and Miti were born at the S.M.G.S. Government Hospital. Its proximity to Pakistan, just thirty-three kilometres away, made formal wars more real for Jammu than Kashmir. Jammu had eight police stations overseeing border areas and only two stations dedicated to the city itself. Additionally, Udhampur, close to Jammu, serves as the Indian Army's Northern Command headquarters. The city reveres the deity of Bahu Fort as its protector and believes Jammu is also blessed by Vaishno Devi. From when I arrived in the state, devotees have increased at this shrine from 40,000 annually to over 10 million.

Pakistan's early influence in Jammu came through their facilitation of the drug, specifically charas (cannabis), trade. My first-hand experience with this issue came during a raid on the charas kingpin, Lakshmi Das, who had a knack for manipulating the judicial system. We sent my colleague, Veeranna Aivalli, undercover as a buyer to meet Das at his house. After the deal was done, we entered in uniform. Das attempted to flee but was captured by our plainclothes officers outside. We seized many kilograms of drugs hidden in his bedroom and kitchen, yet Das was able to exploit the judicial system and get bail within a month of his arrest. Considering his Pakistan connections, we sought advice from then district magistrate, R.K. Takkar, who recommended re-arresting Das under the J&K Public Safety Act. We did, and this time, the charges stuck.

The plight of the refugees from Chhamb in Pakistan after Partition in 1947 and the Indo-Pak War in 1965 was a tragedy. Unlike refugees elsewhere in India, some of whom reached as high as the prime minister's office, over 50,000 mostly Hindu refugees in J&K found themselves in a legal and constitutional limbo due to Article 370. Contrast this with the Jammu & Kashmir Grant of Permit for Resettlement in (or Permanent Return to) the State Act, 1982, introduced by Sheikh and Farooq Abdullah that proposed that those who had migrated to Pakistan after 1947 and before 14 May 1954 the right to resettle in the state. Without dealing with the existing refugees, who were mostly Hindu, this Act was communal, embarrassing and inappropriate.

Disenfranchised populations are invariably restive and in 1965, while temporarily housed in tented colonies, many refugees refused to return even after the formalization of the Tashkent Agreement and joined forces with refugees from 1947 who were still seeking legitimacy. As a trainee officer in 1966, I had to deal with a student protest in support of these refugees. Despite Section 144 banning gatherings, students gathered and pelted stones at the police from college grounds and nearby roads. Outnumbered, a deputed Punjab armed police battalion resorted to firing, resulting in the deaths of four students and the escalation of the unrest, and army intervention was required to restore order for the first time in the state. Subsequently, senior officers, including Mr Wazir, Mr Khajooria and myself, underwent a judicial inquiry but were cleared of any misconduct.

Due to the lasting stain left by the 1984 riots that swept across north India following Indira Gandhi's assassination, Jammu occasionally saw riots between Hindus and Sikhs. In January 1989, a hardliner Sikh group planned a rally on Guru Nanak Jayanti through Jammu city. As intelligence chief, I suggested this procession should not be allowed to take place and spoke of my concerns to then chief minister Farooq Abdullah in a daily intelligence summary. But the district magistrate permitted the procession, influenced by the group's personal meeting with Abdullah. The rally passed through Jammu's busiest and Hindu-dominated areas, raising provocative slogans while displaying photographs of Indira Gandhi's recently executed assassins. This led to massive stone throwing, the destruction of a bus stand and six fatalities. My worries were anchored in Pakistan's ISI actively encouraging collaborations between terrorists in Punjab and the JKLF. I believe that we are blessed that the nexus never developed.

The diverse geography of high mountains in Doda, picturesque valleys like Kishtwar and the plains of Jammu fosters a rich cultural fusion in the region. Dr Karan Singh's suggestion to form a 'Vishal

Himachal' by merging Jammu, Himachal Pradesh and Ladakh had to be retracted amid widespread protests. He explained, '. . . the state was a wholly artificial creation, its five separate regions being joined together by the historical accident . . . Those five different entities had nothing in common with each other. Because of the lack of commonality between these three divisions, the sooner they are separated, the better it would be for the future.' I disagree for three reasons. First, religious and linguistic diversity create social and political moderation in J&K. Second, Pakistan and China illegally occupy 55 per cent of what was India's territory under the maharaja's instrument of accession. Finally, the institutions of the Indian state are now consolidated in J&K.

Dogri, the language of Jammu, while influenced by Punjabi, boasts its own mellifluous charm and has embraced the Devanagari script for its literary expressions. In terms of other cultural achievements, the late Shivkumar Sharma, who was born in Jammu, transformed the santoor – an Iranian stringed instrument – by reducing the number of strings, thereby revolutionizing Indian classical music and introducing a unique genre. K.L. Sehgal, the famous playback singer and actor, also belonged to Jammu. Similarly, the Pahari school of miniature paintings, though now prevalent in regions like Kulu, Kangra and Garhwal, originated from Basohli near Jammu. These paintings are celebrated for their vibrant use of colours like red, yellow and blue, for the distinctive facial expressions of their subjects, for their themes that blend mythology and local folklore.

Jammu is a very fertile region and produces fine basmati rice and rajma. A personal favourite local food is kalari, a traditional ripened cheese made from cow or goat milk, which has a stretchy and dense texture. It is called maish krej (milk chapati) in Kashmiri. Raw full-fat milk is vigorously churned in an iron pot with a wooden plunger before the milk solids are separated using sour milk called mathar. The stretchy curd is then flattened and placed in a doona (pot made of leaves) and left in the iron pot to solidify. It is then sun-dried to remove the moisture. In many ways, the cheese symbolizes a symbiotic relationship with the milk acquired from Gujjars and Bakarwals, the nomadic shepherds from the Valley.

In December 1971, twenty-five years after India's independence, Jammu's physical integration was completed, and it became the Indian Railways' northernmost outpost. Trains between Sialkot (Pakistan) and Jammu city had stopped at Partition; Pathankot was the last train stop when I reached the state, but after the 1965 war, extending the railway line became an urgent task. This costly railway line had about a hundred bridges and culverts, passed close to the Pakistan border, expanded religious tourism to Vaishno Devi and created the foundation for greater connectivity to the Valley. Soon, trains from Jammu to Srinagar would take three and a half hours. I remember taking nine hours for this same journey by car. The first train from Pathankot to Jammu, which should have taken two hours, took six hours, with the train stopping at six places en route within the territory of J&K from Lakhanpur to Kathua, at Sambha, Vijaypur and Satwari stations, as well as at three unmarked locations en route. T.A. Pai, the railway minister, inaugurated the train, saying each train was a great integrator because it was populated by a mini-India. He prayed every train would come and go with prosperity for the state.

Ladakh

Though Ladakh occupies a huge area, it is home to only 3 lakh people. Despite the Zojila Pass being impassable for months each winter, commercial flights to the region only began in the 1980s. Before it was divided into the Leh and Kargil districts in 1979, Ladakh was India's largest district. Kargil, home to a predominantly Shia Muslim population, was religiously distinct from the Buddhist majority in Leh and also different from the Sunni Muslim majority in the Kashmir Valley.

Ladakh was fully opened to tourists only in 1974. This hesitation is ironic because, as Janet Rizvi suggests in her excellent book *Ladakh: Crossroads to High Asia,* for most of its history, Ladakh's hospitality to traders from Kashmir, Punjab, Central Asia and Tibet has stood in sharp contrast to Tibet, which had 'turned in on itself, refusing access to almost all outsiders except those traders and pilgrims whose journeys were sanctioned by ancient and uninterrupted usage'. Janet is married to a colleague from the J&K cadre, Sayeed Rizvi, and Vina and I shared many good times with them.

For centuries, Leh was a crucial halt on a vibrant trade route, serving as a hub to trade in textiles, spices, raw silk, carpets and, notably, pashmina from Tibet to Srinagar. The lucrative trade attracted the attention of Gulab Singh, who dispatched his celebrated general, Zorawar Singh, to conquer the region. By 1853, Ladakh had been incorporated into the Dogra Empire. The centuries-old trade through the Karakoram came to a halt in 1949 when the border between Central Asia and Ladakh was sealed. The following year, the Chinese army advanced into Tibet, setting off a series of events that eventually led the Dalai Lama to seek refuge in India in 1959. The Sino-Indian conflict of 1962 had multiple causes, but India's asylum to His Holiness was a significant factor.

Buddhism reached Tibet from India, and Ladakh played a crucial role in its spread. By the thirteenth century, the epicentre of Buddhist religious authority had shifted eastward, and Ladakh was subordinate to the great monasteries of Central Tibet and administered a religio-cultural empire extending from Mongolia to Bhutan and Ladakh to the Koko-Nor Lake in present-day China. In one of history's great full circles, the Dalai Lama would visit Ladakh every summer after 1959 and stay at a beautiful camp near Choglamsar village on the banks of the Sindh River. This created a range of security challenges, given the constant uncertainty of China's intentions, complicated by His Holiness's spontaneity with programmes and crowds. But we policemen never complained because every conversation with the ever-smiling Dalai Lama is full of joy and blessings. Sadly, his health no longer permits this annual journey.

As Janet points out in her book, Ladakh's geographic remoteness and social atmosphere feel more influenced by its past ties with Tibet and Central Asia but have had multiple forces of influence. The sport of polo is being kept alive in the Leh area by the Shia Muslims, originally from Baltistan, at Chushot, fifteen kilometres up the Indus. Leh became the headquarters of the German-headquartered Moravian Church in 1885, with the missionaries introducing a new religion and the cultivation of potato, spinach, cauliflower, radish and tomato. They also taught the system of preserving root vegetables in semi-underground chambers for use in the winter. Growing food is still a challenge in the region, and tourism is now the largest industry.

Ladakh has been the frontline of many of India's wars and border skirmishes. In 1962, China occupied the Aksai Chin Plateau and advanced to Chushul on the southern margin of Pangong Lake, whose sky-blue water was made famous by the Bollywood movie *Three Idiots*. The auxiliary force of locals who fought in the 1962 war became the fierce Ladakh Scouts and are amongst our army's most decorated regiments. Aksai Chin, however, has not been returned to India because China needs it to link Xinjiang and Tibet. Kargil bore the brunt of the four Indo-Pakistan wars fought at the Line of Control, which was called the Ceasefire Line until the Simla Agreement of 1971. This line had been left so close to Kargil town in 1948 that a Pakistani army machine gun post overlooked its main bazaar. The Indian army took this post in 1965 but handed it back under the Tashkent Agreement. Thankfully, it was retaken in 1971 and the line of actual control has now been pushed back ten kilometres from Kargil town.

Discontent in Ladakh over perceived biases by J&K's Muslim chief ministers was a sentiment that was echoed in Jammu. However, unlike Ladakh, Jammu benefited from serving as the state capital for six months every year during the darbar move, and it was also the supply line for both Kashmir Valley and Ladakh. I recall a young Ladakhi suggesting that Ladakh would only be understood if the darbar move included a few months in Leh during December when temperatures were 20 degrees below zero. There were significant agitations against this stepmotherly treatment in 1967, 1974 and 1982. The discontent escalated in 1989, leading to violence in Leh and a boycott enforced by the Ladakhi Buddhist Association against Muslims, which lasted until 1993. The establishment of the Leh Autonomous Hill Development Council in 1995 helped alleviate some unrest, but calls for separate governance persisted.

Ladakh was left marginalized, in terms of how it was governed, from an early stage. In 1949, Chhewang Ringzin of the Buddhist Association submitted a memo to Prime Minister Nehru, advocating that Ladakh be integrated with Jammu or become an independent state. The abbot of Spituk Monastery Kushok Bakula reinforced these demands to Nehru in person in 1952. The civil administration and police of the state did not give Ladakh the attention it deserved, and we should have made it a separate entity much earlier. Even in my postings at Kashmir Range and as state police chief, I mostly focused my attention to ensuring the six-month winter stocking of essential supplies was seamlessly organized throughout the highway during the summer months because shortages always create law-and-order issues in an otherwise peaceful region.

Conclusion

The state of J&K has had many rulers through its history, including Hindu, Muslim and Dogra ones. While the different regions of J&K have their own unique religion, language, food and landscape, they have also been tied together by history. And while the state's terrain provided its beauty, the mighty Himalayas make infrastructure creation and economic development difficult. Power has been imbalanced; Karan Singh wrote a letter to Indira Gandhi in 1968, acknowledging that Jammu dominated governance in the royal state before 1947 but lamenting that independence had not created a balanced democracy, but simply moved dominance to Kashmir.

India, Jammu, Kashmir Valley and Ladakh are tremendously and permanently intertwined. When one does well, the others do too. I am sure that the post-Article 370 avatar of J&K as a state will chart a different future. The Valley will return to Kashmiriyat – religious moderation and diversity – and come closer to India's secular identity and far from Pakistan's religious intolerance. Jammu will get over its political neglect and finally exploit its economic potential, and the union territory status for Ladakh is leading to greater devolution of funds, functions and functionaries to Leh. The pain of the last few years needs many balms but the post-370 avatar offers opportunities for peace, prosperity and growth that seemed impossible a few years ago.

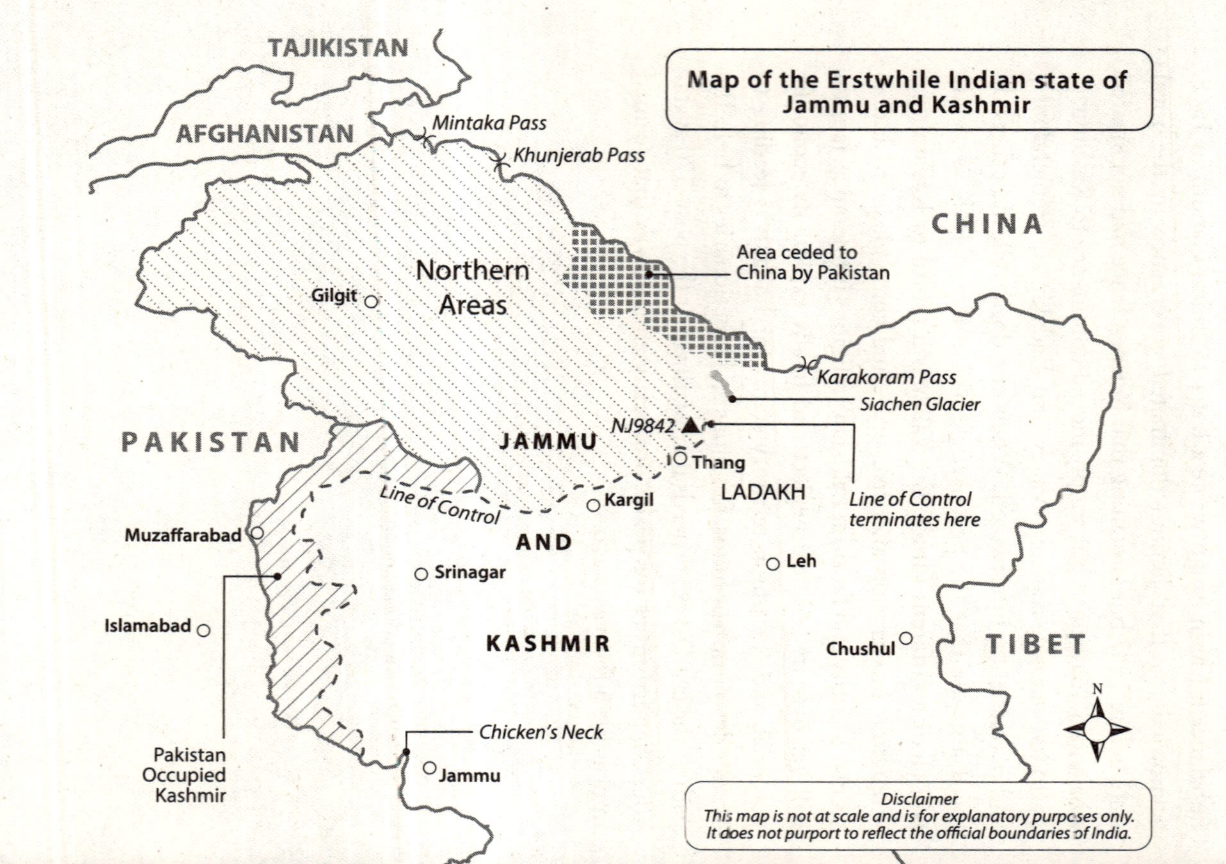
Map of the Erstwhile Indian state of Jammu and Kashmir
TAJIKISTAN
AFGHANISTAN
Mintaka Pass
Khunjerab Pass
CHINA
Area ceded to China by Pakistan
Northern Areas
Gilgit
Karakoram Pass
Siachen Glacier
NJ9842
PAKISTAN
JAMMU
Thang
LADAKH
Line of Control terminates here
Line of Control
Kargil
Muzaffarabad
AND
Srinagar
Leh
Islamabad
KASHMIR
Chushul
TIBET
N
Chicken's Neck
Pakistan Occupied Kashmir
Jammu
Disclaimer
This map is not at scale and is for explanatory purposes only.
It does not purport to reflect the official boundaries of India.

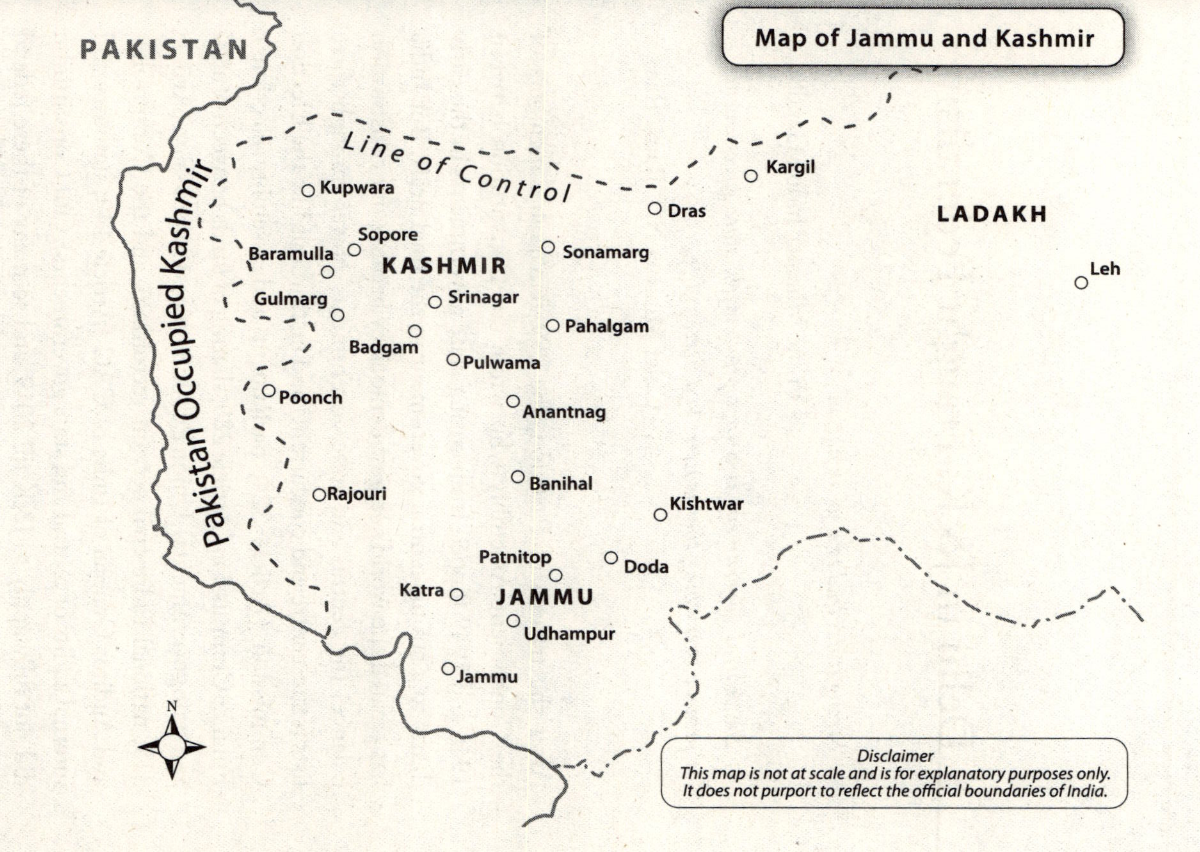
Map of Jammu and Kashmir
PAKISTAN
Pakistan Occupied Kashmir
Line of Control
Kupwara
Sopore
Baramulla
KASHMIR
Gulmarg
Srinagar
Badgam
Sonamarg
Pahalgam
Pulwama
Poonch
Anantnag
Rajouri
Banihal
Dras
Kargil
LADAKH
Leh
Kishtwar
Patnitop
Doda
Katra
JAMMU
Udhampur
Jammu
N
Disclaimer
This map is not at scale and is for explanatory purposes only.
It does not purport to reflect the official boundaries of India.

3

Delhi in J&K: Fraught Federalism

Strong states lead to a weak nation.

– Prime Minister Indira Gandhi

The central government is a conceptual myth; state governments provide everything that matters to a citizen's life.

– Chief Minister N.T. Rama Rao

After the trauma of Partition, the 299 remarkable members of the Constituent Assembly who wrote our Constitution between 1946 and 1949 flipped from strong state governments in the early drafts to a strong central government in the final draft. But India has created the world's largest democracy because our constitution balances the central and state governments' power through three lists (state, centre and concurrent) and institutions like the Election Commission (Article 324; parliament and assembly elections), Finance Commission (Article 280; sharing of funds between central and state governments), Union Public Services Commission (Article 315; national cadre civil servant recruiting), and the Comptroller and Auditor General of India or CAG (Article 149; statutory and internal audits of central and state governments). Our Constitution did not fully apply to J&K till 2019, and so many of these federal central institutions were only partially operational there.

However, history – Pakistan's invasion in 1947, the UN reference in 1948, the adoption of Article 370 in 1950 and Sheikh Abdullah's arrest in 1953 – ensured that the seven pillars of power in Delhi (the prime minister, Parliament, governors, the home ministry, the defence ministry, the external affairs ministry and the finance ministry) have been a constant presence in J&K's society, economy, governance, security and politics.

Prime Ministers

Although the president is the head of state in India, the prime minister serves as the chief executive, and all fourteen of our prime ministers since 1947 have had to deal with importance and urgency of the situation in Kashmir. My gripe is that most didn't recognize that establishing peace and prosperity in J&K required the involvement of local politicians and firm security, but both of these were impossible without a new tone from the top in Delhi. Disruptive as both may be, this new tone was only possible with the removal of Article 370 and cross-border military strikes. But let's first look back.

The involvement with J&K was particularly intense and personal for our first prime minister, Jawaharlal Nehru. He was not born in Kashmir and never lived there, but often called it his homeland. His ancestral connection was amplified by an early fondness that he developed for Sheikh Abdullah after a chance meeting at Lahore Station. He asked Abdullah to come with him to meet Khan Abdul Ghaffar Khan. He would later tell Kashmiris that Sheikh Abdullah was a gift from God and if they didn't follow him, they would be humiliated. Thus began a warm relationship of mutual affection. Abdullah wrote of Nehru in his autobiography, saying, 'There was an innocence of a child in his demeanour which made one love him.' In the same vein, Nehru wrote to Mountbatten, 'There is no doubt Sheikh Abdullah is by far the most outstanding leader in Kashmir.' When the maharaja arrested Abdullah in 1946, Nehru said, 'Does anybody think we are going to desert Sher-i-Kashmir or his comrades because Kashmir state authorities have a few guns at their disposal?' Abdullah's arrest in 1953 must have been particularly painful for Nehru. Deep relationships need multiple reasons to fray, and speculations include a decision to declare Kashmir's independence and question accession, intelligence reports about a growing partnership with Pakistan, concern over communal riots in Jammu and the multiple conversations Abdullah had with foreign governments seeking support. Many saw this arrest as necessary to preserve India's territorial integrity, while others viewed it as a political move to sideline a popular leader. Either way, the case was withdrawn by Nehru a few months before he died in 1964, and Abdullah was sent to Pakistan to explore peace talks.

As a former practitioner of statecraft, I greatly respect historian F.W. Maitland's wisdom, when he wrote: 'What is now the past was once in the future,' because we can never have all the facts or understand the second-order consequences of our decisions. While I am a great admirer of Nehru, as a J&K veteran, I am baffled by three of Nehru's decisions. The first was to bring in the UN after Pakistan invaded Kashmir in 1947, which needlessly internationalized the issue. Later, the office of the United Nations Military Observer Group in India and Pakistan (UNMOGIP) on Gupkar Road in Srinagar became a hotbed of tactical problems for policemen as it was an attractive endpoint for terrorist-sponsored processions to submit memorandums. The second was the implementation of Article 370 and 35A, which poisonously delayed J&K's intellectual, physical and economic integration with the rest of India. The third was what former Foreign Secretary Nirupama Rao calls the 'delusional diplomacy' of 'Hindi Chini Bhai Bhai' in her book *The Fractured Himalaya: India Tibet China 1949–1962*, which led to our defeat in the 1962 war and created wounds in Ladakh that are still festering. Unfortunately, Nehru's idealism often prevailed over realism.

Our next prime minister, Lal Bahadur Shastri, first engaged with Kashmir in 1963 during the first Hazratbal crisis as Nehru's emissary to oversee a special deedar after the Moi-e-Muquddas was reinstated after a week. We are grateful to Shastri for his ferocious response in 1965 that defeated Pakistan's Operation Gibraltar, but I wish the Tashkent Agreement had not returned the captured Haji Pir Pass to Pakistan. The Indian control of this pass would have substantially reduced terrorist infiltration in later decades.

Indira Gandhi's appointment as prime minister after Lal Bahadur Shastri in 1966 introduced another prime minister with personal connections to Sheikh Abdullah. Her memoir, *My Truth*, reflects her respect for Abdullah, noting their first meeting in 1934, highlighting his resistance to feudalism, opposition to the Muslim League and embodiment of secular ideals. Indira Gandhi did not release Abdullah from detention immediately, but her victories in the 1971 Indo–Pakistan War, the signing of the Simla Agreement with Bhutto and the Pokhran nuclear test gave her confidence around Kashmir. This led to the signing of the Delhi Accord in 1975, negotiated by Foreign Secretary T.N. Kaul and adviser G. Parthasarathy, which eventually saw Abdullah reinstated as chief minister in 1975. However, this reconciliation was short-lived as pressure from hardliners in Abdullah's party forced him to return to his pre-1953 rhetoric and Congress party dissenters whispered conspiracies to Indira.

The election of Morarji Desai in 1977 shifted political dynamics once again. Desai persuaded Abdullah to end his alliance with the Congress, supporting Abdullah's public claims about the lack of free and fair elections in J&K and his controversial decision to reject All India Service Officers in 1977. Following a brief stint of Governor's Rule under L.K. Jha, Abdullah won the 1977 assembly elections. It should also be noted that Morarji Desai had a peculiar relationship with Pakistan. He refrained from criticising the execution of Prime Minister Bhutto and was curiously honoured with Pakistan's highest civilian award, the Nishan-e-Pakistan, by General Zia-ul-Haq.

The birth defects of the Janata Party government ensured its collapse, and Indira Gandhi returned to power in 1980. She never forgave Abdullah for his opportunism of 1977, and tensions simmered before boiling over with a loud warning shot in 1981. Aided by the CRPF, a chartered planeload of income tax officers arrived in Srinagar to raid his family and close associates. Indira had already dismissed twenty-nine state governments (the S.R Bommai Judgement from the Supreme Court later restricted the use of this constitutional provision), but she actively considered using it against the Sheikh. While his public posturing against Indira and the central government continued, Abdullah began rolling back his extreme posturing by taking the salute on Republic Day in 1982 at Bakshi Stadium in Srinagar and started inducting All India Service officers in J&K again.

A few days before Abdullah's death, Indira Gandhi made a trip to visit the ailing Sheikh at his home to put the past behind them. Both leaders were rivals but respected each other, and Indira was advised by B.K. Nehru that peace was to be found through a frank conversation with Abdullah 'without hurting his ego or vanity, both of which he has in abundant measure'. It was her first visit to Kashmir since the 1977 parliamentary elections. The visit was important for both; Sheikh Sahib did not need but sought the support of the prime minister in the choice of his successor, and the prime minister wanted to judge the volatility of the state, given the upcoming transition of leadership, for herself.

Indira Gandhi made another attempt to partner with the National Conference and Farooq Abdullah for the 1983 Assembly elections. When these attempts failed – some may say backfired since Farooq partnered with arch-enemy Mirwaiz – she parked herself in the state for two weeks and campaigned extensively. At a campaign event in Iqbal Park (named after the famous Kashmiri poet Allama

Iqbal, who wrote the wonderful song 'Saare Jahan Se Acha'), there was a deplorable incident of some National Conference and Awami Action League rowdies lifting their pherans to display their nudity. Indira never forgave Farooq for his alliance with the Awami Action League, winning the election, and attending an Opposition meeting hosted by N.T. Rama Rao and hosting one in Srinagar in 1983. Indira wanted to leverage the discontent of National Conference leaders against Farooq. Still, she needed a more pliable governor than her uncle B.K. Nehru, who refused to dismiss a chief minister without due process. Nehru was hurt but accepted his transfer to Gujarat. The new governor, Jagmohan, obliged Indira by using his constitutional authority to legitimize a coup by Farooq's brother-in-law, G.M. Shah, in July 1984.

Rajiv Gandhi became prime minister with a record parliamentary majority on the sympathy wave fuelled by Indira Gandhi's brutal and tragic assassination. He overcame his mother's anger against Farooq who supported the seven-month Governor's Rule after the G.M. Shah's government fell in March 1986. He used this to negotiate with Rajiv, returned as chief minister for 136 days in November 1986, and they jointly fought the general elections in 1987. In my extensive road and helicopter travels with both leaders as state intelligence and security chief, I sensed their accord was a partnership between two leaders and not between two parties, and it was doomed to fail politically and administratively. Both dynasts had foreign wives and discussed non-political issues more than welfare, economics or terrorism. I often wonder if Farooq's political career would have been different if Indira had been around longer than her suave but inexperienced son. I heard Farooq's side of the phone conversation that led to reversing the defeat the National Conference suffered in the Amira Kadal legislative constituency. The partnerships between Indira Gandhi and Sheikh Abdullah, Rajiv Gandhi and Farooq Abdullah, and Sonia Gandhi and Omar Abdullah reflect the twin challenges of J&K politics – dynasty and soft separatism.

Rajiv Gandhi shrunk his parliamentary supermajority within five years – he was a gentle but inexperienced soul who surrounded himself with loyalty rather than competence. In one of history's exciting counterfactuals, if Rajiv Gandhi had not lost the parliamentary elections, then Jagmohan would not have been appointed to his disastrous second term that catalysed Farooq's resignation, accelerated unrest and emboldened terrorists. My talented J&K cadre police colleague Radha Vinod Raju, who became founding chief of the National Investigative Agency, investigated Rajiv's tragic assassination. Raju was a gem and made pioneering achievements for the police in taking on militancy.

Prime Minister V.P. Singh engaged little with Kashmir, but appointing Congress rebel Mufti Mohammed Sayeed as home minister was a mistake. Like many Congressmen from Kashmir, Mufti was not a grassroots politician, and in over two decades, he only won one by-election from RS Pura in Jammu, his legitimacy coming from his proximity to Indira Gandhi. Pakistan sensed V.P. Singh's government was too weak to be decisive and accelerated cross-border infiltration.

I was grateful to Prime Minister P.V. Narasimha Rao for his support during the Hazratbal siege of 1993. He called me away from the annual All India Conference of Director Generals/ Inspector Generals of Police in 1995 for an individual meeting at his Motilal Nehru Marg residence. This conference – meticulously organized by the Intelligence Bureau – allows India's law-and-order leadership to compare notes and gain broader situational awareness. Importantly, it reminds us of the nation's expectations of us. The prime minister lived up to his reputation: he listened more than he spoke, asked intelligent questions and reminded me of my duty to bring terrorism under control so assembly elections could be held successfully. I brought up the issue of radical solutions like the hot pursuit of terrorists into Pakistan Occupied Kashmir, but he did not react. I did not gather the courage to ask him about the Babri Masjid demolition in 1992, but *Half Lion*, a biography of him by Vinay Sitapati, suggests that he lost control of events and regretted its impact on the psyche of Indian Muslims. It certainly had significant implications for all of us on the ground in Kashmir because it provided Pakistan's terror factory with new propaganda with which to claim recruits. After him, the short stints of prime ministers Vajpayee, Gowda and Gujral were unhelpful for Kashmir as they were too busy with ensuring the survival of their governments.

Prime Minister Vajpayee's second stint was important for Kashmir for the extremes of war (Kargil) and peace (the Agra Summit). Pervez Musharraf was the arsonist posing as the fireman in both situations and, as the architect of Kargil, he should not have been invited to Agra. I respect Vajpayee as a poet, person and politician – he studied in Kanpur around the same time as Deen Dayal Upadhyay, a student of my father's – but he faced many challenges as a leader. I heard that the influential national security adviser and principal secretary Brajesh Mishra had convinced Vajpayee that the Nobel Peace Prize was within his reach if India made peace with Pakistan. This instinct for peace and insaaniyat (humanity) was honourable, genuine and deeply felt. However, Vajpayee's biggest weakness was overlooking the gap between the words and deeds of Pakistan, Musharraf, the Hurriyat and the Hizbul Mujahideen. Effective action requires a clinical assessment of a situation, and breaking the thermometer never helps cure the fever. My colleague Home Secretary Kamal Pandey asked me to join talks between Farooq Abdullah and the Hizbul Mujahideen in 2000 when I was the chief of CRPF, but I excused myself. I disagreed with the negotiations not because they were terrorists on the other side – which they were – but because the people we were talking to were neither in charge nor willing to change. As they say in Kashmiri, 'Illat galih tah aaadat galin nah.' (The sickness may go but the habits will not.)

Prime Minister Manmohan Singh mostly viewed J&K through the lens of peace talks. Peace is always desirable but his lack of response following the terrorist attacks on Mumbai in 2008 was a bad decision. The terrorists from Pakistan were getting live instructions from their Pakistani handlers, and Kasab's capture gave us hard evidence of Pakistan's involvement. And yet, we did nothing. I have read former National Security Adviser Shivshankar Menon's explanation of the army's hesitation to carry out cross-border operations. However, I don't believe it, and many army generals I know confirm this is neither true nor fair. Pakistan's deep state machinery began to count on India's passive responses to extreme provocations – but India's retaliations were inspired by the Cold War, which wasn't fought with nuclear weapons and where neither side would indicate their red lines. Maintaining a strategic equilibrium with Pakistan requires signalling India's red lines with Pakistan's terror factory. Manmohan Singh is a fine human being whose instinct for peace is understandable because a leader deals in hope – however, hope is not a strategy.

I have never met Prime Minister Narendra Modi – I only remember him as one of the organizers of the Rath Yatra 1992. I also remember him standing with Murli Manohar Joshi to unfurl the Indian flag at Lal Chowk on Republic Day in 1992. But I appreciate his Kashmir strategy – surgical strikes by army on Pakistan, air force attacks on Balakot, the separation of Ladakh and the abrogation of Article 370. Many of these actions reflect the consensus view of his party. The removal of Article 370 was in the BJP's manifesto for over fifty years, but I sense a new tone from the top and choice of team members matters. In the US, I often heard the phrase that policy is personnel. Thus, picking a non-foreign services officer as his national security adviser and a political organization man as home minister brought the cognitive diversity, skills and experience to sell taking on short-term pain for long-term gains, when in the past, the desirable was often shot down as undoable.

Governors

Public opinion, politicians and the S.R. Bommai Supreme Court judgment of 1994 have rightly circumscribed governors' ability to dismiss elected governments. But J&K has the dubious distinction of Governor's/President's Rule having been imposed the most times in the history of any Indian state: eight. Before the abrogation of Article 370, the central government could apply President's Rule only after six months of Governor's Rule. The name of the position may have changed over the years, but the powers and functions have remained the same.

Until recently, governors also functioned as the constitutional head in J&K because of Article 370. The first governor, Karan Singh, was called Sadr-i-Riyasat (a title formally changed in 1965). He was viewed with suspicion by the people of the Valley (as the heir of Maharaja Hari Singh) and Jammu (for participating in his father's exile to Mumbai). Some people also believe his dismissal of Sheikh Abdullah in 1953 was done to avenge his father, but that is not fair, because there had been radical changes in Sheikh Sahib's rhetoric and actions. Singh's autobiography is worth reading for anybody trying to understand J&K's history.

In 1967, Singh left the state to join Indira Gandhi's cabinet, and J.N. Wazir was appointed governor for two months (he had previously been chief justice of J&K). Bhagwan Sahai, formerly the governor of Kerala and lieutenant governor of Punjab, became the governor for five years from 1967 to 1973. After the Delhi Accord of 1975, Governor L.K. Jha first imposed Governor's Rule in 1977 for 105 days after Indira Gandhi's loss in the election.

B.K. Nehru succeeded Jha and accompanied Indira Gandhi to the infamous political rally in 1983. He was also present at the cricket ground during the notorious match between India and West Indies, where National Conference goons, their Awami Action Committee partners and women's college students were cheering for Pakistan even though that team was not playing. As the tensions between Indira Gandhi and Sheikh Abdullah escalated, Nehru bore the brunt of the anger on all sides. I remember meeting Nehru in 1981, during the income tax raids instigated by Indira in 1981, a warning for Abdullah from Indira. He had called me to explain my investigation of the violence and the relative roles of the Central Police Forces and the J&K Police. His view was similar to mine – there was enough blame on all sides and the governor convinced Indira to back down from dismissing Sheikh Abdullah.

After the 1983 elections, Indira's patience with Farooq Abdullah ran out, and she plotted to replace him with Sheikh Abdullah's son-in-law, G.M. Shah. The principled B.K. Nehru refused to dismiss Farooq without a confidence motion or vote in the assembly. She transferred him to Gujarat and replaced him with the pliable and obedient Jagmohan, who followed her orders. I was impressed by Nehru, who knew Indira enough to call her 'Indu' in front of us but chose integrity over family and loyalty. My wife Vina had many delightful conversations with Governor Nehru's charming wife Fori (she was Hungarian and born Magdolna Friedmann) and particularly remembered her advice about separate bathrooms being the key to a successful marriage!

Jagmohan was appointed governor twice, first in 1984 for about five years and then again in 1990 for 125 days. Jagmohan's first term was politically productive for the Congress Party when he legitimized the fourteen dissidents who broke away to form the National Conference (Khaleda) and appointed Shah chief minister. Jagmohan later, however, dismissed this government. He also used this term productively and ensured that the Airport Road was built in Srinagar. He used the legislative powers of the assembly to take over the Vaishno Devi Shrine from Dr Karan Singh's Dharmarth Trust, and this decision was highly popular. Ultimately, he was a man of buildings and roads, not hearts and minds, as became evident from his short second term.

In January 1990, Jagmohan took oath for a second time after being appointed by Union Home Minister Mufti. He arrived in the Valley making pompous claims of crushing the Pakistan-sponsored militancy but left the state to separatists and militancy within a few months. His tenure started with the Gawkadal massacre in 1990 when dozens of civilians died. Before exiting the scene, Farooq Abdullah had already told his colleagues that Jagmohan was like Kakar Khan, Kashmir's most brutal ruler from Afghanistan, and was the demolisher of Turkman Gate. He told National Conference leaders to fend for themselves. Jagmohan had good intentions, but like Don Quixote, he was charging at windmills and proposed simplistic solutions to a complex problem. Jagmohan was hard-working but his rudeness, impatience and inability to listen did not suit the complex combination of religion, terrorism and political vacuums in the state. He often irritably ignored or dismissed the opinions, information or analyses of most people, rarely stepping out during his second term. The only time I attended a coordination committee meeting at Raj Bhawan, I mentioned hearing open cries at Batamaloo Bus Station of 'Sopore, Kopore, Apore', a call to travel across the border. Jagmohan angrily said, 'Why doesn't your police do something, and give the BSF and army some concrete information?' He added, 'If I can promote you, I can demote you.' Since I was not the police chief, I requested the home adviser to excuse me from future meetings. As they say in Kashmir 'Anis haavan sarri wath be-aklas nah kanh.' (We can show the blind the way but nobody can show the way to someone without understanding.) Jagmohan never called me for any further consultations.

The most dangerous lies are the lies we tell ourselves, and thoughtful leaders counter this by surrounding themselves with people who act as hearing aids, seat belts or mirrors. Jagmohan didn't do any of this and so his weaknesses overpowered his strengths during his second tenure of 125 days. In his book *My Frozen Turbulence in Kashmir*, his claim of having single-handedly saved Kashmir for the country is ironic because his second tenure significantly expanded the terrorist population in the state from the hundreds to thousands.

The most tragic occurrence during Jagmohan's tenure was the exodus of the Hindu Pandit population in the Valley. Of course, he is not responsible for this migration – the terrorists were. In his book, Union Minister Saifuddin Soz suggested that Jagmohan encouraged Kashmiri Pandits to leave, and I disagree with him. Pakistan's psychological operations, a flood of guns and targeted assassinations created panic in vulnerable minorities. I didn't like Jagmohan because his lack of moderation often converted a problematic situation into an impossible one, but the ethnic cleansing of the Valley may have been impossible to stop without moving the Pandits into security enclaves.

I hope Jagmohan, later in his life, reflected on whether any alternative actions had been possible. I know many policemen like me hang our heads in shame about our collective failure to prevent the migration of many innocent Hindus whose presence in the Valley was significant, symbolic and stabilizing. His receiving the Padma Vibushan for 'civil service' was insulting to most people in the Valley and a decision I personally found baffling. I avoided contact with Jagmohan – civil servants are better off avoiding perception-starved people like him in power – but the two times that I dealt with him were important and controversial. The first involved a summons to Raj Bhawan in 1984 when, as a willing accomplice in the G.M. Shah coup against Chief Minister Farooq, Jagmohan asked me to forecast the consequences of his plans.

The second is more controversial. Jagmohan dedicated many words in his book and many public speeches to blaming me personally for the tragic CRPF firing on the procession carrying Mirwaiz Maulvi Farooq's body from Sher-e-Kashmir Institute of Medical Sciences (Soura Hospital) to his ancestral home Mirwaiz Manzil in Bohri Kadal. As the head of law-and-order operations without a specifically demarcated charter of duties, I generally confined myself to severe incidents of terrorism. I was in the Police Control Room when we received a wireless message about terrorists shooting Mirwaiz at his private residence in the Nageen area. His followers were taking him to the Soura Hospital nearby for urgent medical attention. My colleague Masud Ahmad Chaudhary and I proceeded towards the affected areas, but large crowds had already started collecting outside the hospital. We met Police Chief J.N. Saksena on the way, who informed us Mirwaiz was dead, and his followers had taken charge of the body.

On reaching the Soura Hospital, we found a sizable crowd of mourners carrying Mirwaiz's body on their shoulders, shouting religious slogans. These agitated supporters and mourners had forcibly taken possession of the body from the Soura Hospital personnel without conducting the post-mortem, a legal requirement in a murder case. They were determined to take him to his abai (ancestral house), known as Mirwaiz Manzil located in the Bohri Kadal area behind the Jamia Masjid area. Emotions were running high, and it was clear our attempts to enforce a previously declared curfew would only escalate into violence.

As the senior officer on the ground, I decided the explosively high emotion was best handled by allowing the procession to voyage through the city with security lining the road rather than intercepting or stopping it. Pakistan had killed him through Hizbul Mujahideen, and I felt there would be considerable benefits in allowing the crowds emotions to be released. After consulting with other senior police officers, including Srinagar police chief Masud Chaudhary, I relayed my decision by wireless to the police control room and all forces enroute. But Jagmohan's habit of not listening led to him to overrule my decision, and without any situational awareness, he issued orders to an outnumbered CRPF detachment to stop the procession at all costs and enforce a strict curfew. The CRPF had no choice but to open fire, and over twenty civilians died. These regrettable deaths added more tragedy and pain to the existing tragedy.

By the end of the day, the governor and police chief blamed the J&K Police and me for the firing. As I have said earlier, there is enough blame to go around, and while we can put the incident down to the fog of war, but in retrospect, we all should have done things differently. Governor Jagmohan and Police Chief Saksena had little crowd-handling experience and violated the basic rule of trusting the person in the line of fire. My experience had taught me that sometimes getting out of the way of an angry crowd with security forces lining the road to prevent spillovers can defuse immediate emotions. The needless panic and civilian deaths had more than one painful consequence. It diffused the anger with Pakistan and Hizbul Mujahideen for killing a Kashmiri leader. But Jagmohan, as always, believed the sole blame lay with others, and he insisted I be punished with a posting to the Mazagaon Docks in Mumbai. I spent six months in Delhi without a job before being rehabilitated by George Fernandes, who was also Kashmir affairs minister, in the Railway Board.

The day after Mirwaiz's assassination, J.M. Qureshi, the security advisor to the governor, called me to inform me that while the high-level enquiry into the firing would follow its course, I should directly take charge of the law-and-order arrangements through the J&K Police for Mirwaiz's funeral arrangements. I sensed that after the firing incident, the governor and police chief had decided on the central security forces maintaining a subdued presence both en route and at the funeral. A Muslim must be buried soon after the person's death, but Mirwaiz's murder under mysterious circumstances and the raw emotions of his supporters meant the final burial arrangements only took place three days later. Ironically, Mirwaiz's burial in the new burial ground of the Eidgah area, where most of the local militants or so-called 'martyrs' were buried, meant his final resting place possibly shared space with the same people who had murdered him. Mirwaiz's last burial procession (supurd-e-khak) proceeded with peace and dignity and in complete accordance with religious rites.

Jagmohan's replacement was Girish Chand Saxena, a retired police officer with a moderate temperament who had been the chief of the Research and Analysis Wing (RAW). He managed to cool tempers in local circles after Jagmohan but finally ended up only reacting rather than acting. In his occasional meetings with us, the governor would emphasize the ultimate strength of the Indian state and philosophically suggested that in the long run, India would find diplomatic solutions to Kashmir and militancy. He served two terms, in 1990–93 and 1998–2003.

Governor General K.V. Krishna Rao was governor for two stints, for six months in 1989 and five years from 1993. I first met the general in the early 1970s when he was 26th Division commander in Jammu. I did not connect with him personally then, but I felt the respect you feel for leaders who know what they are doing. His professional and unconditional support for my setting up a special operations groups that returned the J&K Police to the fight against terrorists was something none of his predecessors had imagined or championed. He was also crucial to restoring democracy with parliamentary and assembly elections in 1996. Later, as the director general of CRPF, it was often my pleasure to meet him at his home in Hyderabad. India and Kashmir owe a lot to this soldier who not only brought democracy back but also governed stoically during the most challenging years of militancy.

After I moved out, Lieutenant General (Retd) S.K. Sinha served as governor from 2003 to 2008, and N.N. Vohra, a retired IAS officer from the Punjab cadre, served two terms over 2008–18. His time in Kashmir saw Governor's Rule imposed four times. Satya Pal Malik became governor in 2018 and lasted only fourteen months, but he signed off on the abrogation of Article 370. G.C. Murmu took charge as the first lieutenant governor in October 2019 and left in

August 2020 when BJP leader and former union minister Manoj Sinha took charge. He seems to be patiently creating the conditions for the essential path to elections, statehood and normalcy.

All India Civil Services

Officers from the IAS and IPS allocated to J&K can usually relate to an old adage – people in the middle of the road will get hit by trucks from both sides. As members of All India Civil Services recruited by the Union Public Services Commission (UPSC), we trained together at the academy in Mussoorie and had batchmates spread across the country. Also, our highest-ranking jobs are in Delhi, and the Department of Personnel and Training controls our service records and conditions, and our destinies are hugely controlled by the central government. But we spend most of our careers in our state cadres, reporting directly to the state government.

The All India Civil Services have been essential to the strength and efficiency of India's federalism. There were two perspectives on the civilian bureaucracy inherited by independent India. Pandit Nehru believed the Indian Civil Services were 'neither Indian nor civil nor a service', while Sardar Patel thought they were a 'steel frame' for India. Either way, our constitution envisaged UPSC-recruited officers allocated to state cadres would spend their early careers in the field before some of them moved to policy roles in either the state or centre. However, because of J&K's special status, the allocation of All India Service officers to the state was only enabled by a parliamentary act in 1959. Consequently, the first UPSC-recruited officers from the academy arrived in 1961 for the IAS (R.K. Takkar) and in 1964 for the IPS (me).

When I arrived, the lower and middle hierarchies in all the civil services were governed directly by the state rules of compulsory 'domicile' and 'state subject's status' for all the appointees. Most of these were politically affiliated and favoured appointees. Even after the parliamentary act, appointments were still predominantly and heavily loaded in favour of 'local' or 'promoted' officers through the special provisions in J&K. All the initial appointees inducted in senior positions in these two principal governance services were made through the constitution of the state cadre. They were generally exempt, during their selections, from the otherwise strict guidelines and rules applied to the induction of such officers anywhere else in India. Moreover, the state followed no rules for cadre or non-cadre officers for the senior district level or sometimes even divisional appointments. Despite this, I had several professional role models including R.K. Takkar, K.D. Sharma, P.N. Sharma (who became a minister after my retirement), chief secretary P.K. Dave, Surendra Nath as inspector general of the police and P.R. Khurana as deputy inspector general of the police .

I must qualify my point about preferring local people whom you know because curating your team should be the prerogative of every leader, and we trust people we have worked with before. Also, punishment for not falling 'in love' or 'in line' with political diktats is not new or unique to J&K. After the publication of an unflattering article about Chief Minister G.M. Sadiq in the local edition of *Nayi Duniya* by Nazir Samnani, Surendra Nath, the state police chief, called me and told me to tell my talented IAS batchmate, Ashok Jaitly, then the district magistrate of Jammu, to have Samnani detained under the state Public Safety Act. Jaitly refused, saying the article was well within the norms of the freedom of the press. He was transferred to Ladakh, and the home secretary, Mr Ghulam Rasool Renzu, carried out these orders. However, Samnani's detention was revoked a day after he tendered an unconditional apology.

E.S. Modak, an IPS officer of 1941 from Maharashtra cadre, was appointed as the police chief and was deputed to the state by the Union Home Minister Y.B. Chavan in 1966. His first action as police chief made a deep impression on me. He organized a two-day conference of all police officers of the rank of superintendent of police (SP) only to listen to them – he did not speak at all. As the lone probationary officer in the state, I felt lucky to be invited and realized that his inclusiveness and silence were powerful leadership tools I should later emulate as and when I was chief. Unfortunately, frequent law-and-order incidents in Jammu, including the student protests in Jammu and communal riots connected with the Parmeshwari Handu inter-marriage case in Srinagar, meant he was sent back to his home state early. Chief Minister G.M. Sadiq, otherwise known to trust his bureaucracy, in a rare occurrence reportedly curtly responded to his request for an explanation with, 'You have made a mess of the law-and-order situations in the state.' The state did not bid him farewell, but I visited him in Jammu before he left and his advice was, 'My boy, try to leave on deputation soon; this is not a state but operates like a private limited company.'

Initially, the state government mostly ignored the existence of the State Public Service Commission. I was amazed that Ghulam Rasool Renzu, the state home secretary under Chief Minister G.M. Sadiq, had been the speaker of the state assembly. Similarly, political patronage was instrumental in the rise of Peer Ghulam Hassan Shah, who rose from the rank of ASI to be the first Muslim and longest-serving chief of state police, from 1980 to 1985. He was 5 feet 5 inches tall, had a strong understanding of politics and deep relationships cultivated over decades since being involved in recovering the holy relic of Hazratbal in 1963. The other example was A.M. Watali, who superseded many police officers, including A.K. Suri (an injustice overcome with his later appointments as the J&K police chief and head of the Railway Protection Force in Delhi). Thankfully, Watali survived when terrorists attacked his house in 1987.

While less hierarchy and more local people rising to the top of services is a good idea – the police commissioners of New York and London often grow into their roles after being beat cops –

my broader point is about rising through merit and transparency rather than political alignment. P.N. Haksar first perfected the art of 'committed' civil servants for Indira Gandhi, but this was later replicated by many state politicians. Today, it is widely accepted that the principal secretary to the chief minister is more powerful than the chief secretary. This is hardly new; I have heard a story – and it is probably fictional – about Punjab chief minister Partap Singh Kairon calling the chief secretary and saying he wanted him to select three people for his office: suchha (honest, educated and public facing), luchha (cunning enough to handle his finances and be an enforcer), and tuchha (loyal and non-ambitious who will give him the gossip). Sheikh Abdullah's preference for 'committed' civil servants drove his 1977 decision to stop accepting IAS and IPS officers from outside the state for the J&K cadre. This decision was only reversed five years later in 1982.

The challenges of being in the J&K Cadre brought all of us All India Services Officers closer. People underestimate the support of friendships when you are far from your family, and all of us benefited personally and professionally from sharing our joys and sorrows. The WhatsApp group we are all on today is called 'JK family', and Vina and I were grateful for our lifelong relationships with Ashok and Neeru Suri, Veerana and Suvarna Aivelli, Vinod and Achhama Raju, Gopal and Vimla Sharma, Paramdeep and Jasjit Gill, Rajan and Neena Bakshi, Bharat and Ranjana Vyas, Ashok and Kiran Bhan, Azhar and Mumtaz Nomani, S.S. and Quodisya Ali, Amar and Daya Kapoor, Kuldeep and Indu Khoda, Rajendra and Vijaya, and so many others. Vina was an important glue for this group. She was a lot more personally connected to many of them. This was not necessarily because she was the oldest but because she was a great listener with high empathy and unending warmth.

I also recognize that All India Civil Servants were not homogeneous. There was a clear difference between what journalist Shekhar Gupta calls HMT (Hindi-medium types) like me and

EMT (English-medium types), usually Stephanians like Ashok Jaitly, S.A.S. Rizvi and Hindal Tyabji. It would be churlish of me not to accept that we envied their confidence, fluency and polish. These were the decades when the understanding was that you had to be Western to be modern. But these differences did not mean that we were divided. Ashok, his charming wife Jaya, Vina and I became good friends and badminton partners in our rookie years in Jammu. I hope their son Akshay's front teeth have recovered from the damage caused by my panicked jump off a camel at Kana Chak, the famous fair in Jammu, when he was three years old.

Despite all the relationships we built, it was easy to feel like an 'outsider'. As a rookie officer in 1965, I was in Jalandhar for work when one of my batchmates visiting Jammu for his military attachment was told I was away in Hindustan. Most All India Service direct recruits faced local, political, social and administrative resistance from the state's established and fully supported local senior gazetted officers. Jealousy among local officers meant rumour-mongering about 'outsiders' was common. The saddest reminder of this was the reaction of local officers and legislators to the establishment of the Rajatarangini Cooperative Housing Society in 1988, spearheaded by my IPS colleague, Veerana Aivalli. The society aimed to help All India Service officers assigned to the J&K cadre purchase a flat. The initiative showed promised and some land was almost finalized, but the ferocious attack in the assembly – senior minister Ali Mohammad Sagar called us traitors and referred to us as officers of the East India Company – was supported by many local officers. Farooq demonstrated his inability or unwillingness to defend us officers publicly even though he had indicated his support earlier. The society soon wound down operations under instructions from Farooq Abdullah via Mehmood Rehman, the president of the Rajatarangini Residential Association, suggesting it would cause him political harm. The irony of Indian civil officers' inability to live where they served did not even cross

Farooq Abdullah's mind. This land apartheid was hardly new; Hari Singh had introduced the concept of a state subject in 1927 through a royal decree which affirmed 'in matters of grants of the state scholarships, state lands for agricultural and house building purposes and recruitment to state service, state subjects of Class 1 should receive preference over other classes . . .' The National Conference was right that the maharaja brought in the law, but even Hari Singh had ensured anybody he brought from outside to serve the state could buy land there. Examples on Gupkar Road included the homes of Sardar Effindi, Dr Mathura Dass and the Kapurs. Sonawar had the homes of the Nandas, Chopras, Khoslas and Rattans.

Being sandwiched between the central and the state governments became common for those of us directly recruited to J&K. In 1984, when Jagmohan summoned me for input for a report to Delhi about the law-and-order implications of dismissing Chief Minister Farooq Abdullah, local officers were quick to suggest disloyalty on my part. But I had anticipated this challenge and, before accepting the meeting, had kept the chief minister in the loop through his principal secretary, Mehmood-ul-Rehman, about the summons from the governor. When income tax officers escorted by the CRPF conducted raids on Sheikh Abdullah's relatives and associates in 1981, the chairman of the Central Board of Direct Taxes, Mr Kuruvilla, furiously told me that as Kashmir police chief, 'You must do your duty and protect my people or face consequences from the prime minister,' even as the chief minister said 'The state police must resist actions by central forces without the constitutional requirement of consent by state governments.'

After the abrogation of Article 370, the status of J&K as a union territory meant the erstwhile J&K cadre had been dissolved, with all officers reallocated to the Central or Arunachal Pradesh-Goa-Mizoram and Union Territory (AGMUT) cadre. Nostalgia is usually like amnesia, so I need to be careful in idealizing the erstwhile J&K cadre. The new AGMUT Cadre means many officers now serving in J&K have never lived there. Unlike other small union territories where the political, religious and geographic context is more straightforward, J&K is best served by All India Service Officers who have served there for decades. I pray that the restoration of statehood for J&K will start with creating a cadre of officers who spend decades developing what Germans call Fingerspitzengefühl or the 'intuition in your fingertips' developed from doing the same thing for a long time. What matters in public administration more than technical knowledge are language fluency, relationships, intuition and judgement, which come from marination in the situation over many years rather than a few years as a policy tourist.

The Home Ministry

Of the central ministries in Delhi, the home ministry had the earliest engagement with J&K during its negotiation of the instrument of accession with Maharaja Hari Singh. The ministry's surface area of engagement with the state increased after 1947 because of Article 370, governor appointments, Governor's Rule, the Intelligence Bureau, the paramilitary forces and special grants from the central government.

The special constitutional status of J&K was a mistake at best and poisonous at worst. Arguably, it was both, and unarguably, it was a temporary provision. The implementation of Article 370 in 1950 was hardly uncontroversial; I speculate the provision was fuelled by Pakistan's brutal attack on Kashmir after Partition, Sheikh Abdullah's credibility after helping the Indian army defeat Pakistan and India's mistaken request for UN intervention. Sheikh Abdullah's warm relationship with Pandit Nehru – nourished by a shared rivalry with Jinnah, a dislike of maharajas and a preference for socialist economics – may have helped, but this window was small. Nehru approved Abdullah's arrest and diluted Article 370 in 1953.

The home ministry shepherded the dilution of Article 370 through forty presidential orders starting in 1953. However, what remained was substantial, and the state was only fully integrated with India physically and legally in 2019. The post-abrogation days and weeks required careful handling of law and order, and many people were worried about terrorism. Then, J&K police chief Dilbag Singh handled the situation with great strategy, coordination and determination. I knew Dilbag as the district chief of Anantnag during my days as police chief; the area was a terrorist hotspot, and Dilbag showed his early potential by leading from the front.

The most deep involvement of the home ministry in J&K was appointing governors and supporting them eight times in Governor's or President's Rule. We have covered governors in an earlier section; the conflict between their position on the ground in the state and their role as Delhi's primary representative ensured this job has never been easy. Those who worked closely with the home ministry were the most successful.

The Intelligence Bureau is an integral part of India's domestic security apparatus. Its beautiful office-cum-residence on Gupkar Road has been occupied by many talented, quiet and competent officers like S.N. Mathur (who was a part of the first batch of IPS in 1948), S.P. Singh, A.K. Chowdhary, K.P. Singh, R.C. Mehta and Ajit Doval. They knew their job was best done in the shadows rather than the limelight and recognized the importance of separating opinion and bias from fact in their reports to Delhi. In the last few years, I have been distraught with one of the occupants of that IB home in Srinagar. I disagree with many things in the book written by former RAW chief A.S. Dulat, *Kashmir: The Vajpayee Years*. But most of all, I disagree with his writing a book with a Pakistani deep-state player (ISI chief). During the early stages of militancy, he held a high-profile convention of the Intelligence Bureau at the Sher-i-Kashmir Convention Centre, and it may not be a coincidence that many Intelligence Bureau field agents were soon targeted by terrorists.

He was clueless when the J&K Police unearthed Pakistan's sinister terror plans in 1988 and his subsequent attempts were mostly terrorist appeasement. Terrorists and separatists recognized this opportunity, and security forces often found themselves randomly and instantly shifting from hunting some terrorist to protecting them. I recognize the value of grand strategy but as the ancient Greek general Thucydides said, any army that creates too much distance between its thinkers and doers will have its thinking done by cowards and its fighting done by fools. My hesitation in talking to terrorists does not stem from bloodlust. The subedar major in my grandson's favourite movie, *Lakshya*, says, 'A soldier in uniform understands war is hell more than anybody else.' But the people Dulat insisted on talking to not only had bad niyat (intentions in the mind) but also bad zehniyat (intentions in the heart and soul). The peace efforts of the late 1990s and 2000s lacked the clear recognition that they would be handicapped without trying to change the rules of engagement with Pakistan. Recent changes like cross-border strikes, the removal of Article 370 and giving Ladakh an independent identity now create a different context for talks, if any, and Dulat's opposition to most of these overdue changes is baffling.

The home ministry's direct control of paramilitary forces like the CRPF, BSF, Indo-Tibetan Border Police (ITBP), and Seema Suraksha Bal (SSB) has given it a substantial presence in J&K. During the initial years of militancy, the BSF took the lead in dealing with militancy, but over time, we realized their training and weaponry instincts were best suited to their original border control mandate. The massive induction of CRPF in the Valley was a significant shift. As police chief, I was particularly grateful for the professionalism and firepower of central forces. The objective in having the police handle terrorism meant we only drew on army support occasionally and attached CRPF platoons to every SOG team.

The recent abrogation of Article 370 and 35A was handled competently by the home ministry, as evidenced by the Supreme Court judgement upholding the action in spirit, letter and procedure. A fundamental requirement of society is 'law and order', broadly defined to include crime, peace, citizenship, territorial integration, religion and national security. A strong and capable home ministry has been essential in integrating India. The book *Governance by Stealth: The Ministry of Home Affairs and the Making of the Indian State* by Subrata Mitra wonderfully documents the history of the ministry's success in 'maintaining public order with the minimum use of force and finding ways and means to minimize resistance to public authority.'

The Ministry of External Affairs

India's letter to the UN Security Council on 1 January 1948 asking for intervention in Kashmir was a mistake. It made Kashmir a pawn in the larger game of Cold War chess with thirteen resolutions being passed on Kashmir (the last was in December 1957) and seven resolutions during the two wars in 1965 and 1971. The UN ignored the diverse aspirations of different parts of Hari Singh's kingdom, like Jammu, Ladakh, Kashmir, Gilgit, etc., and converted it into a bilateral dispute between India and Pakistan, where religion favoured Pakistan's claims. This needless internationalization of Kashmir was compounded by bad luck. Pakistan's willingness to crawl when asked to bend by the West just as the Cold War was starting and India's pursuing geopolitical non-alignment made our life in Kashmir and at the UN more difficult.

The UN Security Council Resolutions of 1948 formed a five-member commission to go to the subcontinent to help the governments of India and Pakistan restore peace and prepare for a plebiscite to decide the region's fate. The book *Danger in Kashmir*, written by a commission member, Joseph Korbel (coincidentally

US Secretary of State Madeleine Albright's father), details the events leading to a resolution asking Pakistan to withdraw its forces from Kashmir and asking India to reduce the number of its troops. But most Western Cold War resolutions supported Pakistan, and India was grateful to the USSR for their consistent veto of this support. Nehru regretted his decision within a month, writing to Vijaylakshmi Pandit, 'I could not imagine the Security Council could behave in the trivial and partisan manner in which it functioned,' and believed the UK and US had 'played dirty'. Cold War calculations ensured the UN's thirteen resolutions on Kashmir supported Pakistan, and they even passed one against the formation of J&K Constituent Assembly in 1951 when J&K Deputy Prime Minister Bakshi wrote to PM Nehru, 'The UN observers don't confine themselves to their legitimate function of watching the ceasefire line but in greater part act as agents of Pakistan.'

India's mistake in involving the UN in 1948 led to the UN resolution of 1949 establishing the United Nations Military Observer Group in India and Pakistan (UNMOGIP), which spends over $10 million annually (funded from the UN general budget) for 110 people (Croatia, Korea, Thailand, Argentina and the Philippines are the most significant contributors). The mandate is to observe, report and investigate complaints of ceasefire violations and rotate every six months between Srinagar and Muzaffarabad. But as a long-time neighbour of the UNMOGIP on Gupkar Road, I always thought their presence was an irritating reminder of Pakistan's duplicity between word and deed, and that this office must be shut down. I vividly remember following the shameful press conference at the UN headquarters addressed by Amanullah Khan in April 1990, eulogizing armed struggle, militancy and martyrs, but we could do nothing.

The Ministry of Defence

Colonel (and later Major General) Akbar Khan, the sutradhar of Pakistan's invasion of Kashmir in 1947, like most terrorists, turned on his masters. He was arrested for the failed Rawalpindi coup in 1951 that tried to overthrow Prime Minister Liaquat Ali Khan for his supposed mishandling of Kashmir. However, Akbar Khan's book, *Raiders in Kashmir*, reflects the widely held delusions among Pakistan's military that Indian masses are 'superstitious, servile and debilitated' and that Indian soldiers are 'weak and cowardly'. If it were not for the swift and bold actions of the defence ministry and the Indian army on the night of 26 October 1947, Kashmir would not be part of India. Seeing the statue of young Major Somnath Sharma outside Srinagar Airport always swells my heart with pride. He saved the airport from being captured by the kabailis (marauders), and his sacrifice enabled the air force and army to bring in troops and push the Pakistanis back. I hope they rename the airport after him some day.

J&K's complicated relationship with its two neighbours – Pakistan and China – makes the presence of central defence forces in the area vital. Wars have ensured the civil administration needs to work closely with these forces to tackle any challenges posed by these countries. I experienced this first-hand when I was police chief of the Jammu district during the 1971 war when the Pakistan air force bombed the Chamb-Jaurian region of Jammu in retaliation for their losses in East Pakistan. This escalation was no surprise to us. The general commanding officer, Major General Zorawar Chand Bakshi, who had local connections, had held extensive briefings with the police and voluntary forces to prepare us for the situation. This anticipation also meant we had enough time to safely evacuate civilians. The war of 1999 in Kargil was different (because both nations had nuclear capabilities), but it was brilliantly and bravely fought by the Indian army despite the geographical location posing a huge strategic challenge.

India's other strong and cantankerous neighbour is China. The first attack by China in India took place in the Aksai Chin region in Ladakh in 1959 when CRPF personnel had constructed a camp in the area, and the Chinese army captured their scouting team. A group tasked with finding the missing scouts exchanged fire with China, and nine personnel died on 21 October 1959. To honour their martyrdom, police forces across the country organize a commemoration day parade on the same day every year. A police memorial has also been constructed at Hot Springs in their honour, and I visited this memorial to pay my respects to the martyrs on the fortieth anniversary of this event in 1999. Later, tensions escalated into war between the two countries in 1962, with China invading parts of Ladakh before unilaterally declaring a ceasefire.

In J&K, the army and police have a complicated relationship with each other, sometimes requiring high-level intervention by the defence and home ministries. In August 1980, an ugly clash escalated; an army truck carrying soldiers in civilian clothes had a minor traffic accident in Badshah Chowk. The locals filed a complaint, and the traffic police arrested them. They were later released and returned to Badami Bagh barracks, but they returned in a few hours with hockey sticks and iron rods to settle their scores first with the civilians and then the traffic police personnel. Senior policemen who intervened were attacked recklessly by the army. District police chief Javed Makhdoomi got a fractured leg, and district police chief Mr Watali sustained head injuries. This serious incident was the first of its kind and caused a loss of prestige for local security officers. Sheikh Abdullah could not afford these kinds of clashes and promptly ordered a high-level joint enquiry by army and police representatives into the incident and tasked it with giving recommendations to prevent any future conflicts.

As a consequence, on 1 September 1980, which was also my

birthday, I received orders for a surprise move as police chief of the Kashmir zone, a first for a non-Muslim outsider officer like me. Sheikh Abdullah had been consolidating the support of Kashmiri Muslims and his control over the administration by only posting trusted Muslim officers to critical positions. However, the previous month's incident and pressure from Delhi forced him to recognize that local officers were arrogantly disregarding the army and the central paramilitary forces. Thus, my big career break in the Valley came because the state police and administration needed a traffic cop to handle the increasingly tense intersection of the army, police and locals.

The next big army and police confrontation happened within a month of Governor General Rao's second term in 1993. An armed local Muslim policeman suspected of being mixed up with the local militants was shot dead in a hot chase by the army during a night patrol at Hazratbal. This death took on communal overtones, and some police units, joined by local militants and politicians, took out a large procession in the main streets of Srinagar. We prevented the situation from escalating, but the mob was unwilling to call off their protest and took Police Chief Bedi, Ashok Suri, and me hostage in the Control Room. We talked to the protestors through the night and calmed them down. Early next morning, the protestors were disarmed, and forty of their leaders were arrested. We followed up with two formal inquiries: one into the policeman's killing by the army and the other into police strike ringleaders and took action, leading to their dismissal. It is a security nightmare to imagine two armed forces of the same country fighting, and I do look back with gratitude on what was avoided that day.

The military and central forces are deployed in Jammu and Kashmir via the provision of it being a constitutional 'disturbed area'. With the abrogation of Article 370, the personnel of the Central Armed Police Forces (CAPF) and the 'armed forces of the Union of India' stationed in Jammu and Kashmir and Ladakh are protected from arrest under the Code of Criminal Procedure. The sixty-five battalions of Rashtriya Rifles were available to assist in security management, and without them, we would not have contained Pakistani terrorism in the Valley. The Indian army and air force have established broad and deep supply chains, roads, landing strips, cantonments, and presence on the ground.

The Ministry of Finance

A successful federation needs both the union and states to have enough resources for their constitutional roles. More than 80 per cent of J&K's spending comes from Delhi, which makes the state government what the Kashmiris call 'avaizan aasoon' (always dependent). The state would not even be able to pay its salaries without the central government. Thus, J&K politicians have always promoted government service as an industry with over 4 lakh government employees for a population of 80 lakh.

In the larger picture. Kashmir is an economic infant with low economic complexity. There is no wage premium in handicrafts; less than 5 per cent of the fruits and nuts in the state are processed, and it accounts for less than 0.7 per cent of India's gross domestic product (GDP). There is only one listed company and only one company with a paid-up capital of Rs 10 crore; thus it is hardly fertile soil for economic vibrancy. The economy in J&K is predominantly dependent on agriculture and allied activities. For export, Kashmiri saffron is the most famous and valuable, along with agricultural produce like apples, cherries and pears, as well as manufactured goods like handicrafts, rugs and shawls. The Jammu and Kashmir Bank (J&K Bank), one of India's oldest private sector banks, was set up in 1938 and is 70 per cent owned by the state government but is in poor health. In 1971, HMT Chinar, a subsidiary of the manufacturing company Hindustan Machine Tools (HMT), was the first public sector enterprise in J&K. After a few years, militancy and migration (most workers in the factory were Kashmiri Pandits, and they migrated to Jammu) affected their operations, and the factory closed down in 2013. In 1980, Cadbury set up a flagship plant with the latest French machines to press apple juice from fallen apples (otherwise a waste for farmers) in Doabgah near Sopore during Sheikh Sahib's government. However, operations wound up within a year because of unreasonable local pressure. The plant was briefly handed over to the HPMC but is currently abandoned. In recent years, however, tourism has been improving.

In 1981, Indira Gandhi led the central government and used the finance ministry to send a message to the state government. They were preparing for the Darbar move when a planeload of 275 central officers arrived in Srinagar to physically investigate a dozen homes and offices belonging to Chief Minister Sheikh Abdullah's staunchest supporters and political associates. Armed contingents of the CRPF were waiting at the airport to accompany individual parties on their raids. The income tax department had never conducted an enquiry in J&K, and locals were not used to any questioning by central agencies and offered extensive resistance. However, they were quickly separated into single rooms with their telephones being disconnected. The income tax officers were well armed with prior intelligence from local informants, including detailed maps of the inner premises. The raids, however, saw much resistance from the public. As the raids proceeded, news leaked, and angry mobs of civilian supporters barged into raided premises and grabbed the incriminating documents, unaccounted valuables and account books from the investigating teams. The situation was not improved by income tax officers unprepared for the cold weather as they wandered into nearby markets to buy woollen sweaters. Since it was not tourist season, they stood out as the 'raiders from Delhi'.

Conclusion

The only thing worse than having and executing the wrong strategy is being confused about your plans. Successive pillars of power in Delhi told us on the ground in the state to be patient, that they were experimenting with talks with terrorists, supporting various local politicians and making geopolitical progress. Kashmiris make the distinction between tahammul (patience rooted in the fortitude to handle adversity) and sabr (patience rooted in strategy and used to create strength in Kashmir). Sabr is always advisable in strategy, but only after bold actions change the game. Without the decisions that only Delhi could take – abrogating Article 370, cross-border strikes and separating Ladakh – the problems that plagued J&K could have yet continued for a long time.

History shows the impossibility of the two notions: J&K run from Delhi or J&K run with complete autonomy from Delhi. Prosperity needs peace, and peace needs the competitive politics that has emerged in other Indian states. J&K does not have the financial or security resources to stand on its own feet as a mountainous border state. Central assistance and involvement must continue, but many Indian states – particularly in south India – demonstrate the possibilities of contested federalism with economic development without separatism. I am hopeful for the future of J&K as peace returns, integration increases and the role of Delhi reduces to what it is in other states in the daily life of the state government as it normalizes.

4

Politics in J&K: Separatism as Strategy

The enemy of my enemy is my friend.

– *Arthashastra*, Chanakya

'Ghaattijaar scha naati ti baziri hayi mael.'
(Wisdom is not mutton that is it can be purchased from the market.)

– Kashmiri proverb

India was one of the first nations to grant all its citizens universal franchise right at the adoption of its constitution, even though its poverty, diversity and size made it an improbable democracy in 1947. Most other countries brought in voting rights based on the citizens' wealth, land or education, with some Swiss women gaining suffrage as late as 1972. India has now created the world's largest democracy on the infertile soil of the world's most hierarchical society due to our constitutionally enabled competitive politics, fair elections, contested federalism, social reform and economic growth. India and Pakistan, born at the same time, have had very different destinies for many reasons, but one of them is that about three million people win some kind of Indian election.

Pakistan didn't have a national constitution till the 1970s, has never had a prime minister serve a full term and hand over to another, changed their national capital three times and has suspended their constitution multiple times. As Bernard Crick pointed out in his classic 1962 book *In Defence of Politics*, democracy is impossible without brutal, loud and competitive politics. India's politicians are hardly perfect but are elected for a fixed term, forced to fight competitively for votes and are constantly disrupted. Even in our first national election of 1951, the Indian National Congress that got us our freedom received only 45 per cent of the votes polled.

Politics in J&K began with the formation of the Muslim Conference in 1931, which morphed into the National Conference in 1939 and then merged with the Congress in 1965. The Plebiscite Front was formed in the 1950s and dissolved in 1975 when Sheikh Abdullah became a Congress chief minister. However, the National Conference was revived in 1977 when Sheikh Abdullah broke with Congress. The Jamaat-e-Islami fought elections in 1971, and the National Conference partnered with their arch-rivals, the Awami Action Committee of the mirwaiz in 1983. This partnership broke during the 1987 elections when the Awami Action Committee joined hands with the Muslim United Front (and later with the Hurriyat Conference). In 1984, the National Conference split between the two Abdullah siblings, and the Congress aligned with the National Conference again in 1987. The BJP aligned with the Jammu and Kashmir Peoples Democratic Party (PDP) in 2015. It is worth noting that some of J&Ks troubles come from national parties putting party interests ahead of national ones.

A large part of the politics in J&K is the awkward dance between the Nehru family (Jawaharlal, Indira, Rajiv and Rahul), the Abdullah family (Sheikh Mohammad, his son Farooq, his daughter Khalida's husband G.M. Shah and his grandson Omar Abdullah), and the Mufti family (Mufti Mohammad Sayeed and his daughter Mehbooba). In 1947, Sheikh Abdullah became the first Kashmiri in 358 years to govern Srinagar since the conquest by the Mughals. He ignored the traditional faultline of Jammu vs Kashmir but amplified the issues of autonomy vs integration and spent years in detention. The uneasy relationship between Delhi and the state governments began with the controversial dismissal of the Kerala government by Prime Minister Nehru in 1959. Indira Gandhi would go on to use this provision twenty-seven times against state governments, but J&K has the dubious distinction of being the state where Governor's Rule was imposed the greatest number of times.

Politics in J&K have traditionally had much lower competitive intensity, diversity and churn than the rest of India because soft separatism was a profitable political strategy here. Of course, like other Indian states, there are no eternal allies or perpetual enemies in Kashmiri politics – there are only permanent interests. In politics, you have to have loyalty to yourself, your party, the people who voted for you, but also to your country. Since these interests are often in conflict with each other, politicians need to be clear about putting their country first, and many politicians from J&K have lacked this clarity.

Newer politicians from J&K have failed to contain or control terrorism in Kashmir because they promoted a soft separatism gift-wrapped as demands for autonomy, thus creating a distraction and hiding their administrative incompetence. Traditional J&K politicians have long skilfully derived power not from governance but by exploiting a combination of historical, geographic, religious and geopolitical factors. Despite being a politically conscious, close-knit society, the politics of J&K have hardly been normal by Indian standards.

Even as J&K Congress party chief, in 1981, Mufti disrupted a meeting convened by Vasanth Sathe, the union information minister, to rename Radio Kashmir as All India Radio (ironically, he didn't hesitate to fight parliamentary elections from Uttar Pradesh). Farooq

Abdullah ignored requests to control pro-Pakistani sloganeering at a 1983 India–West Indies cricket match while smugly suggesting it would improve his bargaining power with Delhi. After organizing a public ceremony for the surrender of 200 militants with their arms when he returned as chief minister in the 1996 elections after a long hibernation, he stated that he did not want to hold any such events in the future.

Royal Diwans

The diwans (the heads of the royal bureaucracy or prime ministers) played an important role in most princely states, and J&K was no different. The rulers in some states such as Travancore, Baroda and Mysore were fortunate, or wise, enough to have competent people like Mirza Ismail, Madhav Rao, C.P. Ramaswamy Aiyar, etc., to help their post-Independence states/regions develop better infrastructure, higher human development indicators and greater prosperity. Unfortunately, J&K had a series of unremarkable diwans, including Daljit Singh, Hari Krishan Kaul, Janak Singh, Kailash Haksar, etc. However, two notable diwans of the Kashmir state helped with writing our constitution, serving on the Constituent Assembly, and these were N. Gopalaswami Ayyangar (six years) and B.N. Rau (one year). Ram Chandra Kak, another diwan, was unhelpful to India's cause. He is partly the reason why Maharaja Hari Singh did not sign the accession documents before the British left India. Mountbatten often reminded people Pakistan did not exist till 14 August 1947. If Hari Singh had done what the 560 other rulers had done, I wouldn't have been able to write this book.

In 1947, as Lahore High Court judge Mehr Chand Mahajan was preparing to take up a position in the Shimla High Court, he received a letter from the maharani of Jammu and Kashmir about a promise he had made to interview for the role of prime minister of the state. Keeping his word, he took over amid the Pakistani attack and played a vital role in the integration of the state into India. Mahajan shared a close bond with Home Minister Sardar Patel and ensured that Sheikh Abdullah took over as prime minister after him in 1948. Mahajan returned to law and served as the third chief justice of the Supreme Court of India. He may have made a more significant contribution to India and J&K as a member of the Radcliffe Commission, which was tasked with demarcating the India–Pakistan border. His interventions were crucial in ensuring that Gurdaspur (in present-day Punjab) would be a part of modern India. This district is an essential link between J&K and and the rest of India, facilitating road and train connectivity. Previous proposals that had given Gurdaspur to Pakistan would have made it much harder to integrate J&K in India.

Prime Ministers (1953–65) and Chief Ministers (1965–1975)

Sheikh Abdullah was prime minister for five years before being arrested in 1953, after which his deputy Bakshi Ghulam Mohammad took charge as prime minister and head of the party for a decade. Bakshi was born in 1907 to a midwife mother and an unemployed labourer father in the centre of Srinagar. After finishing Class 8 at the missionary-run Tyndale Biscoe School, he became a teacher in missionary schools but soon began working to mobilize the youth to secure civic and political rights. Sheikh's loyalists viewed him as a traitor after 1953, but during the early years of the National Conference, Bakshi's realism balanced Abdullah's idealism and provided the scaffolding required to grow and run not only a movement but a political party and the administration. General Thimayya, the commander of army operations in Kashmir, said, 'Bakshi frequently saved Abdullah from the consequences of his naivete. Sheikh Abdullah might be considered the Nehru of Kashmir and Bakshi as the Patel.' Similary, Nehru told Patel, 'The most efficient person is Bakshi Ghulam Mohammad, who gets things done, though in doing this he does not always follow the rules and regulations.'

Intelligence Bureau reports describing Abdullah as vacillating in the unambiguously pro-Indian position he had taken in 1947, saw Bakshi as 'unambiguous, predictable, stable and pro-India'. I never met Mr Bakshi in a professional setting, but I encountered him as a student when I came to Srinagar to play football in 1959. A surprise visit became even more delightful when he responded to our light-hearted request by arranging a lovely trip to Pahalgam for us. Bakshi's reputation suffered because of his brother's corruption, but his tenure saw peace, calm centre–state relations and essential infrastructure building, such as beautiful tourist huts in the Pahalgam, Kokernag and Gandhinagar areas of Jammu. He was a pragmatic politician who believed that the interests of the Kashmiri people were safer with India than with Pakistan. In 1963, Bakshi was removed under the Kamaraj Plan, under which senior Congress leaders resigned to take up organizational work in the party. J&K lost out on a pro-Indian Muslim leader, and this, I believe, was a mistake.

Khwaja Shamsuddin succeeded Bakshi for four months, but his tenure never recovered from the theft of the holy relic from the Hazratbal shrine. Ghulam Mohammed Sadiq replaced him, with Shamsuddin remaining part of the state assembly. When I arrived in the state, Sadiq was in power as prime minister from 1964 to 1965 and then as chief minister from 1965 to 1971. Both the positions of prime minister and Sadr-e-Riyasat (president of the state) were changed to chief minister and governor during his tenure to integrate the state with the rest of the country. Though initially a supporter of Sheikh Abdullah, Sadiq had switched loyalties after the former's arrest in 1953 and formally broke away from the National Conference to form the Democratic National Conference in 1957 (however, it merged with National Conference in 1960). He later joined the Congress in 1965 and formed that party's first government in the state.

A stern and quiet man, Sadiq was an armchair politician and not interested in the political projection of his personality. He left most of the administrative governance to his chief secretary and police chief. He would hardly grant interviews to ministers, members of Legislative Assembly (MLAs) or other political characters. Consequently, there was little political interference in issues related to security, law and order and police management, which made him a great leader to serve under as we had the autonomy to be fair. He inducted many officers from the All India Service into the state government as he decisively pursued the integration of the state. To set an example for other politicians, he agreed to the arrest of his son Rafiq Sadiq when he overreached his authority to interfere in a police case.

He was a rare Kashmiri politician who was honest and had the full support of the central government. He had a frail figure though – his health was failing and he died in December during the 1971 war at the Post Graduate Institute of Medical Education and Research in (PGIMER) Chandigarh. We brought his body to the chief minister's residence in Jammu before it being quietly sent by road to Srinagar in the night. His remains were placed at his residence in Gagribal for religious rites attended by many people before being buried in his ancestral graveyard in Magarmal Bagh, Batmaloo.

Syed Mir Qasim succeeded Sadiq. He was a mild-mannered politician with no large political base except in the Anantnag district where his hometown of Dooru and constituency of Verinag were located. His autobiography suggested the Sheikh's politics influenced him in Class 11 to organize a protest against a local landlord, but I often heard Mir Qasim boast that he influenced the Jamaat-e-Islami to marginalize Sheikh Abdullah. As Anantnag district police chief, I had noticed the Jamaat often claimed political cover for their actions by claiming him as a godfather. He was part of the breakaway faction of the National Conference led by Sadiq but later re-joined the party. The support he received from Delhi and Indira Gandhi meant his tenure as chief minister lasted three years, and he readily handed over the reins of his majority government to Sheikh Abdullah after the Delhi Accord. After resigning, Qasim stepped back from politics and spent more time with his children in the US. He died in 2004 in Delhi, but his mortal remains were brought back to Dooru for burial.

Sheikh Abdullah

Sheikh would often say 'Hamne to Kashmir ki hukumat Lal Chowk mein pari pai' (We found Kashmir's government lying in Lal Chowk), referring to his role as emergency administrator when the maharaja of Kashmir moved to Jammu after the Pakistani invasion in 1947. He would also say, 'Kashmir ka muqadar pichathar lakh mein bech diya tha' (Kashmir's destiny was sold for Rs 75 lakh), a reference to the Treaty of Amritsar signed between the British and Gulab Singh, the general who betrayed Ranjit Singh, who described himself as 'zar kharid' (a slave bought with gold). He was a unique politician who was known in three distinct ways 'kunba parast' (obsessed with giving family power and positions), 'Baba-e-Quom' (father of the nation), and 'Sher-i-Kashmir' (Lion of Kashmir).

I think that the five most important landmarks in Sheikh Abdullah's life were not getting a government job in the 1920s (leading to a career in politics), supporting Indian troops in 1947 (stemming from a dislike of Jinnah and the idea of Pakistan), getting arrested in 1953 (many plausible reasons), returning as chief minister in 1975 (without getting anything in return for twenty-two years of struggle and detention), and nominating Farooq Abdullah as his successor (over the claims of his son-in-law G.M. Shah). He was a pragmatic chief minister who changed the political history of Kashmir.

Sheikh Abdullah was born after his father died; his great-grandparents were Saprus (a Kashmiri Pandit clan), and his family were shawl merchants in Soura outside Srinagar, where he later built a magnificent medical institute. He spent forty-nine years married to the formerly divorced Begum Akbar Jehan of Shadimarg of the Tangmarg district, who had a Slovak-British father and Gujjar mother. They had five children: Khalida, Farooq, Tariq, Mustafa and Suraiya.

Among the first Kashmiris to pursue higher education, his MSc at Aligarh Muslim University in the 1920s sparked his political consciousness. The Sheikh believed Maharaja Hari Singh's rule was unfair, incompetent and oppressive. A biographer estimates he spent sixteen years, six months and twenty-two days of his life as a prisoner or in detention. However, his politics were synthesized in his co-founding of the Muslim Conference after Maharaja Hari Singh's forces fired on peaceful protesters in 1931 (which was marked as Martyrs' Day and was a state holiday until recently). He was a powerful orator who understood his largely rural and oppressed people as is clear from a speech in 1933, where he said, 'It is not your motherland cannot provide you with roti, its every corner is filled with treasures, but what can we do if our hands and feet are tied, and those who control our fate have no pity on us? What kind of azadi is this, that 90 per cent of the people of Kashmir, which was once the centre of knowledge and talent, cannot recognise the alphabet? Oh, poor brethren, this is a painful tale, but as long as God and your love are with me, we will continue to work towards our goal together.'

The Muslim Conference transformed into the more secular All Jammu and Kashmir National Conference in 1939 to ensure people from varied backgrounds and religions could join the movement, with Abdullah suggesting that 'communal politics doesn't suit the temperament of the people of this state'. Although 173 of 176 delegates at the Muslim Conference convention had approved the renaming, a significant faction broke away from the National Conference in 1941 to revive the Muslim Conference under Chaudhary Ghulam Abbas. Jinnah described the National Conference as a 'band of gangsters' and thought the Sheikh was a 'rotten egg' with secular ideas who would oppose integration with Pakistan.

Those who revived the Muslim Conference were primarily religious and social conservatives from Jammu and included an anti-Abdullah group from the Valley led by the mirwaiz of Srinagar's Jama Masjid. During Jinnah's 1944 visit to the Valley, Jinnah certified the Muslim Conference as being representative of 99 per cent of the state's Muslims. In contrast, Indian National Congress leaders like Jawaharlal Nehru, Maulana Abul Kalam Azad and Khan Abdul Ghaffar Khan attended the National Conference's annual convention in 1945. It is possible to imagine a different outcome for J&K if the Sheikh had not shepherded the emergence of the National Conference from the Muslim Conference because then Kashmir valley would have met the Mountbatten criteria for accession (the will of the people and geographical contiguity).

Abdullah's opposition to the maharaja struck a chord with Nehru, who convinced him to join the All-India States' Peoples' Conference in 1941 – the umbrella organization agitating in two-thirds of India ruled by maharajas – and became its president in 1946. This role expanded his orbit. He was arrested after starting the Quit Kashmir agitation against the maharaja in 1946, which Jinnah opposed and described 'as a movement of a few renegades that had nothing to do with Muslims'. In August 1947, after meeting Maharaja Hari Singh under a chinar tree, Mahatma Gandhi visited Soura to meet Begum Abdullah and assure her Sheikh Abdullah would be released soon, and his facilitating Abdullah's release from jail a few months before the Pakistani invasion is a massive contribution to the Valley being part of India today.

The maharaja jailed Sheikh often but ironically handed him leadership as 'emergency administrator' after Pakistani terrorists enforced the maharaja's hasty retreat from Srinagar to Jammu. The 1947 raid by Pakistani terrorists was unsuccessful for three reasons. The first was Sheikh Abdullah and the thousands of volunteers mobilized by National Conference leaders like Bakshi Ghulam Mohammad and G.M Sadiq, including a women's unit. His inspiring slogans of 'hoshiyar, khabardar, hum hain taiyar' boosted the people's morale as he led from the front. The second was the raiders themselves – memories of their looting, rape and murder would remain for decades. The third and final reason was the bravery of the Indian army. Abdullah's speech to the United Nations in 1948 was clear: Kashmir could not be anything else other than a part of India. He added, 'I had thought all along that the world had got rid of Hitler and Goebbels but . . . I am convinced they have only transmigrated their souls to Pakistan.'

However, his secular instincts were and are still debated. Governor B.K. Nehru believed 'he was secular in so far as he did not believe in unduly discriminating against Hindus, but his loyalty was to the Muslims whose interests were always uppermost in his mind.' He presented himself as a devoted Muslim who believed in Islam as the sole means to spiritual salvation but believed it had taught him to fight for the rights of all his fellow citizens, regardless of their religious affiliation, and to protect the honour of his Hindu mothers and sisters as he would his Muslim mothers and sisters. His 1933 speech reiterated this belief, 'I am Muslim, but I see Hindus and Muslims with the same eye in worldly affairs and want them to live and work happily together.' Years later, Tarachand Bhat described Abdullah as a man 'whose conscience was Muslim, his heart was Kashmiri and his brain was secular.'

Prime Minister Sheikh Abdullah (1948–53)

Sheikh Abdullah founded the National Conference to fight feudalism, and he joined India because of its ideals of secularism, socialism and suspicion of the landed ruling elite of Pakistan blocking his plans to transfer land from the traditional feudal oligarchy to peasants. His Naya Kashmir Manifesto of 1944 was visibly leftist; their flag was red and in 1947 they named the downtown square with a clocktower Lal Chowk, or Red Square after the original in Moscow. Their slogan was 'Alyaban halla kari, dushman chall kari' (When the plough moves, it tears apart the enemy) and a plough was prominently used in their party flag. Abdullah ensured over 700,000 people from the peasant class became small landowners after he came to power, and transferred over 1 million acres of land, which were expropriated from landlords without compensation.

The primary accomplishment of his prime ministership was the transformation of agriculture in the state and improving incomes in rural areas as the Naya Kashmir Manifesto in 1944 had promised to abolish parasitic landlordism without any compensation and to transfer land to landless tillers and cooperative farming associations. As prime minister, Sheikh Abdullah was a pragmatic politician; he abandoned the most radically communist provisions of his 1942 Naya Kashmir memorandum and believed the Line of Control (LOC) should be India's national boundary because the people in the territory occupied by Pakistan were not Kashmiri in language, culture, music or food.

Political Exile (1953–75)

In 1947, in a speech at Lal Chowk, Abdullah used a Farsi couplet by Amir Khusrau, 'Mun tu shudam tu mun shudi, mun tun shudam tu jaan shudi' (I have become you and you, me. I am the body, you the soul), to describe the special bond between him and Nehru. But over the next five years something caused a rift between the two leaders, leading to Prime Minister Abdullah's arrest in 1953.

We will never really know what led to the arrest, but the earliest signs of a change of heart was his ferocious fight with N. Gopalaswami Ayyangar during the drafting of Article 370. He was unhappy with the final draft passed by the Indian Constituent Assembly because it brought Kashmir under India to a greater extent than in his agreement with Nehru and violated 'the discharge of his duty to his people'. Sardar Patel angrily responded, 'Whenever Sheikh Sahib wishes to back out, he confronts us with his duty to the people. Of course, he owes no duty to India or to the Indian government . . . who have gone all out to accommodate him.' US ambassador Loy Henderson was surprised by how openly Abdullah began talking about the Valley's independence as the only solution to the Kashmir conundrum.

Abdullah's speech at RS Pura in Jammu in April 1952 described the demand for 'full integration' with India being 'unrealistic, childish and savouring of lunacy'. The final blow came in June 1953, when a sub-committee of the National Conference suggested independence as an option for the state's future. This suggestion seemed like a long distance to travel for the personality covered in the short biography written by his friends B.P.L. and Freda Bedi, who suggested that Abdullah, the lion-hearted, was Mahatma Gandhi's spiritual heir. After a meeting at Abdullah's house with National Conference workers, where Nehru criticized the organization, Abdullah heatedly retorted he was the prime minister of the state, and Nehru angrily replied he was the prime minister of India. Nehru wrote to Maulana Azad: 'I fear Sheikh Sahib's mind is so utterly confused he doesn't know what to do.' I believe the corruption, nepotism and administrative incompetence during his prime ministerial years cost Abdullah the control of his party, cabinet and colleagues (Bakshi, Sadiq and Masoodi). This led to him playing the separatist, anti-India and religious cards.

On the morning of his arrest in August 1953 by Senior Superintendent of Police (SSP) L.D. Thakur (one of the best people I have reported to), the then twenty-two-year-old Sadr-i-Riyasat Karan Singh invited Sheikh Abdullah to his residence for a forty-five-minute chat. In his autobiography, Dr Singh suggests the conversation revealed that Abdullah's mind and intentions had moved from a position of clearly endorsing Kashmir's accession to India as final and irrevocable into expecting some sort of international pressure to be brought upon India to grant virtually independent status to Kashmir. Dr Singh reflected that the Sheikh 'looked upon himself as a Kashmiri who happened to find himself in India, I considered myself an Indian who happened to find himself in Kashmir.' It should also be noted that this arrest became feasible because Deputy Prime Minister Bakshi was around and willing to facilitate matters. Dr Singh felt Bakshi's 'whole stance vis-a-vs the accession [to India] was . . . more amenable to strengthening the relationship between the state and centre and less charged with the Kashmiri chauvinism so sedulously fostered by Sheikh Abdullah.'

Tragically, the relationship between India and Kashmir that Abdullah imagined was similar to what had existed between the princely states and the British Empire, precisely the structure he had spent his early life fighting against. The 'personalized sovereignty' of the empire had ended with the British's departure and the birth of our constitution. The charges for Abdullah's arrest included disruption, corruption, nepotism, maladministration and establishing foreign contacts, which threatened the peace and security of the state. After his removal as prime minister in 1953, Abdullah spent most of his time in detention, though he was released three times before being rearrested in 1958, 1964 and 1968. In August 1955, Abdullah's followers formed a new organization called the Jammu and Kashmir Plebiscite Front because New Delhi had hijacked the National Conference brand.

After Abdullah was released by Nehru in 1964, he travelled to Pakistan to explore peace and meet with Ayub Khan. When asked by a journalist if he was going to Pakistan as an Indian citizen, he replied, 'I am going as Sheikh Muhammad Abdullah; I am going as a human being.' He had identified himself in his passport application as 'Kashmiri Muslim' rather than Indian. Nothing came of this visit even though he presented Ayub with a santoor made of of Kashmiri walnut wood and said, 'Pakistan has ultimately got its saviour after its share of trials and tribulations.' In April 1965, Ayub Khan asked the director of Pakistani Intelligence, Ayub Awan, to contact Sheikh Abdullah and offer him support and cash. Awan approached Abdullah when he was visiting Saudi Arabia and told him he had heard about Operation Gibraltar, and that the Kashmiri people would not welcome Pakistani soldiers but if he were to 'call upon them to rise, their response could be overwhelming.' He was arrested on his return. His political ambiguity took ten years to disappear; in fact, in a 1971 interview with the *Rahnuma-e-Deccan*, he supported the Pakistani state against the movement in East Pakistan.

The 1975 accord Abdullah signed with Indira Gandhi was a huge break from his past private positions and public rhetoric. Many people were involved in the 1975 accord, but D.P. Dhar and P.N. Haksar played vital roles in the final agreement. An election was proposed in 1975, but Abdullah's return to power was accelerated by Chief Minister Mir Qasim stepping down and lending Abdullah the support of the Congress legislators. The Congress proposed a coalition with the National Conference, but Mir Qasim and Mufti Mohammad Sayeed sabotaged its chances of success. The coalition was proposed again in 1983 but it only succeeded in 1987. With great difficulty, Sheikh Sahib convinced party hardliners like Fakr-e-Kashmir Mirza Afzal Beg to dissolve the Plebiscite Front and sign an agreement with Indira Gandhi's Congress party. His small government with only four ministers ensured that the governance of the state effectively showcased what Kashmiris had lost during Abdullah's incarceration.

Many people were baffled by this agreement, which had little to show for Abdullah's years of imprisonment, protest and exile. We must remember historian Marc Bloch's suggestion that history is the science of men in time, as it could have been a multitude of factors that drove this compromise including Abdullah's seventieth birthday approaching, West Pakistan's brutality toward East Pakistani Muslims, India's victory in the 1971 war, the Simla Agreement making Kashmir a bilateral issue, the US's defeat in Vietnam, India's friendship agreement with the USSR, Farooq Abdullah's feedback from a Pakistan visit in 1974 and India's nuclear test. Some locals believe the 1975 accord began the end of Abdullah's legacy since it made no provision for the revocation of any of the twenty-eight constitutional orders issued in the name of the president of India or the 262 union laws made applicable since 1954. I disagree.

Chief Minister (1975–82)

Sheikh Abdullah, the Sher-i-Kashmir, knew politics was the art of the possible and forged compromises when required. But he was a man of conviction. Despite being chief minister with Congress support and having predominantly Muslim party workers, Sheikh Sahib didn't implement emergency provisions or jail any Jan Sangh or RSS leaders during the Emergency. He supported RSS candidate Vaid Vaishno Dutt in the Jammu Municipal elections to defy Indira. Much later, Sheikh threatened to counter Islamic fundamentalism in 1980 by becoming a 'mullah', while banning a proposed international conference of the Jamiat-e-Talaba in Srinagar.

The 1975 Accord was fragile, but after Indira Gandhi lost power in 1977, Congress politician D.D. Thakur recounted some discussions about her starting the fight back by getting elected to the Lok Sabha from J&K. And Sheikh Abdullah was willing to help. Despite protests from G.M. Shah, he offered to vacate the Srinagar seat won by Begum Abdullah in 1977. But those plans went nowhere, and the relationship with Indira began to sour. Abdullah broke with the Congress to contest the state elections on a revived National Conference party platform. He returned with a resounding win and extremist parties like the Jamaat-e-Islami saw their five seats of 1972 come down to one. The Morarji Desai government in the centre had promised free and fair elections without any rigging. The Jamaat-e-Islami sought to capitalize on the situation and aligned itself with the Janata Party both at the state and national levels; Sheikh Abdullah responded and said a vote for the Jamaat would be a vote for the Jan Sangh.

Under Abdullah's leadership, the National Conference became more assertive in the Valley and other Muslim-dominated parts of Jammu, Kargil and Ladakh. Due to his failing health, Begum Abdullah and his Kautilya-esque political strategist Mirza Afzal Beg led his campaign. Beg used to carry a green handkerchief and rock salt (from Pakistan) to signal they would open the road to Muzafarrabad if they came to power. He won the election but was unable to deliver youth mobilization despite using promises and slogans for freedom, self-determination and plebiscite. During this time, the state government stopped appointing All India Service officers to critical positions in the administration and preferred local officers instead. While I knew that competence would prevail over loyalty, I began to explore options for a deputation to Delhi. In time, however, when Sheikh Sahib sidelined Mirza Afzal Beg and needed someone to competently handle Beg's stronghold of Anantnag, he appointed me district police chief in 1979.

When Indira Gandhi returned as prime minister in 1980, she did not forgive or forget what she thought a betrayal and considered dismissing Sheikh Sahib's government, saying, 'Hindus of Jammu are feeling insecure.' Sheikh Abdullah wisely responded, 'The war among parties must not harm our national interests. My ancestors were Hindus. In Kashmir, we have the same blood; all are brothers and continue to have the same culture. Such remarks surprise us all, and if the country's prime minister makes such a charge, people outside the state will take it seriously.' Despite his rhetoric, Abdullah consistently neglected Jammu, ignoring the sound advice of former National Conference member Professor Balraj Puri, who detailed these issues in his book *Jammu: A Clue to the Kashmir Tangle*. I had extensive discussions with Professor Puri about his book but the Sheikh increasingly isolated himself and Puri later wrote, 'Sheikh's 'misfortune is that he is never criticised. He is either abused or eulogised.'

Indira did fire a warning shot in retaliation. In 1981, a contingent of income tax officials arrived to target Sheikh Sahib's confidants in Srinagar. He saw the raids as a personal attack and undemocratic, and he suggested that the motivation behind them was 'to disrepute the lawfully constituted government, to create terror and to erode the authority of the state government. You cannot enforce your law without informing the legally constituted government.' When he arrived in Srinagar from Jammu a day after the raids, he was visibly unhappy. He was the first to leave the aircraft and wanted me to brief him immediately in the airport VIP lounge in the presence of Ghulam Ahmad, his principal secretary and Peer Ghulam Hassan Shah, his police chief. He interrupted my briefing angrily, suggesting the income tax officers had behaved illegally and rudely and were guilty of behurmati (indecent insults) in their behaviour towards the women family members of those raided and demanded legal action.

I apprised the chief minister that there had been indiscretions on both sides, in which income tax officials had also been attacked and injured, including the daughter of Brigadier Sailo, the chief minister of Mizoram, who was a part of the group and had lost a tooth. The income tax officials alleged this had happened after Dr Farooq Abdullah, then member of Parliament from Srinagar, appeared on the scene and said to the boatmen at the Dal Lake, 'Ichu nebruk' (These people are outsiders). While Prime Minister Gandhi was behind the raid, local police officers like Watali, who did not fully understand federal jurisdictions, worsened the situation. It was clear that Sheikh Sahib was convinced by my balanced conduct in handling the difficult and legally complex situation. After the raids, the local sympathy for Sheikh's defiance of Delhi was so high that on Martyrs' Day in 1981, one of his bitterest political rivals Maulvi Farooq, who was the chief of the Awami Action Committee, carried out a peaceful procession emphasizing that Kashmiri identity was a cause uniting all the parties.

During Sheikh Abdullah's tenure in 1979, the government hosted an international cricket match for the first time in Srinagar between the Australian cricket team led by Kim Hughes and the North Zonal team. When the game between India and Australia was announced, a JKLF group in London sent a threat to the Australian squad, stating J&K was disputed territory and they would cause harm by disrupting the match and ruining the pitch. The Australian board headed by Donald Bradman panicked and wanted to move the game elsewhere, but former governor Dr Karan Singh, then union education and sports minister, asked them to reconsider. The Australian deputy high commissioner Mr Powell agreed to fly to Srinagar to assess the situation. The chief minister was confident of his government's abilities and their control over the security situation. He had recently arranged for his son Farooq to be nominated as the president of the J&K Cricket Association and felt the success of this match would be important in establishing credibility for Farooq. At the end of a meeting with the Australian team and Farooq, Sheikh Sahib smiled at me and told me in Urdu to accompany Farooq and the deputy high commissioner to the stadium, take them around the city and 'report back to me if they find any traces of the JKLF'.

Convinced about the strength of the security arrangements, the Australian High Commission gave the green signal, and the team arrived on schedule for their three-day visit. Sheikh Abdullah attended the incident-free match with the crowds enthused by the match and cheering the Indian team. The game ended in a draw, even though Indian cricketer Arun Lal got out after scoring 99 runs. Sheikh Abdullah came for the prize distribution ceremony and told Farooq Abdullah and me that he had thought that football was the only game that inspired the youth of Kashmir but was happy cricket was also becoming popular. The inimitable umpire Swaroop Kishen made my day by signing a bat with the inscription 'Think, Pause, Decide', which is great advice for anybody. I truly wish that the Cricket Association president Farooq Abdullah had internalized this advice in his tenure as chief minister.

Sheikh Sahib always had his ear to the ground. When protests broke out across Kashmir after the death of Pakistan president Zulfikar Ali Bhutto in 1979, he made a goodwill visit to the Arwani village in the Pulwama district, a stronghold of the Jamaat-e-Islami, where sweets had been distributed at Bhutto's hanging, accompanied by my colleagues M.A. Shah, Farooq Ahmad and me. Mobs had razed the village to the ground and even destroyed the lone bridge connecting them to the national highway. The mob anger was intense: many had travelled long distances from places like Tral, and three arsonists had fallen into the Jhelum and died while setting the bridge on fire. He held an open meeting with the victims – mainly Jamaat-e-Islami followers – who complained about the attack. He patiently listened to the villagers' complaints but said they should accept this loss as 'khuda ka keher' (God's havoc) being bestowed on them. His dislike for the Jamaat-e-Islami was palpable, but he still promised relief and resettlement measures.

One consequence of these riots was that the three districts of the Valley were bifurcated. One-third of the large Anantnag district I was heading at the time was sliced away to form the Pulwama district, which was in the news many years later for the attack on CRPF jawans. Zulfikar Bhutto's death exposed the clear social-political-religious divide in the Valley between the followers of Jamaat-e-Islami and Sheikh Abdullah's National Conference. Jamaat-e-Islami supporters – widely spread out in the district of Anantnag and the jurisdictions of Kulgam, Qazigund, Shopian, Pulwama, Tral, Awantipora, Bijbehara and Pampore – were happy and distributed shiri (sweets) at every stage of Bhutto's death sentence being confirmed.

The Jamaat-e-Islami of Kashmir owed complete allegiance to the ideology of Maulana Maududi, its founder, an architect of the Islamist movement and the mentor of Zia-ul-Haq, then president of Pakistan. This divide was not only political but religious. The Jamaat-e-Islami were followers of Wahhabi fundamentalism, which contrasted with Kashmiri Ahle-et-Quad (those who believe in saints and shrines). For the latter, Bhutto – a champion of the Kashmiri cause – had been murdered by the chief martial law administrator Zia-ul-Haq through a managed judicial process. Many Kashmiris reacted to Bhutto's hanging in mystifying ways. They attacked the office of the UN, came to burn my home in Anantnag and stoned the residence of the chief justice of the J&K high court Mia Zalauddin for not stopping Zia. Ironically, the Kashmiris rioted again, and more than a dozen people were killed, when Zia-ul-Haq died in an air crash in August 1988 because 'India was responsible'.

In 1982, the state assembly passed a resettlement bill to 'provide for the regulation of the procedure for grant of permit for resettlement in or permanent return to the State of the permanent residents'. This controversial legislation for people who had migrated to Pakistan between 1947 and 1954 and wanted to return was supported by the National Conference and the Valley residents and opposed by the Congress and the Jammu residents. State parties supported and national parties opposed. The bill passed, but President Giani Zail Singh sent it to the Supreme Court for presidential reference, leading to a two-decade-long legal battle.

A five-member bench returned it unanswered, long after Sheikh Sahib's death, in 2001.

Sheikh Abdullah, like all humans, was imperfect. He forced Nehru to banish Maharaja Hari Singh to Mumbai and replace him with Karan Singh. He made feeble attempts to win over the people of Jammu and Ladakh. He would often use religion in politics as, for instance, he led the Eid prayer at Eidgah in downtown Srinagar, instead of the mirwaiz, to send a message to Indira Gandhi in 1980. His initial genius lay in recognizing that politics and Islam in Kashmir were anchored and connected through sacred spaces and so, he exploited a nineteenth-century feud between the families of Mirwaiz Hamadani based in Khaniq-i-Mualla and Mirwaiz Yusuf Shah based in Jama Masjid to carve up the city and take control of its shrines. The two mirwaizs feuded over defining 'true Islam'; the mirwaiz of Kashmir labelled his opponent as a mushrik, or sacrilegious saint worshipper, while he himself was charged with being a Wahhabi who was against Kashmiri Islam, for whom saint worship was important. This strategy allowed Abdullah to stake his claim to speak for Muslims in Kashmir and create a powerful political platform through these sacred spaces.

After Sheikh Abdullah took charge of the trust that administered Hazratbal, his biographer Chitralekha Zutshi describes his Friday speeches as 'melodious multilingual oratory that expressed his support for shrine worship combining rhetoric on justice and freedom from oppression and exploitation for the masses'. As chief minister, he banned inducting national civil servants into the state government and preferred 'committed' state officers instead. He didn't make the National Conference a cadre-driven meritocracy but gifted the party to his family as if it were private property.

Since political aspirations and the mass religious mobilization of Kashmiri Muslims were linked, Sheikh Abdullah's towering personality had already subsumed and obtained the support and broad acceptance of all the groups as the lone custodian of the

'Kashmiriyat' identity. His chief ministership saw peace, though I wonder if luck played a major role since Pakistan needed time to recover from the formation of Bangladesh before it organized its terror factory. It only got its act fully together by the late 1980s under Zia. Kashmir's masses also believed Sheikh Abdullah possessed supernatural healing powers. During his rare appearances at public meetings, especially in rural areas, a big challenge for the police was men and women with small children jostling to obtain this blessing with a touch of his hand. Adult men and women who could reach him for contact or a handshake considered themselves divinely blessed.

Martyrs' Day celebrations, held on 13 July every year, became a politico-religious event, with rival Sher and Bakra factions taking out parallel processions that ended at the Mazar-i-Shuda (Martyrs' Graveyard) in Khanyar with religious prayers and speeches. The 1977 state elections accentuated the religious-political divide between Sheikh Abdullah and the mirwaiz's followers. The mirwaiz's Awami Action Committee had won two seats in central Srinagar, including one by Abdul Rashid Kabuli. In 1979, the mirwaiz's followers had decided to boycott the function and not allow Sheikh Abdullah's convoy to pass. Tensions were high, and the Awami Action Committee issued threats against the chief minister. Additional forces were deployed to enforce a curfew, control stone pelting and contain the mirwaiz's followers. Sheikh Sahib's procession travelled without interruption from Mujahid Manzil, the headquarters of the National Conference, through Bohri Kadal to Mazar-i-Shuda, where he offered prayers and made a speech. Many police officers, including me, had to get stitches due to stone-pelting injuries. My colleague Hamidullah Khan, understood the Sher-Bakra divide deeply, and his relationships on all sides of this divide created a civil face that allowed police firmness in dealing with the violence. Sheikh was pleased by the police efforts and visited me to enquire about my injuries.

Sheikh Abdullah used his pulpit at the Hazratbal shrine during the Milad-ul-Nabi fair and on Eid at Eidgah to deliver a message of unity amongst Kashmiris. As chief minister, he would travel to the Valley three times each winter. The first trip, in December, was anchored around his birthday on 5 December, with public celebrations hailing the Baba-e-Qaum and addressing a Friday gathering at the Hazratbal shrine. The second trip was as chief guest for the Republic Day parade in Srinagar – his predecessors would attend the parade in Jammu where the governor was the chief guest. A third trip in March was to oversee arrangements for the restarting of schools and the darbar moving back. Sheikh Sahib personally monitored two things: the adequate supply and reasonable price and quality of sheep meat, and the availability of ingredients for local bakeries to ensure the uninterrupted supply of sachwaru, bakarkhani, etc. Unlike his successors, he was aware of the needs of the masses and knew how to lead them.

In 1981, I accompanied Sheikh Sahib to the annual saffron auction on the outskirts of Pampore town, Kashmir's most important centre for saffron production. He received 15 per cent of the yearly auction value as a donation to the J&K Muslim Auqaf Trust, which was headquartered in Hazratbal. The sympathy generated by the income tax raids targeting the J&K Muslim Auqaf Trust and the Nawa-i-Subh publishing house run by the National Conference meant that donations had increased by about three times, but Sheikh Sahib had begun making reconciliatory signals to Delhi. We can perhaps attribute these signals to the reminders of mortality that only get louder with the relentless march of time.

As Chitralekha Zutshi observes in her excellent biography of Abdullah, 'He had an instinct for people and gravitated towards those with ideas, to whom he listened, and from whom he learned. These individuals – Iqbal, Nehru, Ghulam Ahmad Ashai, Prem Nath Bazaz, B.P.L. Bedi, Mirza Afzal Beg, Bakshmi Ghulam

Muhammad, Ghulam Muhammad Sadiq, Chaudhury Ghulam Abbas, Mohammad Sayyed Masoodi, Mridula Sarabhai and Jayaprakash Narayan to name a few – became critical to his political education, and in a sense, defined his political persona. Gradually, with their help, he became a professional politician adept at drawing on multiple ideologies to shape a narrative around himself, one he honed and jealously guarded. He also instinctively understood Kashmir, Kashmiris and what he thought they needed, and that became the singular ideology that directed him throughout the vagaries of his political life.'

Succession

Sheikh Abdullah's last days involved a tortuous decision about his successor, particularly because his worldview did not envisage picking somebody from outside the family. The only credible non-family successor, Mirza Afzal Beg, had been expelled from the party in 1979. Beg had grown up in Anantnag, where his landlord family had been granted the title of 'Mirza' for their services by the Mughals. His law degree from Aligarh Muslim University was helpful in his years as founding president of the Plebiscite Front in 1955, negotiating the Delhi Accord in 1975 and winning the 1977 elections. Beg's expulsion from the party must have been hard for Abdullah, who had once said they were so close they should be buried together in one grave. This left only two choices, and Governor B.K Nehru thoughtfully framed it as a choice between a fool (his son Farooq) and a rogue (his son-in-law G.M. Shah).

The succession that took place in September 1982 on Sheikh Sahib's death had been set in motion a few months earlier when Sheikh Abdullah had obtained G.M. Shah's resignation from his cabinet after he was absent at an official function on 15 August and Sheikh Sahib had inducted Farooq into his cabinet as the minister of health. In a few weeks, an ailing and emotional Sheikh Abdullah handed over the leadership of the National Conference to Farooq Abdullah at Iqbal Park in Srinagar, saying, 'The crown I am placing on your head is made of thorns. My first wish is you will never betray the hopes of your quam. You are young enough to face life's challenges, and I pray God gives you the courage to fulfil your responsibility to the people I have nurtured with pride and to whom I have given the best years of my life.' The crowd responded excitedly, 'Ameen!'

Sheikh and Begum Abdullah were seated on the balcony of a government-owned hotel when a procession carrying Farooq Abdullah in a flower-decked open truck from the party headquarters in Mujahid Manzil reached Lal Chowk. Senior National Conference party functionaries in the crowd reminded me that this was the same balcony on which Nehru had backed Sheikh Abdullah and joked about this anointing echoing the ceremony held for Prince Charles in England a few years before that. They were implying bad omens. The political and constitutional path for Farooq Abdullah's succession was settled smoothly by D.D. Thakur, who was the senior cabinet minister in Sheikh Sahib's last government. Unfortunately for Farooq, Thakur later turned on him and cut his chief ministership short. It was clear that Farooq had inherited power but not stature.

During his final years, people began to refer to Sheikh Sahib as 'kunba parast'. Sheikh Nazir, his nephew and political secretary, lived on the same premises as him. G.M. Shah, his eldest child Khalida's husband, was a senior minister in his cabinet and lived in an adjacent plot provided by Sheikh Sahib. Dr Farooq Abdullah, his eldest son, was given an independent house on Gupkar Road and made the president of the National Conference. Tariq Abdullah was made chairman of the State Transport Corporation and also given a separate, private house on Gupkar Road near Farooq. Sheikh's youngest son, the unmarried Dr Mustafa Kamal, was given Begum

Abdullah's original ancestral property at Shadimarg and set up a medical practice near Gulmarg. His youngest daughter, Suraiya, married into the affluent Matto family and lived near Nageen Lake. She was later the principal of the Government College for Women (superseding many more deserving candidates), and her husband was a doctor who later headed the Government Medical College in Srinagar. His habit of putting family first began early. In 1950, Prime Minister Sheikh Abdullah threatened to resign when Sardar Patel pursued his father-in-law Michael Harry Nedou for his activities in slowing down the integration of the central Indian states in his position as adviser to Yeshwant Holkar of Indore. However, Nehru intervened, the allegations were dropped and Abdullah inducted his father-in-law into his cabinet as minister of tourism. A frustrated National Conference party worker once described the strong Sheikh's weakness for his family to me using the Kashmiri proverb 'Ku-liyaa ka'-mue humu-rowve-nakh? Pannuv mayvan!' (O tree, who made you bow down? My own fruits!)

A few days before Sheikh Abdullah's life ended, I accompanied Prime Minister Indira Gandhi for what ended up being a reconciliation with him at his house in Srinagar behind the Nedous Hotel. It was a small gathering, and only Intelligence Bureau Chief T.V. Rajeshwar, Begum Abdullah, Sheikh Nazir, Gulzareen Khan (his ever-present personal security officer of Afghani descent) and I were present in the room. During this meeting, the prime minister suggested that Sheikh Sahib should make Farooq chief minister within his lifetime, but he kept silent. When Begum pushed him to respond to Indira, he feebly murmured 'Imanchu pata' in Kashmiri, or that she knew the problem, which was the increasingly forceful succession claim being made by G.M Shah. Indira Gandhi stored that information in her mind for later use when she turned against Farooq Abdullah.

Funeral

After his heart attack in June 1982, Sheikh Sahib grew frail and was confined to his residence. For the first time, he had foregone participating in the Eid prayers at the Eidgah and the politically important Martyrs' Day event. I was surprised to receive a message that Sheikh Sahib and Begum Abdullah wanted to privately visit a friend in the Hazratbal–Nageen Lake area and needed me to accompany them. They visited the familiy of Haji Ghulam Mohammad Butt, the owners of famous Claremont houseboats that were situated at the corner where the Nageen and Dal lakes meet. I was saddened when I realized what this hour-long meeting was for. Under Islamic tenets, a Muslim can choose his last resting place by purchasing and paying for the land. Sheikh Sahib had chosen the northernmost corner of land facing the Dal Lake adjacent to the Hazratbal complex area, and he had come to finalize the purchase from the Butt family personally. Sheikh Sahib was the most outstanding Kashmiri Muslim of the twentieth century, and these were the last stages of his life. The concertina wire, sand bunkers and police platoon now needed to protect his grave from desecration symbolize the tragedy and change in Kashmir since his death.

However, nobody escapes the inevitable. Sheikh Mohammad Abdullah, the lion of Kashmir, who many Kashmiris believed had supernatural powers, succumbed to various age- and heart-related ailments on the evening of 8 September 1982. His unquestioned political strength and towering legacy meant that Kashmir exploded with grief – an emotional tumult of mourning, followed by the tribute of an unprecedented funeral procession from the Polo Ground in Srinagar to his final resting place in the Naseem Bagh area where a memorial musallam (grave) would be built according to his wishes. Politically, the Valley would never be the same without him. I remember President Giani Zail Singh openly weeping at his death in Srinagar, telling me, 'I have lost my leader,' referring to Sheikh Sahib's presidentship of the All India State Peoples' Conference, which had agitated against undemocratic royalty being allied with the undemocratic British.

The police were responsible for the funeral arrangements till the burial. The deep sorrow and emotions of the Kashmiri masses needed an outlet, but it had to be contained within a structure to ensure that he received a befitting and honourable last journey. Sheikh Sahib was a national figure, and last respects were paid by the president of India, Giani Zail Singh, many union ministers, chief ministers and national leaders of Opposition parties, including Atal Bihari Vajpayee. Prime Minister Indira Gandhi came to Srinagar twice that week, once to look up the ailing Sheikh and the other for his burial. It was a send-off few leaders get.

Soon after Sheikh's death, Dr Farooq Abdullah was installed as acting chief minister and gave a calming speech on the radio. Events were moving fast, and many decisions about the funeral needed to be made. Farooq served as an effective bridge: a family member, acting chief minister and president of the National Conference. Despite all the arrangements, the crowds had become unmanageable by 11 a.m. the next day. You could see the people's agony as they stood weeping and beating their chests. It became difficult to maintain order, and by midday, cordons around the dias where the body was kept were being broken regularly. However, the police eventually got the situation under control. According to Muslim religious rituals, the body must be buried soon after the sacred rites. Keeping Sheikh Sahib's body in state for the people to pay homage was a first for a Muslim in Kashmir. We appeased the waiting crowd by requesting the principal of the Regional Engineering College in Srinagar to install a close circuit TV with a view of the body. These TV units mounted on three police buses calmed the emotions of a large number of people waiting in line at the Polo Ground.

The policemen also did their best and performed their duties for more than forty-eight hours straight without flinching. It was more than an official commitment on their part; it was a dedicated tribute to their late home minister, whose heart reached out to them, giving them his best. No food was cooked in many houses in homage to Sher-i-Kashmir. The size and emotion of the crowds made it impossible for us to take Prime Minister Gandhi and other guests from Delhi to the burial ground by road. So we improvised and used one of Dal Lake jetties to transport them by motorboats and shikaras on the day of the funeral to avoid further security and traffic chaos. In his first letter in office, Dr Farooq Abdullah wrote to the director general of police in J&K, Ghulam Hassan Shah, and complimented him and all the officers for their work in the days after his father's death. But for us, the work had been a reward in itself.

As Maroof Shah insightfully observed in an article in *Greater Kashmir*, 'The Sheikh's life embodies Kashmir's tragic story – its divided self. He was torn between secularism and religiosity, federal and central, national and regional, Quom and Paradise. Living in a land of gods, Kashmiris feel homeless.' As Chitralekha Zutshi notes, the most tragic divide lies in Sheikh Abdullah's legacy of being perceived as a 'prophet, guide and harbinger of freedom on the one hand and a traitor, opportunist and demagogue on the other.'

A hundred years ago, sociologist Max Weber identified three sources of authority. The first was the authority of the eternal yesterday, i.e., sanctified through past legitimacy. The second was the authority of extraordinary personal charisma. The third was the authority of a statute's legality based on rationally created rules. Sheikh had all three sources and used them to deliver ambitious visions in healthcare (the Soura Institute modelled on PGI Chandigarh), tourism (the convention centre modelled on Swiss infrastructure) and pride (the Hazratbal modelled on Medina). But his successors have run out of authority because they haven't fought terrorism like Sheikh Sahib did. I remember multiple instructions from him when I was police chief of Anantnag, Srinagar and Kashmir to deal with them firmly. Dr Farooq Abdullah's suggestion that unemployment and poverty birthed terrorism got a sharp retort from Internal Security Minister Chidambaram: 'If that were true, then large parts of India would have been disturbed.'

Begum Akbar Jehan Abdullah

Sheikh Abdullah's wife Begum Akbar Jehan played a significant role in Sheikh Sahib's success and worldview. Given his long stints in prison, she practically raised her family on her own. Many people also suggested Begum made essential decisions in Sheikh Sahib's old age, held the family together during his detention and was critical in his succession decision. Most importantly, she was a great influence in his decision to sign the accord with Indira Gandhi in 1975 so he could live peacefully and comfortably towards the end of his life even though in the early 1950s, she had been saying that 'there was no reason why Kashmir should not be independent like Switzerland'.

Begum Akbar Jehan's grandfather, Michael Adam Nedou, a Croatian architect, emigrated with his family from Dubrovnik to Lahore to open the first of a small chain of elite hotels in Lahore in the late 1870s. The next one was built in Gulmarg in 1888, and he built Srinagar's first luxury hotel and finest confectionary shop twelve years later. Its guests included explorers Sven Hedin, Francis Younghusband and Heinrich Harrer. Harry Nedou, Begum Akbat Jehan's father, spoke Urdu fluently, converted to Islam and later married Mirjan, a Kashmiri woman. The tall and well-built Nedou served Yeshwant Holkar as a military adviser, aide-de-camp and part-time bodyguard for two decades. These activities caused friction with Sardar Patel, who suspected he was spying for Pakistan and plotting with Bhopal's Hamidullah to drive a 'dagger into the heart of India' by preventing Indore and other central Indian states from acceding to the Indian union. For the Abdullah family, personal finances were an issue in the early years and Sheikh Sahib's autobiography acknowledges his wife's family help during lean times.

Begum Akbar Jehan had a keen interest in politics and even took over the responsibility of campaigning in 1977 when her husband was unwell. During this time, she emerged as an image of social and cultural renaissance, especially for ladies and the youth, as she publicly came out without purdah, an essential development in the otherwise conservative society of Kashmir. She also undertook charity work in the state for the upliftment of women and the backward Gujjar and Bakarwal Muslim nomadic tribes, upholding her mother's legacy. In her later years, she would keep an eye on her son's government and was sometimes vocal about Farooq Abdullah's government's shortcomings while paving the way for her grandson Omar to join electoral politics.

For my part, I enjoyed the custom of conveying Eid greetings to her in person; my children were thrilled with the food, new clothes and Eidi money. I also visited Farooq Abdullah every Eid. After Sheikh Abdullah's death and the emergence of militancy, Begum Abdullah moved in with her son Farooq Abdullah at his residence on Gupkar Road, where she lived until her death in 2000. Just before the darbar move to Jammu in 1989, I visited Dr Farooq's residence to greet him on his lawns. I expressed my desire to greet the elderly Begum Sahiba because I knew she was getting on in age. Ushered into the residential drawing room, the gracious and motherly Begum Akbar Jehan accepted my Eid greetings with shukrana (polite thankfulness). I felt this would be my last meeting with her, and I raised the politically sensitive subject of militancy by asking how Sheikh Sahib would have dealt with the situation. Begum Sahiba, deeply aware of Kashmir's political developments, was sad and melancholy about the rumours of threats to desecrate Sheikh

Abdullah's grave and the terrorist leader Hamid Sheikh's father being called Baba-e-Quam. Begum Abdullah said, 'Nashukre Kashmiri; mere shauhar ne inko izzat bakshi.' (Ungrateful Kashmiris; my husband won them respect.) If Begum Akbar Jehan were alive, she would recognize Kashmiris were enacting what historians call the reverse biblical curse, where instead of the father's sins imposed on future generations, the sins of the next generations are imposed on the father.

Farooq Abdullah

Farooq was different from his father; he was flamboyant, humorous and extroverted, and on most days he did not have the seriousness, discipline and strategic thinking that statecraft demands. I often heard jokes that as chief minister Farooq Abdullah was the second-most powerful man in J&K – the most powerful was the last person he spoke to. He was what one could call kaan ka kacha, and to be fair, his fickle-minded or perfectly weathervane reputation was not undeserved. We often had to get his signature on file as soon he gave us a decision, or else somebody else would get to him, and he would change his mind. His principal secretary, Mehmood Rehman, often told me, 'Prepare to make your point to Farooq in three minutes, or you will lose your opportunity.'

The former American president Barack Obama wrote in his memoirs, 'It's said every man is trying to live up to his father's expectations or make up for his father's mistakes, and I suppose that may explain my particular malady.' These lines could have been written by Farooq, who became chief minister ninety minutes after his father's death. His time in London and Jaipur did not prepare him for the challenges of leading a state like Kashmir. He failed to take many of the challenges of his political journey seriously and didn't view his father's legacy as a privilege and honour. He did not have his father's powerful political intelligence to say different things in Delhi, Jammu and Srinagar, though, this capability seems to have improved in the last few years.

Upon assuming leadership, Farooq boldly announced a complete overhaul of his cabinet during a large public condolence meeting on 12 September at Iqbal Park in Srinagar. This was portrayed as a break from the past, emblematic of a young leader's desire for fresh beginnings and innovative thinking and indeed, every leader should have the liberty to assemble their own team. The final years of Sheikh Abdullah's administration had seen a shift towards nodding heads replacing competing ideas, consensus stifling diverse opinions and a preference for loyalty over merit.

However, Farooq's abrupt public announcement to dismiss the cabinet proved problematic. Effective politics often requires gradual, evolutionary changes rather than abrupt revolutions. This swift action inadvertently created numerous adversaries as nearly all the dismissed ministers later united against him. This move highlighted a tendency towards impulsive decisions, a characteristic that defined his political journey. Many party workers joked in private, invoking the Kashmiri saying, 'Aes kholni bronh ghatsi dhemaagh kholoon.' (Before opening your mouth, open your brains first.)

Farooq soon inducted new ministers in his cabinet with the goal of a corruption-free government and efficient administrative machinery. He also chose one of my IPS colleagues, the very competent Veerana Aivalli, who had previously served in the Central Bureau of Investigation (CBI), as his new state vigilance chief with the mandate to take decisive action against corrupt political and administration officers. However, Farooq's enthusiasm for anti-corruption measures diminished soon, and he transferred Aivalli.

Shortly after he took over, Farooq was inaugurating a newly constructed building complex at the Pampore police station on Sheikh Sahib's birthday when, in the presence of the director general of police (DGP) Pir Ghulam Hassan Shah, he announced he was considering promoting me to succeed Shah as the new police chief to encourage young officers. This incident was an early indicator of Dr Farooq's weakness for drama and his unwillingness to think deeply about public announcements. His statement only created bickering and uneasiness in the local police leadership, and my appointment as police chief would have been highly premature then. It happened in due course, thankfully, almost a decade later.

Farooq Abdullah's Transition to Chief Minister

In the first few months of office, Farooq would make odd and towering promises on all fronts without any plans about how to execute them. It may have been necessary for a young leader who had succeeded his iconic father to create a splash, but this only created dissonance and dissent. Farooq worked hard to expand his party's influence, even in the Muslim-majority districts of the Jammu region, such as Doda, Rajouri and Poonch. His attempts to consolidate and expand the National Conference's influence in the Jammu region created friction with the Congress leadership, which viewed this as challenging their base. Although Indira Gandhi had supported Farooq's installation in the family succession rivalry, she watched the emergence of Farooq as a leader who was trying to balance conflicting interests and accommodate the priorities of Jammu and Ladakh, areas where her Congress party was the most dominant political force, with some unease.

Much later, in 1987, Farooq Abdullah tried to stop the annual darbar move when he issued orders to keep the secretariat in Srinagar open through the year. The decision resulted in an agitation led by the Jammu Bar Association, which several political parties, including the Congress, later joined and Farooq was compelled to rescind the decision within a month. During this month, I constantly assessed the political fallout of this decision and submitted a report to Dr Farooq. Knowing the repercussions of such a polarized decision, he responded sternly when asked about his thoughts on the information: 'Yes, sir, I have read, and I don't care a damn if the government falls over this issue.' He landed in Srinagar and immediately drove to a remote rest house ahead of Ganderbal, saying he did not want to be disturbed. This bravado was short-lived as then Union Home Minister Buta Singh flew to Srinagar and asked for Farooq to return. Dr Farooq reversed his decision after a closed-door meeting between the two leaders. This backdown was inevitable but needlessly provided his opponents like Maulvi Farooq talking points about 'accepting central interference'. Protests in the Valley continued, and Farooq deputed Education Minister Mohammad Shafi and me to convince the leadership of the Bar Association – Mian Abdul Qayoom Khan and Mohammad Shafi, musclemen of Maulvi Farooq – to back down. It took multiple visits to Maulvi Farooq's house, but the protests were finally called off in two weeks.

While the government operated from Jammu, Farooq Abdullah took two quick five-day visits in December and March to continue being in touch with the people's problems. G.M. Shah, Farooq's bitter rival, never gave up his ambitions along with his nephew Ghulam Mohi-ud-din Shah, who had been replaced by his bachelor nephew Sheikh Nazir as general secretary of the National Conference when Farooq Abdullah took over. Although the rebels did not openly challenge Farooq's leadership, they secretly continued to project the impression that the government was weakening. 'The times of Sheikh Abdullah's dominant political consolidation of Kashmir's political legacy were now over. However, Farooq Abdullah continued to project a dynamic image, make dramatic rhetorical announcements and attempt to emerge as the consolidated leader of all three state regions. While in Jammu, he said whatever was needed to ensure good ties with the central government, without whose all-round support he would and could not efficiently run the state.

The reinstallation of Dr Farooq Abdullah's government – after his party won forty-six out of the seventy-five seats in the State

Legislative Assembly Elections of 1983 – happened at the Banquet Hall in Raj Bhawan in Srinagar on 12 June. The ferociously fought elections – Indira Gandhi campaigned for a few weeks as a sitting prime minister in a disturbed state – saw Farooq Abdullah lead the National Conference to victory. This relationship continued to deteriorate with increased bitterness during the 1983 state assembly elections. The 'Double-Farooq Alliance', an agreement between Farooq Abdullah and Maulvi Farooq, had helped to keep peace in Srinagar at this time.

Governor B.K. Nehru was fond of Abdullah and administered the oath of office to the chief minister and his cabinet members. The confidence and celebration amongst the members of the new government amidst the local guests was indicative of the new government's hopes. Farooq Abdullah continued consolidating his political ground in Kashmir by mobilizing the public. At the next Martyrs' Day function and Milad-un-Nabi, week-long celebrations around the Hazratbal shrine premises saw massive public participation. Dr Farooq assumed charge as the chairman of the Hazratbal-headquartered J&K Muslim Auqaf Trust; this legacy from his father helped consolidate and publicly project his religious base. He also cleverly and strategically used the Independence Day celebration at Bakshi stadium in August to dial down some of the bitterness between him and Indira Gandhi.

Alliances

Farooq Abdullah's political rivalry with Indira Gandhi's central government resulted in a continuing deterioration of the centre-state relations. His attendance at the first conclave of the regional alliances in Vijayawada in May 1983, hosted by N.T. Rama Rao, attracted the ire of the prime minister. He added fuel to this fire when, in October 1983, he hosted a conclave of fifty-nine Opposition leaders (which saw tremendous public support) in

Srinagar, representing seventeen non-Congress parties to discuss centre–state relations. The day before the conclave, he had expelled his brother-in-law G.M. Shah from the National Conference. During this time, while addressing a public meeting in Srinagar, Indira Gandhi saw not just public disorder but also a low turnout compared to the Opposition conclave meeting at the same venue that received substantial public support. She had already made a public statement about the disappointing anti-India and pro-Pakistan sentiments at the recent cricket match between India and West Indies. She began receiving input from local Congress leaders about developments involving Dr Farooq in the state.

As the centre–state relationship worsened, so did Farooq's relationship with Kashmir's administrative setup and party workers. The new government seemed to have contradictory objectives; it wanted to consolidate and strengthen the administrative machinery, but political and local compulsions meant giving out-of-turn promotions to local Muslim officers. Farooq was losing political and administrative ground within the National Conference, G.M. Shah was gaining lost ground, and support from Congress for Farooq was also weakening. He responded by turning up the autonomy rhetoric to dangerous levels. J&K assembly speaker Choudhary Mohammad Aslam reached out and asked me to convince Farooq Abdullah to tone down his shrill demands, saying, 'Indira Gandhi jo uske azeem walid ko 1975 mein nahin de sakti thi, wo is shohda ko kaise milega?' (What Indira Gandhi couldn't give his great father in 1975, how will this amateur get it?)

Politicians everywhere face conflicting pressures from hardliners, party workers seeking favours and funders seeking payback. But the skilled ones strike the right balance between opportunism, long-term strategy and public service. Farooq tried to be a man of all situations, often leading him to waffle on his political and administrative positions. He was easily influenced instead of seeking out multiple perspectives, synthesising his view and then executing it with conviction. However, in popular perception, his charismatic personality overtook many of these shortcomings.

Soon after India and West Indies had played their iconic World Cup Cricket final in Srinagar in October 1983, both teams came back for a one-day match. The game, played at the scenic Sher-i-Kashmir Stadium, showed Farooq's carelessness in controlling anti-India sentiments. The ground had a capacity of 35,000 and was beautifully bounded on all sides by the tall chinar trees. This was the second international game ever being played in Kashmir after the 1979 India North Zone vs Australia match. The stakes were even higher at that point. Farooq was still the president of the J&K Cricket Association, but now he was also chief minister. It was a challenge for the newly formed government to organize the match, and as zonal police chief, I was responsible for maintaining order. I had taken adequate precautions with multiple rehearsals and detailed briefings with the state police units and central paramilitary forces. Yet, this match ended up being different from the one Sheikh had hosted in 1979 amidst threats from the JKLF.

The early signs were not good; the crowd started booing loudly at the Indian team's good batting performance and trying to push the outer fence. Surprisingly, the loudest hooting and shouting came from the exclusive girls' gallery of the Women's College, where big cut-out photos of Pakistani Cricketer Imran Khan were displayed, much to the surprise and annoyance of the Indian cricket team players and their supporters who had come from outside the state to cheer them. Dr Farooq's sister, Suraiya, was then the principal of the Women's College. Sentiments ran high; India's opening batsman, Srikanth, hit the West Indies bowler for a six into the stands. Some spectators from Haryana were rejoicing, but local spectators physically manhandled them, and minor incidents continued up to lunchtime.

During lunch, a policeman's intuition for trouble kept me taking rounds of the field. I noticed two spectators jumping the gallery fence and running towards the pitch. I don't think I have sprinted that fast since my student days as I reached the pitch and broke my baton on one of the intruders. Before I reached the second intruder, he hit my legs with some stumps, but I pushed him over. I whistled for reinforcements to arrive. Meanwhile, two more troublemakers had jumped the fence. After arresting all four, I summoned the secretary of the J&K Cricket Association, M.L. Nehru, to ensure the pitch was returned to its original condition. Indian captain Kapil Dev was hesitant about getting back on the pitch, but I assured him the damage to the pitch was minimal and play could resume. The West Indies finally won by using the 'rain rule'. I was relieved the match wasn't abandoned because of the disturbances but was embarrassed to have Wesley Hall, the West Indies Sports Minister, a famous former fast-bowler, tell me the West Indians had never had such cheering even in his hometown of Barbados. Sunil Gavaskar later wrote, 'Being hooted at after a defeat is understandable, but this was incredible.'

In the days before the match, I had requested Farooq Abdullah to issue firm instructions through his National Conference party leaders to mobilize and organize ground checks on anti-Indian sentiments since emotions were still high after the bitter 1983 elections. Although Farooq supposedly issued instructions to help the police through his cousin Sheikh Nazir, the general secretary, I could see that the instructions were not percolating down the line. It was even more disappointing when, under political directions to the police station staff, even those miscreants who had disturbed the playfield area during lunch were shown some leniency and were initially booked under ordinary criminal laws instead of the stringent preventive detention laws for their anti-national acts. But we continued to work behind the scenes; the JKLF's demands from when they kidnapped diplomat Ravindra Mhatre in 1984 included freeing the seven separatists we still had in custody for disrupting the cricket match.

I felt Farooq was wrong in treating this incident lightly and called Inspector Rashid Baba, the security officer in charge and Farooq's trusted assistant, to understand why he had not conveyed my security worries. Baba assured me he had fully shared my apprehensions but was surprised Farooq had returned home from the match in a very relaxed mood and had suggested that the match troubles helped in getting Indira Gandhi to realize how it was impossible for them to govern Kashmir without him. However, he miscalculated; these incidents did not go unnoticed, and Indira Gandhi returned from her trip overseas to strongly condemn the state government's inability to control the pro-Pakistani elements in the state. Farooq is wonderful social company but often ignored the Kashmiri proverb of 'Vaav vachhit naav traavin' (Sail the boat after paying attention to the wind direction) and wrongly judged situations or second-order effects.

To add to Farooq's woes, in 1984, the following year, the Indira Gandhi-led Congress government in Delhi appointed Jagmohan as the J&K governor, cutting short the tenure of her uncle B.K. Nehru. At the time, I was surprised to receive a call asking me to meet the governor, and my survival antenna dictated I should check with the chief minister's office before going, which I did. At the meeting in Raj Bhawan, I immediately sensed that a plan to oust the chief minister was underway. The governor asked me about the state's prevailing law-and-order situation, recent cricket match, assembly elections, and Farooq's personality, local popularity and governance capabilities. He directly asked what the fallout on the law-and-order situation would be if Farooq were dismissed. Giving the governor honest feedback, I told him the chief minister was losing ground amongst the public and his administration but believed he could still establish his democratically legitimate majority on the floor of the assembly.

I decided to meet Farooq a week later because the local rumour mill and the grapevine were moving fast. I made a morning appointment at his residence on Gupkar Road, a few hundred metres from my Rose Mount home. I told him that since I had served his father and also his state government in difficult times, I was apprehensive about the future of his government after Jagmohan's probing questions. I probably stepped over the line and mentioned that the Kashmir grapevine was predicting a change of chief minister by Eid, and he must watch party dissidents. He dismissed my advice, saying if anybody dared to touch his widely popular government, there would be a revolution and unending violence in Kashmir. I left his residence feeling that he was needlessly overconfident when an urgency to save his government should have been the appropriate response. That fatal flaw of all humans – willful blindness – held him back. A few days later, I was amazed and frustrated when he undertook shallow public spectacles of traffic checking in Pahalgam and a motorbike ride with actress Shabana Azmi.

Ironically, the thirteen National Conference legislators defecting with G.M. Shah drove past Farooq's house on Gupkar Road to reach Raj Bhawan. Farooq remained unaware until a call from the governor asked him to come to the Raj Bhawan urgently. Dr Farooq, who returned to his residence for legal consultations before submitting his resignation, is said to have pulled up his intelligence advisor, Abdul Rahim Nanda, for not providing the requisite intelligence. As Sumantra Bose points out in *Kashmir at Crossroads*, this coup has interesting parallels with 1953 with Indira Gandhi, Jagmohan, G.M Shah and Farooq Abdullah in the roles of Jawaharlal Nehru, Karan Singh, Bakshi Ghulam Mohammed and Sheikh Abdullah.

G.M. Shah cut short the extended tenure of the police chief Peer Ghulam Hassan Shah who honourably resigned instead of joining as transport commissioner. However, Shah's government was in power for less than two years, and this failed experiment significantly improved the relationship between Farooq and Rajiv

eikh Abdullah takes the salute on 26 January 1982, at Bakshi Stadium in Srinagar. his was a clear departure from his attending the official function at Maulana Azad adium in Jammu, the winter capital, where the governor takes the salute. It was his last major public appearance before his death.

Security briefing with the Dalai Lama in Jammu in 1988 before his month-long stay in Leh

Said-Ullah Lone, the first police officer killed by militants in 1989

Receiving President Venkataraman at the Srinagar airport with Chief Minister Farooq Abdullah after the iconic Rajiv–Farooq Accord

With Governor General K.V. Krishna Rao surveying Hazratbal the morning after the militants surrendered in 1993

Inspecting arms recovered in an SOG operation

With Chief Minister Farooq Abdullah at the state secretariat along with the organizing committee for the football tournament in 1983 in memory of Sheikh Abdullah

Presenting a memento to Prime Minister Vajpayee at the CRPF diamond jubilee parade in 1999. Deputy Prime Minister L.K. Advani attended the parade as well. The visit helped provide additional funds and resources for CRPF expansion.

My police colleagues (L to R) Azhar Nomani, Ali Mohammad Watali, me, Naeem Akhtar and R.V. Raju at a traditional Kashmiri wazwan in 1980

With my wife, Vina

Gandhi's central government. They soon signed the Rajiv–Farooq accord, and in 1986, Farooq returned as chief minister. In the state elections held the following year, the National Conference emerged as the single largest party and formed a government in coalition with the Congress.

Farooq Abdullah's coalition government under the Rajiv–Farooq accord was formed under uneasy political compulsions of both political parties after the last three years of frequent government changes and political instability in the state. The competing rival claims of the two parties made unified political power problematic because of their dominant presence in the two respective regions, the Congress in Jammu and National Conference in Kashmir. The Congress had schemed with dissidents to displace Farooq within a year of winning a massive majority in the 1983 elections. Now, the same government was back. However, the personal equation between the two young leaders cemented their agreement to end Jagmohan's direct rule. Farooq brought me back as his intelligence chief. In 1990, when Jagmohan was appointed governor again by Mufti Sayeed – primarily to spite his arch-political rival Farooq – it was a disaster, and Jagmohan hardly left the Raj Bhawan during his less-than-five-month tenure. But his appointment triggered Farooq's resignation as chief minister, and by this time, Rajiv Gandhi had lost his supernormal majority in the national parliament. The next few years saw some of the most challenging militancy in the state.

The 1987 elections are often called unfair. One of the most controversial constituencies was Amira Kadal, in the heart of Srinagar, where the hotly contested election was between the National Conference and the Muslim United Front, which included anti-establishment groups like the Jamaat-e-Islami. On the day of the counting, Abdullah summoned me to his Gupkar Road residence, where I was present when Prime Minister Rajiv Gandhi called suggesting that a win for Muslim United Front candidate Mohammad Yusuf Shah, who was leading, could pose serious trouble for the government, and Farooq should fix the situation. Dr Farooq instructed Deputy Inspector General of Police Watali to visit the counting centres and passed similar instructions to the divisional commissioner and district magistrates to ensure the victory of his coalition candidates. When results were declared, the National Conference candidate Ghulam Mohiuddin Shah, who had been trailing all day, was declared the winner. I reiterated this to Farooq then – and still believe – that although their vote share might increase, the Muslim United Front would not get more than six seats so there was no reason for heavy-handed interference. Mohammad Yusuf Shah is now known as Pakistan-based Syed Salahuddin and heads the United Jihad Council and used to lead the Hizb-ul-Mujahideen.

Farooq returned to power in 1996, an election we will discuss in much more detail later. His tenure saw controversy around corruption with fund misappropriation in the Rural Development Fund in the Anantnag district. There were rumours the district development commissioner had funnelled money out of the central J&K treasury to fund militants. This led to the arrest of more than half a dozen gazetted officers and their dismissal by the governor. Later, during Abdullah's tenure, the accused were reinstated. I am sure the government followed the due process of law, but political considerations often outweighed punishing law-breaking and corrupt civil servants.

Corruption is not unique to India or J&K – democracies have to fund elections – but there are two kinds of corruption. Political scientist Mancur Olson believed roving bandits (rent-seeking leaders who don't care about the future) were more toxic than stationary thieves (profit-sharing corruption is still wrong but at least builds a more prosperous future). His elegant distinction is highly relevant to India and may even partly explain the economic divergence between north and south India. It certainly explains a lot about J&K.

Dynastic politics continued in the National Conference with Farooq's son Omar joining the party and even forming the government in 2009. After the abrogation of Article 370, the National Conference, along with the Peoples Democratic Party (PDP), Communist Party of India (Marxist) [CPI(M)], and the Jammu and Kashmir Awami National Conference led by Khalida joined hands to form the Gupkar Alliance to campaign for autonomy for the state. Farooq's political position was weakening, and he created a diversion with the many stormy state assembly sessions where autonomy and terrorism were prime discussion points.

Farooq has always had big shoes to fill. His love of life, positivity, and energy are endearing, but governing J&K requires strategic sense, moderation, discipline and persistence. I have not worked with his son Omar, but my colleagues tell me he is a decent, if not decisive, man. However, the broader issue of dynastic succession across many political parties in India is the lack of grassroot connections, judgement or maturity among dynasts that only comes with years of experience. The expansion of dynasties in politics arises from money power, brand strength, networks, feudal mindsets, etc., but it is dangerous for democracy. I hope the massive expansion of meritocracy in many areas of Indian society — cricket, cinema and business – is soon replicated in politics. The courage in your heart, sweat on your brow and strength of your back should matter more than your surname. The younger Abdullahs have lived off, but significantly diminished, the legacy of Sheikh Abdullah.

G.M. Shah

Ghulam Mohammad Shah (Gul Shah or G.M. Shah) was an ambitious man who had nursed chief ministerial ambitions for decades. This wish came true only briefly and required family treachery: he was married to Sheikh Abdullah's daughter Khalida and had to depose her brother. Born in 1920 in Srinagar, Shah participated in the struggle against the maharaja and was founding general secretary of the Plebiscite Front in 1955. As an administrator, his tenure saw divisive politics and communal violence. Governor B.K. Nehru felt he was 'corrupt, lecherous, arrogant, ill-mannered, unpleasant, pro-Pakistan, anti-India and anti-Hindu', and suggested he physically assaulted his wife to get what he wanted from Sheikh Sahib. He was not bright; I remember locals thinking of him as dim and corrupt, and saying of him, 'Akli kani kangri khoar' (To have the empty wicker basket of a kangri instead of brains) and 'Yeth ye'd tcchhu-ne zanh ti iwaan yad.' (This stomach never gets filled up.)

Shah believed he was senior, more experienced and worked harder than Farooq. He thought Sheikh Sahib should have designated him as successor. But he undermined his case early on. He was once caught in a traffic jam outside the secretariat in 1981 where the traffic sub-inspector Gulam Mohammad Wadoo tried to clear the way for Shah's stuck motorcade. Shah came out of the car and slapped him repeatedly in public. It snowballed into a police strike because Wadoo threw his cap down and said he would resign from public service. The incident received press coverage, since many journalists were around, and since Shah was already unpopular with the general public, a crowd of 5,000 people soon gathered. Sheikh Abdullah was forced to promise action against Shah and urged the policemen and the public to end their protest. He called the protest leaders to his office and turned his cheek towards them, asking them to vent their anger on him. Out of respect for their leader, the police officers dispersed, but the incident left the Sheikh embarrassed and cost him political capital. He had the people's pulse, and this incident reinforced they would not accept Shah.

The last straw was when Shah openly rebelled against Sheikh Abdullah's decision to nominate D.D. Thakur to take the salute at Independence Day celebrations on 15 August 1982. He believed it was his right to take the salute and sulked by leaving for a secluded irrigation rest house in Saler, ahead of Ganderbal, with another minister, G.N. Kochek. Sheikh Sahib insisted they should attend the ceremony and told me to have police officers hand-deliver a wireless message asking them to come back. But they ignored the message. The parade went well, and as per tradition, a large reception was held on 16 August at the Emporium Park. We ensured that Sheikh Sahib attended in a wheelchair and towards the end of the event, it was announced the chief minister had recommended to Governor Nehru that two ministers be dropped from his cabinet, and Farooq would be inducted as a minister the next day at 11 a.m.

Shah got his revenge against Farooq in 1984 when he broke the National Conference by forming National Conference Khalida (his wife's name) with thirteen legislators. With the outside support of the Congress Party, he formed a government that lasted twenty months. Shah dealt with severe challenges to law and order in the months of the darbar move with the repeated imposition of curfew and extensive deployment of central forces to enforce it. The public began calling him 'Gul Curfew'. However, despite Farooq Abdullah's National Conference's bitter undercurrent of political challenges, Shah's government initially had the support of the governor, the central government and the Congress Party, which had installed it.

Srinagar remained disturbed through Shah's government, especially in the areas in the centre of the city, where Farooq Abdullah received the support of Mirwaiz Maulvi Farooq and his Awami Action Committee supporters under the 'Double Farooq Alliance' in the 1983 elections. A large National Conference faction and Sheikh's wife, Begum Akbar Jehan, still supported Farooq. This meant the new Shah government was considered a puppet, an unfair encroachment on Kashmir's polity and divisive to Kashmir's consolidated legacy of Sheikh Abdullah.

The Congress Party eventually withdrew support as the law-and-order situation collapsed, especially in Anantnag and other neighbouring districts where Hindu temples were being attacked and desecrated. Although Shah was supposed to be a firm administrator, the lack of broad political support during his tenure ended up seeing decisions that were peevish, reckless and vindictive towards the bureaucrats who had served with Sheikh Sahib and Farooq (including evicting me from my house). Governor Jagmohan, who had eagerly dismissed Farooq, now enthusiastically dismissed Shah. Rajiv Gandhi and Farooq Abdullah welcomed the fall of the Shah government, which eventually led to their accord and brought Farooq back to power.

His last years were sad and spooky, and locals say every Friday, he would visit his family graveyard to inspect his chosen and already dug grave. Sometimes, he would descend into the pit and lay down on the soft soil and order changes for more elbow or headroom so the fit would be perfect when he was finally laid to rest.

Mufti Mohammad Sayeed

Mufti Mohammad Sayeed was born in Bijbehara and entered politics in the 1950s. He changed his party, role and position many times. He used a religious title for political prominence but was not a popular leader in Kashmir's conservative circles and society. His opponents targeted him by calling him 'Wily Fox' (because he changed parties many times) and 'Mufti Whiskey', as he enjoyed imported scotch and Dunhill cigarettes. He was elected to the J&K assembly from Bijbehara in 1962, was made minister in the state government and later made his Lok Sabha debut from Uttar Pradesh.

When Sadiq Sahib took over as chief minister in 1964, Mufti became his senior minister. He benefited from Sadiq's undermining the National Conference and renaming it the Pradesh Congress Committee. Nehru didn't want to undermine the National Conference and in 1963 warned against establishing a branch of the Congress in Kashmir, but Mufti benefited from this platform and became the president of the state Congress unit in 1972 for a decade.

He was closely involved in later backroom manoeuvres that undermined the Sheikh–Indira accord. We were neighbours for decades in Tulsi Bagh, and although he went along with it, he never fully reconciled with Indira Gandhi's decision to bring back Sheikh Abdullah in 1975, working with dissenters to undermine him. I remember him hosting a wazwan for Prime Minister Indira Gandhi during the 1983 election campaign. His ambition was to become the state's chief minister and not the home minister (the role that destiny gave him first). He used this dinner to increase the already high levels of mistrust between Indira and Farooq and primarily invited party functionaries who supported his ideas like Makhan Lal Fotedar. He was appointed minister of tourism in the Rajiv Gandhi government. He was a prominent Congress leader in the state, but the party never formed a government under Sayeed's leadership.

In 1987, he quit the Congress after Gandhi's defeat in the Lok Sabha elections and joined Jan Morcha led by V.P. Singh to become the first Muslim home minister in the union cabinet. While he was home minister, tragedy struck as his third daughter Rubaiya was kidnapped by JKLF separatists, only to be released in exchange for five terrorists – Abdul Hamid Sheikh, Sher Khan, Javed Ahmed Zargar, Noor Kalwal, and Altaf Butt – publicly. At the time of the kidnapping, the relationship between the centre and state was complex as Sayeed was the union home minister in Delhi, and Farooq Abdullah was heading the government in the state. It was rare for two Muslim leaders belonging to Kashmir to hold full power at the state and centre, but there were no coordinated efforts to resolve the crisis. The terrorists viewed this kidnapping outcome as a significant success, triggering a ferocious increase in violence, assassinations, kidnappings and bombings. During his tenure as union home minister, Mufti's home state faced another tragedy – the exodus of Kashmiri Pandits.

Sayeed joined hands with the Congress again under P.V. Narasimha Rao's government, which he left in 1999. Along with his daughter Mehbooba Mufti, he formed the Jammu and Kashmir Peoples Democratic Party (PDP) in 1998, which became a strong competitor to the National Conference. Unfortunately for the state, just like the National Conference, the PDP's governance and birthing were also based on dynasty. The PDP formed governments in a coalition. In the 2002 assembly elections, even though the National Conference emerged as the single largest party, the PDP allied with the Congress and decided to share the chief ministership between Mufti and Ghulam Nabi Azad. The alliance lost the next election to National Conference, and Omar Abdullah took charge of the state. In the 2014 assembly elections, the PDP failed to get a majority again and allied with the BJP, which was a partnership born with contradictions. However, the two parties agreed on a common minimum programme to ensure the smooth functioning of their government. However, the fault lines were visible on several issues, including the revocation of Article 370.

With the death of Mufti in 2016, his daughter Mehbooba Mufti took charge but lost power because her soft stand on separatism meant she could not control the growing terrorism. She never forgot to visit the houses of terrorists killed by security forces, and her soft separatism infected her party. In the apple cradle of Shopian they say, 'Chhounth voutshit tshu chhounth rung rattaan.' (The apple gets its colour by seeing apples around it.)

Syed Ali Shah Geelani

Syed Ali Shah Geelani, the first patron of the Askari (militant) wing of the Jamaat-e-Islami, was a master of soft separatism. Born in Sopore, he worked as a government teacher before joining the

Jamaat in 1950, rising to be its chief (Ameer-i-Jamait), and was a three-time member of the J&K assembly (1972, 1977 and 1987). He was initiated into politics by Moulvi Mohammed Syed Masoodi, the general secretary of the National Conference, but unlike the ninety-year-old, bedridden Masoodi who was assassinated by the Hizb-ul-Mujahideen, they proclaimed Geelani as the Rehabar-i-Inqalab (Guide of the Revolution).

There were no surprises there; he believed 'our fate and future are linked with Pakistan', and often suggested that 'to say the role of the gun is over is to not only contradict reason and reality but speak of insanity and self-deception'. He also believed that 'the burning of Charar-e-Sharief shrine was part of the major plan of post-Partition, anti-Muslim India'. His only statement that made me smile was his call for public resistance against the J&K Police Special Operations Group that were 'ruthless instruments of counterinsurgency'.

Many politicians, including Omar Abdullah, have attributed the rise of militancy in the state to his role in politics. He was the president of the All Parties Hurriyat Conference, who later formed his own political party and was responsible for organizing many strikes and shutdowns in the Valley even though he spent many years under house arrest. Earlier, he would often visit me to get officials transferred from postings, and he remained an important escort for Pakistan's exported terrorism.

In 1988, Geelani, along with three other members of the Muslim United Front, used the deliberative privilege of the state assembly in Jammu to scream about alleged atrocities of the central paramilitary forces and the state government. I sent a note to Dr Farooq requesting him to ask Geelani to condemn terrorism, knowing full well he would not. Dr Farooq's challenge to Geelani was met with racy, rhetorical and provocative Urdu expressions, but Geelani refused to condemn violence and said the voice of the

Kashmiri people was being suppressed. Shortly after this assembly session, Geelani and his Muslim United Front legislators resigned in Kashmir.

Geelani had ensured he never had direct links with terrorists and was never caught by the J&K Police. However, I could sense his involvement during the kidnapping of Doordarshan director Farooq Nazki's brother-in-law in 1990, who was quickly released, much to the curiosity of everyone around. In 1992, Nazki had even received a call asking for his resignation as director in exchange for his brother-in-law's release. Later in 1993, Nazki, who was a friend, told me he reached out to Geelani – his old teacher – and camped at his house until he did something. Geelani eventually agreed and wrote a rukka (a small note) with the following text: 'Janeman, humara maqsad pura hua. Riha karen.' (Darling, our mission is complete. Release him.) This note reached Sopore through relay messengers, where the terrorists released the hostage unconditionally and safely.

During the 1996 elections, Geelani gave calls to boycott the elections and appealed to the public to refrain from participating. There was a police barricade outside his residence, but even with tight security, people found innovative ways, including wearing the traditional attire of the pheran and burkha, to enter the house. His brother, a teacher in a government school in the Botingoo village in Sopore, ignored these calls, continued taking on government poll duties, and paid the price for it with his life as the Hizb-ul-Mujahideen assassinated him. Geelani, however, refrained from condemning or acknowledging the incident.

It is ironical that while Geelani for many years refused to declare his nationality as Indian, he continued to draw a pension as a former MLA, making me remember the common idiom, 'Sau sau chuhe kha ke, billi haj ko chali.' (After eating hundreds of rats, a cat goes on a pilgrimage.)

Abdul Ghani Lone

Abdul Ghani Lone left the Congress to form the separatist People's Conference Party in 1977 and was dedicated to restoring 'internal autonomy' in the 'disputed territory'. But Lone had begun laying the foundations of separatism much earlier as education minister in the Mir Quasim government; he packed educational institutions, university and the judiciary with Jamaat cadres. He creditably won the Handwara assembly seat despite the momentum of Sheikh Abdullah's party. Born in Kupwara, Lone was one of the founding members of the All Parties Hurriyat Conference and was said to have come up with the idea of bringing various separatist organizations under one umbrella. As they say in Kashmiri, 'Hallen baanan, wuquir thaana heeven hevee samkhaan.' (Crooked utensils need crooked lids.)

On 21 May 2002, Lone was gunned down at Eidgah in Srinagar's old town by the Hizb-ul-Mujahideen at a memorial service to commemorate the twelfth anniversary of the assassination of Mirwaiz Moulvi Farooq. I am never baffled by Kashmir's ironies; the holy Eidgah never had any graves till terrorism began, but the mosque management caved and allowed terrorists to be buried there. Edigah now not only has the graves of both Mirwaiz Farooq but also his murderers. Many years later in 2017, on the Muslim holy night of Laylat al-Qadr, the Jama Masjid witnessed the senseless stripping, beating and lynching of police officer Mohammed Ayub Pandith. Islam does not preach such senseless violence, and I am sure khuda's keher will catch up with these terrorists who use holy places to murder in his name.

Mirwaiz Maulvi Farooq

Another player was Maulvi Farooq, the chairman of the All–Jammu and Kashmir Awami Action Committee. Through the years, depending on the political situation, they partnered with the Janata government in the 1977 election and later with the National Conference in 1983 to keep the Congress at bay in the state. He represented one side of the Valley's traditional political fault line of Shers vs. Bakras; The Shers were Sheikh Abdullah supporters who were anchored primarily around Hazratbal mosque and captured the imagination of most moderate Kashmiri Muslims, while the Bakras (named after their beards) were the mirwaiz's radical supporters around Jama Masjid Mosque in Nowhatta. Mirwaiz Moulvi Farooq said, 'More Muslim youth are seen in the mosques because the only place where they get some sort of relief or respect after being humiliated by Indian security forces [seen as Hindu troops] is in places of worship.' He recognized the absence of strong political leadership made the role of religious leaders more significant than expected. I met Mirwaiz Maulvi Farooq many times over the years and always sensed that he was as anti-Abdullah as he was pro-Pakistan.

Hizb-ul-Mujahideen terrorists assassinated Mirwaiz Farooq for meeting with George Fernandes. At this point, the Awami Action Committee also engaged in dynastic politics, with Mirwaiz Mohammed Umar Farooq taking over at the age of seventeen after his father was assassinated. Umar Farooq united twenty-three Kashmiri pro-freedom organizations into the All Parties Hurriyat Conference. He became president of the organization from 1993 to 1998 when he was replaced by Geelani. Farooq took forward his father's agenda.

Jammu's Politicians

The BJP had connections in the Valley but was politically stronger in Jammu than in Kashmir. It started as Praja Parishad and later turned into Jan Sangh, which is the foundation of the BJP. Syama Prasad Mookerjee, who was the founder of Jan Sangh, died in jail in Srinagar. 'Jahan hue balidan Mukherjee, woh Kashmir hamara hain'

(Where Mookerjee was martyred, that Kashmir belongs to us), was a slogan I grew up hearing in Kanpur. Mukherjee's Parliament speech in 1952 made it clear the separate flag and constitution for Kashmir were temporary and wrong, and they must go. Between Jammu and Kashmir, Jammu was a more substantial base for the Congress, and the National Conference had a hold on Kashmir for several decades. Congress had a strong set of leaders from Jammu who enjoyed positions in the cabinet but didn't make it to the chief minister's seat. One usually has to pick sides in politics, but I maintained good relationships with leaders from both the BJP and the Congress, and I saw a host of stalwarts from Jammu contributed to the politics of the state and the country.

Pandit Prem Nath Dogra, known as Sher-e-Duggar, was the president of the Bharatiya Jan Sangh in 1955. He was an MLA from Jammu city and was key to mobilizing people from Jammu towards an integrated Jammu and Kashmir. However, the party could not get a strong foothold across the state because of central leaders like Nehru and Indira, and equally strong state leaders like Sheikh Abdullah. They dominated the political and administrative scene in the 1977 elections when they won two Lok Sabha seats and reached a double figure in the assembly elections. Being a sportsman (a university-level footballer and hockey player), Pandit Prem Nath Dogra was the president of the Olympics association in Jammu. Since I had always participated in sports, he recommended my name to succeed him on the committee. I knew him early in my career when he was kind enough to welcome an outsider to Jammu. I had accompanied Chief Minister Sadiq to his residence in Kachi Chawni to pay our respects to the ailing octogenarian. As a popular leader, when he died in his eighties in 1971, his funeral was attended by thousands across party lines in Jammu.

Thakur Baldev Singh from Kathua district was a member of the Jan Sangh. His family had a defence background, but he returned to his home state. He was elected as the J&K Jan Sangh president in 1967 and as an independent member of the Lok Sabha from the Jammu–Rajouri–Poonch constituency in 1977. He believed that J&K should be a part of India and supported the abrogation of Article 370, and both issues led to him spending time in jail in 1949 and 1952 respectively.

Girdhari Lal Dogra, a Congress leader and former cabinet minister in the state, was related to Pandit Prem Nath Dogra (though they were poles apart in political ideology) and was the father-in-law of the late BJP leader Arun Jaitley. He was the most influential Congress leader in the state. Prime Minister Indira Gandhi made him speaker, and he was finance minister for more than twenty-five years in various J&K governments. Despite the power he wielded, he was humble and grounded; we often met in my office and elsewhere. Never having lost an election from the Hiranagar constituency, Dogra Sahib enjoyed support from the public and leaders across party lines. He was a Gandhian who always wore a white cap and changed land ownership rules in favour of the tiller.

Pandit Trilochan Dutt was a strong Congress leader in Jammu who had a following across religions and castes, especially among refugees in the Jammu and Poonch regions. He was a cabinet member under Sadiq and was known to put in long hours on the ground, keeping everyone working for him on their toes. He held his position with such regard that when the chief minister passed an order related to his ministry that he did not believe in, he resigned and did not take his resignation back even when Indira Gandhi intervened. Later, the government changed administrative rules to ensure the chief secretary informed the ministry when a relevant decision was taken. Dutt's career, like so many Indian politicians', was sabotaged by his son's interference in administrative affairs.

Pandit Mangat Ram Sharma was the deputy chief minister of J&K in the government led by Mufti Mohammad Sayeed during 2002–05 (a post brought back to J&K politics after 1948 when G.M.

Bakshi was appointed as deputy chief minister), the speaker of the J&K legislative assembly and a one-time Lok Sabha member from Jammu–Poonch (1996). His tenure eased the situation between coalition governments, which later became the trend in J&K. He was close to the Gandhi family but was known to be impartial regarding his role as the assembly speaker.

Choudhary Mohammed Aslam was the J&K president of the Congress for seventeen years, served as the education minister in the state cabinet and was the assembly speaker. He was the first Gujjar Muslim nominated to the Rajya Sabha and held his seat until 2008. From Surankote in Poonch district, he contested eight elections starting in 1966 from his home constituency and understood the relationship between the central and state governments. Choudhary Aslam had the foresight during the darbar move agitation to warn Farooq Abdullah about the consequences, but his wise counsel was dismissed lightly, citing political compulsions. He believed Farooq's demand for autonomy would remain unfulfilled.

Mian Bashir Ahmed was not only a politician but also a religious leader. His father and grandfather were religious personalities, and Mian Bashir was commonly known as 'Babaji'. Born in 1923, he was the most prominent Gujjar leader who maintained close relations with Sheikh Abdullah and Indira Gandhi, and contested elections four times from both National Conference and Congress. Mian Bashir played a crucial role in propagating peace, especially during troubled times like the 1965 and 1971 wars, where he rehabilitated people in the tribal belt and border areas. He was awarded a Padma Bhushan in 2008 for his contributions towards the tribal Gujjar, Bakarwal and other oppressed groups of society in J&K.

Conclusion

Journalist M.J. Akbar had once asked, though the Kashmir nose is long, is there no local politician who can look beyond it? Why does compromise always prevail over conviction? Why does greed always take precedence over investment? Why does illusion trap guardians of power so easily? Why is today's petty reward so much more important than the stability of the next ten years? Why is policy so often handcuffed to personal hatred?

There is one answer to his questions: local politicians have treated J&K like a jagir rather than an amaanat. A jagir is personal property you can do whatever you want with; the maharaja of Cooch Behar spent 50 per cent of the state treasury on Cartier items and Rolls Royces. Cooch Bihar is now among the poorest parts of India, unlike Baroda or Mysore, whose current prosperity has much to do with its leaders of long ago. But the idea of amaanat has no room for ownership; you care for something till you hand it to the next generation. A uniquely Kashmiri twist on amaanat was that you were obligated to hand it over in better condition than when you received it. Local politicians have long failed this test. The story they should have told was about the community they wanted to build with the shared ideals of justice that hold us together as citizens. It's a story that tells us we should be better than we are but their soft separatism story peddled envy, inequality and division.

Politics created extended periods of governance imbalances between regions. Post the Islamic conversions in the twelfth century, the rulers focused only on the Valley. The Dogra regime focused on Jammu at the expense of Kashmir. Of the many political divides in Abdullah's personality, like being a Muslim and nationalist leader, the one he failed to reconcile till his death – and cost the state deeply – was representing the people of the Kashmir Post the Islamicalley versus those of the entire state. A commission led by Mukherjee (1966), P.B. Gajendragadkar (1973) and S.M. Sikri (1981) dove into the issue of governance balance without much success because of political preferences, short-termism and self-interest.

Corruption in J&K has been high because of huge government spending, weak oversight and poor accountability. We humorously responded to Prime Minister Vajpayee asking for ideas in our annual closed-door conference of police chiefs to reduce corruption with lyrics from a song from the movie *Amar Prem:* 'Majdhaar mein naiyaa dole, to maajhi paar lagaye, Maajhi jo naav duboye, use kaun bachaye? (A boatsman can stabilize his boat in a storm, but nobody can save the boat if the boatsman is the one sinking the boat?) However, honesty and development are slowly becoming important election issues in Indian politics; I am hoping this trend is replicated in J&K.

State elections have not been the equivalent of what in Kashmiri is called 'Aenus munz punnin shakal haavin' (The mirror that shows the authentic self) because politicians have been myopic. Soon after the 1996 elections that returned Farooq to power, the police arranged a significant surrender of terrorists with arms on Gupkar Road. After the ceremony, he conveyed to me he did not want to attend any more terrorist surrenders. Terrorists had killed thousands of Kashmiri Muslims and brought the 75,000 Kashmiri Pandit families in the Valley down to 650; how could this not be a priority?

Pakistan and India, born at the same time, have very different democracies. Pakistan's queasy relationship with democracy – no prime minister has ever completed a full term – almost seems like a birth defect arising from their two-nation theory and their deep state embracing national poet Muhammad Iqbal's lament 'Jamhooriyat ek tarz-e-hukumat hain jis me logon ko gina jaata he, tola nahin.' (Democracy counts people instead of weighing them.) Pervez Musharraf, then concurrently president, prime minister and army chief of Pakistan, quoted Iqbal and condescendingly decided to 'weigh' citizens by making college degrees compulsory for all election candidates.

In India, an estimated 3 million people win an election, and 22 million people stand for an election. India's democracy is far from perfect, but it has begun delivering outcomes in nation building, social justice and poverty reduction. A new breed of politicians from J&K must emerge for J&K who do the same.

5

Pakistan in J&K: The Terror Factory

Had His Highness of Kashmir (Hari Singh) acceded to India by 14 August, Pakistan did not then exist and, therefore, could not have interfered.

– Viceroy Mountbatten

Yous kaensi hindi khaetri kubbar khanan, so scho panay taeth munz gatcham.
(The one who digs a grave for others falls into it himself.)

– Kashmiri proverb

The Kashmiri term for the gap between word and deed – quol-o-fel – is captured in a Pakistani president telling an Indian president in 1987, 'Hum Hindustan ke saath sirf aman chahte hain.' (Pakistan only wants peace with India.) The earthy Giani Zail Singh responded to Zia-ul-Haq with 'General Sahib, ek kudi do gal ni kar sakdi; aankh bhi maare te ghunghat vi kade.' (A girl can't wink and cover her face at the same time.)

The need to convert Indian Muslims into Pakistanis via what historian Eric Hobsbawm called the 'invention of tradition' was reflected in an amusingly titled book released in 1950, *Five Thousand Years of Pakistan: An Archaeological Outline*. But failures in the founding ideas of any country often get blamed on outsiders; India became an imaginary enemy for Pakistan, and Kashmir became the vessel for this hostility. The idea of Pakistan died at birth when most Muslims chose to stay back in India in 1947 and was buried with Bangladesh's birth in 1971. These birthing challenges combine with what Dr Farooq Abdullah insightfully calls the fitrat (primal instinct) of modern Pakistan – the three As of Allah, America and Army – to sabotage democracy and prevent a more normal sovereign Pakistani identity. Pakistan's army has become a powerful vested interest in an enduring rivalry with India; formal wars are mere interruptions of a non-stop Pakistani jihad in Kashmir since 1947 that accelerated in the 1980s and drew confidence from nuclear weapons.

Pakistan is a constant presence in every J&K Police officer's life because of the factory they have built to export terror. When I was the police chief of the Jammu district in 1971, we eagerly awaited the Indian Airlines flight hijacked from Srinagar, but it never returned because terrorists blew it up at the airport in Lahore. In 1972, we administered 145 square kilometres of Pakistani territory known as the 'Chicken's Neck, which is a narrow strip of Pakistani land that extends into India near Akhnoor, captured by the Indian Army till the Simla Agreement. In 1979, when I was the Anantnag police chief, General Zia's hanging of Bhutto in Pakistan sparked mob anger especially as it was claimed that India was responsible for the execution. In their outrage, they cut down every apple tree in the orchard of the Jamaat's former MLA Abdul Razak Bachru, in his village. In 1983, as Kashmir police chief, I witnessed the cricket match between West Indies and India with mobs cheering for Pakistan. In the early 1990s, I went to the bus stand in Batamaloo only to hear conductors call out 'Sopore, Kopore, Hopore' (Sopore, Kupwara, across the border). As police chief in 1993, the terrorists negotiating with us during the Hazratbal siege were taking orders from Pakistan, and the militants negotiating with me on the phone about kidnapped foreigners in 1995 were Pakistani. For example, the chance rescue of the American John Childs might not have happened because he was trying to hide from our helicopter, believing it was Pakistani. The most personally painful experience was Mast Gul being feted in Pakistan just after burning the sacred Charar-e-Sharief Ziarat.

Pakistan's obsession with J&K began before its birth; Mohammad Ali Jinnah visited Kashmir four times before Partition and spent three months in 1944 making speeches like 'I am a Muslim, and all my sympathies are for the Muslim cause. It's better to live in a hut in Pakistan with the sense of security than to live in a bungalow in India in a shadow of security.' But soon after the announcement of Partition in June 1947, Jinnah sensed Sheikh Abdullah would be a problem and began scheming with Kashmir Muslim Conference leaders to advocate for independence for the state so he could ease its accession to Pakistan later. The dislike was mutual; Abdullah suggested Jinnah was not a true Muslim, had little knowledge of the Quran, and a Muslim leader from Bombay could not decide the fate of the people of Kashmir.

In 1995, my comments on cross-border terrorism at an Interpol conference in Kathmandu were interrupted by the Pakistani delegate saying India should not blame internal rebellions on its innocent neighbours. His comment was particularly cheeky since Nepal was the preferred venue for coordination meetings between terrorists and the Pakistan Army's Inter-Services Intelligence (ISI). This dissonance between what Pakistan says and does began early; they signed a standstill agreement with the maharaja in August 1947 only to buy time to prepare for an attack seventy days later. This duplicity continued in the Simla Agreement and Benazir Bhutto, Musharraf, Sharif, Khan and their successors have diligently carried this dishonourable tradition forward.

The Garrison State

In 1937, American political scientist Harold Lasswell proposed the concept of a 'garrison state', where violence specialists would use or create threats to establish the supremacy of the military over the state and society. A Pakistani military officer echoes Lasswell in suggesting, 'Since there is no other institution to rival our military in organization and discipline, our image grows and reaches a point of predominance and power where we become an object of mass reverence.' Consistent with ancient Roman political advice, 'Panem et circenses' (give them 'bread and circuses', and they will never revolt), Pakistan's garrison state has used India, Kashmir and religion to justify and expand their power and loot the region.

India and Pakistan, born at the same time, have had radically different political and economic destinies because Pakistan's military has directly or indirectly ruled the country for most of its existence. Pakistan's early interests in Kashmir were a fire that would have burnt itself out if the army had not become the country's most powerful institution. Generals Iskander Mirza (1958), Ayub Khan (1958), Yahya Khan (1969), Zia-ul-Haq (1977), Pervez Musharraf (1999), Qamar Bajwa (2022) and currently Syed Munir Shah, do not agree with Samuel Huntington's views in his 1957 book *The Soldier and the State*, which suggests 'a highly professional officer corps stands ready to carry out the wishes of any civilian group which secures legitimate authority.' The army's wealth and power – skilfully investigated in *Military Inc.: Inside Pakistan's Military Economy* by Ayesha Siddiqa – is symbolized by the allotment of ninety acres of prime land to former army chief Raheel Sharif; civilian outrage received the terse military response 'every four-star general gets a similar allotment under a constitutional provision with the decision made by Army General Headquarters.' This disagreement is unsurprising. Later J&K chief justice Dr A.S. Anand told us his request in the 1990s to an Oxford University librarian for a copy of the Pakistani constitution got the smiling response of 'We don't keep magazines and periodicals.'

Paraphrasing Voltaire, many countries have an army, but Pakistan is the only army that has a country. There are many explanations for why democracy has been weak in Pakistan, including Islam, the Muslim League, their role in the Cold War, American support, etc. But the most important is the uneasiness of the elite with universal franchise. Their National Defence University suggests, 'Political structures based on democratic norms are best served by educated masses, which is lacking in Pakistan', and Lieutenant General Shuja Pasha of the ISI once said, 'Most Pakistanis lack awareness of [their] rights and duties as citizens and the electorate find it easy to be manipulated and identify themselves more with representatives from their ill-educated stock.' In 1958, Ayub Khan said he was forced to impose military rule 'with great reluctance . . . but the fullest conviction that there was no alternative except the disintegration and complete ruination of the country. History would never have forgiven us if the present chaotic conditions were allowed to continue.'

The influential role of the army in Pakistan has two fuels, suggests Professor Aqil Shah in *The Army and Democracy: Military Politics in Pakistan*. First, the perceived threat of imminent war from the militarily stronger India led Pakistan's founding political leaders to subordinate society's needs to the needs of the soldiers. As they diverted precious resources from economic development to warfare, civilian oversight institutions languished while the 'otherwise inchoate' ex-colonial military reconstituted, unified and modernized itself with American assistance. The second, consistent with Jinnah's belief that they had a mutilated, moth-eaten Pakistan, arose from attempts to 'build a viable nation by imposing a policy of national homogenisation on a multiethnic society, which quickly politicised ethnic and linguistic cleavages.' Rather than finding a constitutional power-sharing solution for peaceful accommodation, they retained a highly centralized system which suppressed regional demands for cultural recognition, political representation, and equitable resource distribution. The West Pakistani elites used coercion to integrate the Bengalis and other minor ethnic groups (Pashtuns, Sindhis and the Baluch) while denying the legitimacy of all claims for political representation, participation and regional autonomy based on subnational identities.

India finished writing its constitution by 1950, had its first federal election in 1952 and first reorganized states in 1956. Pakistan's challenge was nationalism without a nation; this bred centre–provincial conflict and delayed their first national constitution till the early 1970s. A military mindset that perceived democratic institutions as conditionally legitimate led to interventions that may have been responses to threats to military interests but were designated civilian failures. The military compensated for Pakistan's conventional weakness with material assistance and training to Islamist militants to fight India in Kashmir, and with nuclear weapons. Not only has this policy triggered a more offensive Indian military build-up, but militant groups like the Tehrike Taliban Pakistan have undermined the state's monopoly on coercion and terrorized Pakistani society, with over 50,000 civilian and security personnel being killed in terrorist attacks since 2004. Pakistan is stuck in a doom loop; patronage networks destroy productive ones, faith replaces realism and purists rout pragmatists.

The ISI's political role dates back to the Ayub Khan era (1958–69) when he placed his total reliance on ISI for internal as well as external intelligence and used it to keep a watch on political activities and evaluate public opinion. Unfortunately, the Pakistan army's incompetence – losing every war it has fought – is irrelevant because it purchases its wealth and power by exporting terror to India, which began with their support of Khalistani terrorists in the 1980s. The plan presented to Ayub in December 1964 was the first active involvement of the ISI in Kashmir. Over time, the ISI would come to be known as the 'Invisible Soldiers of Islam'.

Doubts about Pakistan's niyat (intentions of the mind) and zehniyat (intentions of the heart) creep in often but not enough. We underestimate that since 1988, Pakistan has exported 1 lakh handguns and AK-47s, misled and hurt about 1 lakh youth and 75,000 families in J&K. Only lately have Kashmiris begun to recognize Pakistan as 'ghaebhi boothi rami hoon' (a wolf in sheep's clothing).

Prime Ministers

Pakistan has had twenty-three prime ministers, while India, born at the same time, has had fourteen. While their prime ministers have not been as legitimate or powerful as India's, they all dealt with Kashmir. Before we dive into the formal and proxy wars fought by Pakistan, it is essential to acknowledge that politics has been unable to prevail over uniforms because politicians have often invited military meddling. Bhutto encouraged the army to invalidate the legitimate election win of Mujabir Rehman in 1971 and even supported the army's Operation Searchlight that killed many innocent citizens in East Pakistan. He was the brain behind Operation Gibraltar and Operation Grand Slam, which triggered the 1965 war and is known for his famous speech at the UN promising a '1000-year war' with India. He signed the Simla Agreement with Indira Gandhi and got 90,000 prisoners of war back. Perhaps we should have anticipated this treachery; a fifteen-year-old Bhutto had written to Mohammad Ali Jinnah in 1943 saying, 'Musalmans should realize Hindus can never and will never unite with us; they are the deadliest enemies of our Koran and our Prophet.' He was executed in 1979 by Islamist Zia-Ul-Haq for murder. His daughter started differently but soon fell in line about Kashmir. Benazir called Kashmir the shah rug (jugular vein) of Pakistan a few months before her assassination by terrorists with Islamic or military links (probably both). The Sharifs, Imran

Khan and all other prime ministers have never dared to break the linked dysfunctions of exporting terrorism, army primacy and mass poverty.

Formal Wars

Pakistan's presence in Kashmir since Partition through formal wars and proxy wars (terrorism) is impossible to unpack. When acting commander-in-chief General Douglas Gracey refused Jinnah's order in 1947 to send troops to J&K, the Quaid-e-Azam encouraged a military solution. This duplicity set the tone for decades; the formal wars in 1947, 1965, 1971 and 1999 are merely interludes in Pakistan's non-stop Kashmir jihad.

1947

The dissonance between Pakistan's word and deed was fully displayed in 1947 when Pakistan signed a standstill agreement with the maharaja. Bhopal's nawab Hamidullah Khan even said if Pakistan ever tried to invade Kashmir, he would be the first to take up arms and fight Pakistan. But Pakistan's jihad in Kashmir began seventy days later when the Mujahideen – mostly Afridis from Khyber and Mehsuds from Waziristan, along with members of the Pakistan army disguised in civilian clothes – entered J&K in October 1947. In the preceding month, Pakistan had already imposed an economic blockade by cutting off the supplies of kerosene, oil, petrol and food. The architects of this invasion were Colonel Akbar Khan and Sardar Ibrahim Khan (later the first president of Pakistan-Occupied Kashmir). The colonel met with Prime Minister Liaquat Khan in Lahore soon after writing the plan 'Armed Revolt inside Kashmir' and received intelligence reports from Pakistan's army intelligence chief, Brigadier Sher Khan. The divisional commissioner of Rawalpindi Khwaja Abdur Rahim collected funds and weapons, the North West Frontier province chief minister Abdul Qayoom Khan recruited jihadis, and the Pir of Manki Sharif promised jihadis houris (virgins in paradise). The army supplied food, uniforms, radios, arms and ammunition. The marauders raped, looted and pillaged without mercy; they shot many nuns at the Saint Joseph's Franciscan convent and crucified National Conference leader Maqbool Salim Sherwani in Baramulla. The Indian army's response that pushed the invaders back and forced a ceasefire in December 1948 was brave, challenging and magnificent. The marauders had reached close to Srinagar when the Indian Army, along with Sheikh Abdullah's supporters, drove them back up to the ceasefire line and cleared the Valley.

Colonel Akbar Khan's plan to take Kashmir forcefully ended with the ceasefire of 1948, but he continued to write papers like 'What Next in Kashmir?', 'Keep the Pot Boiling in Abdullah's Kashmir', and 'How to Solve the Kashmir Problem'. His book *Raiders in Kashmir* makes the role of the Pakistani military clear and lays out the details of a plan presented to President Iskandar Mirza with an expenditure of Rs 60 lakh to induct multiple batches of 500 militants each into Kashmir after the ceasefire. He rose to the rank of major general before being arrested in the Rawalpindi conspiracy coup in 1951 and served five years in jail. In typical Pakistani style, his 1970s rehabilitation included participating in planning the genocide in East Pakistan, quelling the Baloch uprising and his appointment as chief national security adviser to Zulfikar Ali Bhutto. Soldiers in Pakistan face almost no accountability for their failures, but in this case, there seem to have been no consequences for treason. Perhaps this is why Pakistan loses all the wars they fight.

1965

The plan that started the second war between India and Pakistan in 1965 was kicked off in 1958 when Field Marshal Ayub Khan set up a Kashmir cell chaired by Foreign Secretary Aziz Ahmad with the defence secretary, the director of the Intelligence Bureau, the chief of general staff of the Pakistani army, and the director of military operations. Aziz told the cell that Ayub had ordered them to prepare two options: one to encourage sabotage activities across the ceasefire line and the second to provide all-out support for the induction of guerrillas into Kashmir. Some of Ayub's advisers felt the plan was too risky but Foreign Minister Zulfikar Ali Bhutto urged him to act boldly and courageously since the Kashmiri people would rise in support.

During the war, I was particularly saddened by the Pakistani air force shooting down the civilian plane carrying Gujarat chief minister Balwant Rai Mehta, a freedom fighter who had spent seven years in British prisons. He had delivered an inspiring lecture during our training at the Police Academy in Mount Abu, reminding us of the expectations of independent India from civil servants, particularly those in uniform. At the time, little did I know that our night patrols in response to cross-border infiltration fears were merely a preview of J&K.

On 8 August 1965, Operation Gibraltar began with ten groups – Khalid, Tariq, Qasim, Salahuddin, Ghaznavvi, Khilji, Murtaza, Babar, Nusrat and Sikandar – of 500 men each. By 16 August, the Indian army had overcome nine groups except Ghaznavi. This disaster led Ayub to launch Operation Grand Slam on 31 August, tasking the Pakistani military with capturing Akhnoor near Jammu. On 6 September, India crossed the international border from Punjab towards Lahore, and in the next seventeen days, India's victory was complete. During the last dark days of Operation Grand Slam, Ayub handed command to Major General Yahya Khan to salvage the situation. Yahya Khan failed, but this did not stop him from removing Ayub in 1969 and overseeing the bloody East Pakistan genocide that fuelled the creation of Bangladesh.

1971

The reactions of a captured Pakistani soldier summarized why we would win the war. The BSF had captured Asian sprint champion Abdul Khaliq and detained him at the battalion headquarters in RS Pura. As a sports enthusiast, I went to meet Khaliq, who couldn't stop cursing and abusing his battalion commandant, who had abandoned him at Suchetgarh without reinforcements of ammunition or soldiers.

The 1971 war began in East Pakistan and didn't have anything to do with Kashmir, but it raised significant questions about Pakistan for people in the Valley. This war's roots were West Pakistan's unwillingness to accommodate Bengali linguistic, political and cultural aspirations. But it was sparked by the refusal to accept Mujibur Rehman as prime minister of Pakistan despite his legitimate electoral victory. The Pakistan army's defeat in 1971 shattered many myths about Pakistan's military. But General Tikka Khan's Operation Searchlight, which brutally unleashed the Pakistani army on its 'own' people in East Pakistan, caused the most damage. Archer Blood, then US consul general in Dhaka, sent a dissent note, now popularly known as the Blood Telegram. He recounted the state-sponsored violence and said, 'Our government has failed to denounce the suppression of democracy. Our government has failed to denounce atrocities. Our government has failed to take forceful measures to protect its citizens while simultaneously bending backwards to appease the West Pakistan-dominated government and lessen any deservedly negative international public relations impact against them.' After the 1971 war, the two tools of Pakistan's Kashmir strategy became ISI and Islam.

Sialkot borders Jammu's borders in the west and Pakistan-occupied (Bhinber) in the northwest. Jammu city is within driving range of Pakistani infantry, firing range of Pakistani big guns and bombing range of Pakistan's air force. We expected the repeated physical and strategic targeting of Jammu, given the experiences of the mass infiltration in the sectors of Poonch-Rajouri and Chhamb-Jourian during the 1965 war. The preparation of the Indian defence forces, BSF, civil administration, Home Guards and police in J&K for the expected war began early, and the Pakistani air force bombing on 3 December 1971 came as no surprise.

We began preparing for the war with a new Jammu police control room, Home Guards and civil defence control room at the central parade grounds complex. It became the fulcrum of civil–army coordination, and joint briefings/drills/rehearsals with local leaders and citizens prevented panic and rumour-mongering. The police control room hosted a briefing by the general commanding officer (GOC) of the 26th Division of the Indian Army (the primary army formation deployed for the defence of Jammu), Major General Z.C. Bakshi, to brief teachers, civil servants, civilians and police officers about the war preparations. The general surprised everyone by acknowledging that in a war zone, fears about loss of life and property given the range of Pakistani guns and air force were understandable but assured this would not happen because mutual deterrence kept each other's air force and armies from targeting civilian areas.

The detailed briefing by this seasoned and confident officer with local connections – in life, often the messenger is more important than the message – with maps of the Jammu and Pakistani sides reassured everyone. A civilian officer worriedly asked him about the sensitive border area about 15 kilometres away at the Kana-Chak, jutting into India and referred to in Pakistan military maps as the Dagger Area. Major General Bakshi delightfully assured him the Indian Army considered this area a 'Chicken's Neck' rather than a dagger and promised this neck would be wrung. He fulfilled this promise, and when asked about Indian losses after the war, he replied that the only causality in capturing the adjacent 145 square kilometres of 'Chicken's Neck' area was a sprained muscle that one of the officers had suffered.

A casual evening playing badminton at the office-cum-residential complex of A.K. Chaudhary, the assistant director of the Intelligence Bureau in Jammu, was transformed with a message from the control room that war had begun. Our lives were changed too over the next fourteen days, with each day stretching to eighteen hours of work. The primary concern during this period was the defence of the vital, six-decade-old bridge that served as the only link between Jammu and Srinagar, as well as the only connection between the old city of Jammu on the north side and the Jammu airfield at Satwari on the south. Despite multiple low-flying sorties by the Pakistani air force aimed at destroying this crucial bridge, all their attempts failed.

This resilience bolstered a widespread religious and mythological belief among the people of Jammu in the protective powers of the revered Goddess Mahakali from the Bahu Fort temple. Vina and Manish were visiting the Devi and took cover during a Pakistani air raid; our driver insisted it was thanks to the Devi that pilots were unable to locate the bridge despite seeing the river, and the bombs landed in the riverbed some 50 metres from the structure. The only direct hit was a 1,000-pound bomb dropped on the Jammu airport runway, which, fortunately, landed on the runway's flanks, causing no significant disruption to the airfield's limited operations. Unlike 1965, when a third of Jammu's population migrated to neighbouring states, this time the preparation and confidence meant that migration was minimal.

The only sector where the Indian Army conceded ground for strategic reasons after the start of the war was in the Chhamb police station jurisdiction, across the River Munawar-Tawi, on the southern side. Chhamb has a tumultuous history, with the area changing hands between the two countries every few years and finally being given to Pakistan post the Simla Agreement. Pakistan aimed to use this vantage point for big artillery guns to target the army brigade headquarters at Jourian in the Akhnoor sector that also linked Rajouri and Poonch. With this intense fighting in this area, large civilian populations exited, and we had to visit these areas often.

The capture of the 'Chicken's Neck' and 3,000 square kilometres of Pakistani territory by the Indian army was exciting but after the war ended, the Jammu district police were responsible for its administration. The fertile area, shaped like a triangle, covering 145 square kilometres, is divided by the creeks of the Chenab River and lies along the international border with Pakistan, extending up to the Marala Headworks. Many Indian civilians from the Kanachak and Akhnoor areas eagerly and excitedly started visiting this sensitive security zone full of many landmines and booby traps. Further, about two dozen Pakistani civilians were captured and handed over to us. We set up three civil police posts, backed by the CRPF platoons, to control civilian access. From our captured forward positions, Pakistan's Marala Headworks was within firing range, and if we targeted it, large parts of the Punjab province would be inundated. Similar to the needless return of Haji Pir Pass under the Tashkent Agreement, I wish we had not returned the 'Chicken's Neck' to Pakistan under the Simla Agreement. Our soldiers captured these small but strategic land areas with immense sacrifices, and India should have retained both for leverage and friction against the Pakistan military.

1999

Preparations by the Pakistan army for the 1999 Kargil War had started months in advance. In May 1998, India conducted a second nuclear test, which made Pakistan respond within a few weeks. It is unclear if Prime Minister Sharif was involved, but Pervez

Musharraf, the army chief at the time, was in charge and began operations in Kargil. In May 1999, when the Indian forces noticed the occupation of some of their vacant military posts, they initiated Operation Vijay, which involved 2 lakh Indian troops. Over the next two-and-a-half months, the Indian army recaptured our territory. The duplicity of Pakistani state while capturing Kargil Heights, an area acceded to India by the Simla Agreement, was evident when Vajpayee was undertaking his friendship bus journey to Lahore. As they say in Kashmiri, 'Hatti khash tah haungani mithi.' (A kiss on the chin but an axe on the throat.)

Pakistan catalysed the needless death of thousands of soldiers on both sides outside a formal war. I was CRPF chief during Operation Vijay; this paramilitary organization has a deep history in Ladakh, with the ten members dying in 1959 defending Indian territory in a Chinese incursion preceding the 1962 war. But this time, the ITBP and BSF led as the CRPF had shifted entirely from border security to internal security.

Zia-ul Haq reviewed an army plan to take over Kargil in the 1980s, but he hesitated because of predictions it would convert to a full-scale war and chose to sponsor terrorism instead. By 1999, Musharraf believed Pakistan's nuclear tests made conventional war unlikely and a lightly masked army operation cutting off Ladakh from India would stop before total war, due to international pressure. The human ability – particularly the Pakistani army's – to delude themselves never surprises me. But a military that has lost all four formal wars it has fought against India and treats its soldiers like firewood should be confined to barracks and shrunk.

A Proxy War

The army in Pakistan needs to keep alive the bogey of India's wish to reverse Partition. It believes it ensures the survival and stability of Pakistan through conventional forces, nuclear deterrence and asymmetric jihadi warfare. Its first attempt at a proxy war came in the 1947 attack on Kashmir; it lost but established cross-border Islamic terrorism as an integral foreign policy tool.

Praveen Swami's excellent book *India, Pakistan and the Secret Jihad: The Covert War in Kashmir, 1947–2004* frames their jihad as having five distinct phases: the first began with Partition and continued until the early 1960s, led by small covert operations to put political pressure on J&K administered by India; the second phase in the 1960s engaged master cells and their subsidiary underground organizations to create mass rebellion conditions in the state; the third phase post the elimination of master cells manifested as al-Fatah until the 1971 war helped create a corpus of trained personnel; the fourth phase manifested itself from the third mainly as the National Liberation Front through the 1970s; and finally, the fifth phase began in the 1980s built on lessons learnt from the CIA in Afghanistan. Each phase of jihad impacted J&K's politics, policy and economy differently.

After Pakistan's defeat in the 1965 war, the ISI became the backbone of their Kashmir strategy. Al-Fatah was the first organization in the Valley to receive weapons, training and sanctuary. But more compelling was the National Liberation Front, which had a military wing headed by Major Amanullah, a political branch headed by Amanullah Khan, a financial wing led by Mir Abdul Qayyum and a rabta (coordination) wing headed by Maqbool Bhat. Contrary to popular belief, Maqbool Bhat was never the co-founder of the JKLF as he was already in jail.

Amanullah Khan became the chairman of the organization and expanded it by setting up units throughout Europe, the Middle East and the US. He appointed Hashim Qureshi as the convener of the unit in Pakistan-Occupied Kashmir in 1982. The other prominent members of this unit were Dr Farooq Haider, Raja Muzaffar and Sardar Rashid Hasrat. Soon, however, the Plebiscite Front distanced itself from JKLF as Amanullah Khan formed it without the consent of their leadership. It is crucial to clear the confusion between the JKLF (Jammu Kashmir Liberation Front) and JKNLF (Jammu Kashmir National Liberation Front), and the two Amanullah Khans. The Amanullah who founded the JKLF in England became more famous. The other was a retired Pakistan army major who, along with Maqbool Bhat, launched JKNLF (Jammu Kashmir National Liberation Front) in 1966 in Pakistan-Occupied Kashmir.

Major Amanullah and Maqbool Bhat crossed the ceasefire line in June 1966 and set up underground cells in Srinagar, Sopore, Baramulla, Bandipora and Anantnag. But in September 1966, Indian intelligence learnt of Maqbool Bhat's presence, and he kidnapped a police inspector, Amar Chand, whom he killed before surrendering. In August 1968, the courts sentenced Maqbool Bhat and Mir Ahmed to death for killing Inspector Amar Chand. But in December 1968, Maqbool Bhat, Mir Ahmed and Chaudhary Yasin, another fighter imprisoned in Srinagar Central jail, broke out of prison and reached Pakistan-Occupied Kashmir after a sixteen-day trek through snow-covered mountains. Treated as heroes in Pakistan, the National Liberation Front (NLF) soon sponsored a series of bomb explosions in Jammu and Poonch at railway stations, ammunition depots, transit camps, etc. Their fame helped them recruit Hashim Qureshi from Srinagar to become the head of the NLF in Kashmir. Qureshi later hijacked an Indian Airlines flight from Srinagar with a toy pistol and hand grenade. Events are unclear, but after celebrating the hijacking, the Pakistan government distanced itself from Qureshi, and he spent nine years in jail there.

In 1970, Amanullah Khan published the paper 'Free Kashmir', advocating for 'a united, neutral, secular and federal republic' of Jammu and Kashmir encompassing the entire territory of the erstwhile princely state. His suggestion that the republic remain strictly neutral between India and Pakistan got him arrested by the Pakistani government and jailed in Gilgit (his birthplace). Maqbool Bhat returned to Kashmir in 1976 to recruit, but with the ISI holding back money, he soon ran short of funds and tried to rob a bank, ended up shooting the bank manager, and was arrested and eventually sentenced to death. In 1979, the NLF morphed into JKLF.

In 1980, the most funded and extended Pakistani interference in Kashmir began at a meeting between General Zia-ul-Haq and Jamaat-e-Islami's Maulana Abdul Bari in Rawalpindi. The Jamaat was founded in 1941 by Maulana Syed Maududi, whose 1920s book *Jihad in Islam* advocated an Islamic state and detailed the vanguard revolutionary tactics that became terrorism. Their student wing had fought alongside the army in Bangladesh, and its official publication, the *Tarjamanul Quran,* supported the Iran Revolution. General Zia soon arranged a series of meetings for Bari with ISI officials who urged him to travel to Kashmir legally on a visa to visit family. General Zia-ul-Haq combined the army with Islam by unleashing the ISI, allowing the Tablighi Jamaat to operate freely within the military, requiring comments on an officer's religious sincerity in evaluation forms, and embracing the Ghazwa-e-Hind (conquest of India) propagated by the Jamaat. In 1987, Pakistan's army raised terrorist funding, set a Nizam-e-Mustafa (Islamic order) deadline, and introduced Afghan Mujahideen leader Gulbuddin Hekmatyar to Hizb-ul-Mujahideen co-founder Mohammad Abdullah Bangroo. Since then, the export of terror has continued unabated.

Between 1980 and 1983, Maulana Bari built influence with the wary founding emir of the Jamaat in Kashmir, Maulana Sa'adud Din. The Jamaat in Pakistan and India operated independently, and Din was sceptical because of the 1965 and 1971 defeats. Bari admonished him, 'If you think the Pakistan army will come and fight in Srinagar to liberate you, it is impossible.' He suggested a new strategy was necessary with him 'doing the fighting and ISI paying the bill and providing other support'. The response was positive, and the next few meetings between Kashmiri leaders and the ISI were held in Saudi Arabia under the cover of Haj to avoid being noticed by Indian intelligence.

In September 1982, the ISI hosted a meeting where Kashmiri leaders travelled to Pakistan via Saudi Arabia with the cooperation of Saudi intelligence – neither Saudi nor Pakistani officials stamped their passports – for 'direct negotiations and final planning'. Maulana Din was out of the loop about this meeting, but General Zia clinched his support in May 1983 when Din travelled as a state guest to Pakistan. The architect of the 1947 attack on Kashmir, Colonel Khan, described the tribal and proxy tactics they adopted as 'a hawk that flies high in the sky, out of danger, until he sees the prey, swoops down on it for one mighty strike and then does not wait around, but flies off to some far-off quiet place to enjoy what he has got.'

After 1983, Zia's instructions from the top ensured that the ISI financially and physically supported a variety of organizations and leaders in Kashmir like the Jamiat-e-Talaba, Mahaz-e-Azadi (Sheikh Tajamul Islam), Islamic Students League and Ansarul Islam (Hilal Ahmad Mir). The JKLF's relative inactivity ended when it kidnapped Indian diplomat Ravindra Mhatre in Birmingham in February 1984 and killed him when the Indian government did not meet their demands to release Maqbool Bhat and pay 1 million pounds in ransom. India's parliament had reinstated the death penalty after years in 1976 and retaliated by hanging Maqbool Bhat a week later. I remember Chief Minister Farooq Abdullah being summoned to Delhi by Indira Gandhi and being given advance notice so he could ensure law and order. In history's uncanny ability to repeat itself, India again ended an eight-year moratorium on the death penalty in 2012 when it hanged Ajmal Kasab, a Pakistani national convicted for his role in the 2008 attacks on Mumbai.

The ISI had ignored the JKLF after its agreement with Kashmir's Jamaat-e-Islami, but Mhatre's murder ensured its director general Akhtar Ahmad Khan sought them out. The ISI and JKLF overcame their differences after Amanullah Khan was deported from the UK and reached Karachi in 1986. They were unnatural partners because for the JKLF, azaadi meant an independent J&K, while for the ISI, azaadi meant accession to Pakistan. Amanullah Khan told the ISI, 'As a Muslim, I believe in the kalima [the proclamation that there is no god but Allah, and Mohammad is his Prophet], but as a Kashmiri, I believe in sovereign Kashmir.' But their partnership kicked off with two bomb blasts at the telegraph office and Srinagar Club on 31 July 1988, despite the delay from the original Martyrs Day start promised to General Zia.

In one of history's great ironies, the architect of modern Kashmiri terrorism, General Zia, died in a plane crash within a few weeks of these blasts. After his death, the ISI worried about their support of the JKLF as the group was nationalist, secular and had no particular allegiance to Pakistan. It began diversifying its support to include groups like the Zia Tigers, Al Hamza and Ansarul Islam. In July 1989, a meeting in Haiderpura in Budgam unified various bodies. The Ansarul Islam was renamed Hizb-ul-Mujahideen (the party of holy warriors), with the first leader being Hilal Ahmed Mir. At the same time, Masood Sarfaraz of the Jamaat-e-Islami formed another group with the same name. Syed Ali Shah Geelani brought the Jamaat-e-Islami and Hizbul together at a meeting in Kathmandu. But the souring with the JKLF continued as the ISI cut off funding in 1990 and facilitated a discussion with Afghan leader Gulbuddin Hekmatyar, who advised Hizbul's Salahuddin to eliminate all his rivals. It should be noted that Gulbuddin's camps were also providing training to the United Liberation Front of Assam (ULFA) militants at the time. In the Hizb-ul-Mujahideen, the ISI found a pro-Pakistan Islamic group that they could back which offered an alternative to the pro-independence JKLF.

Pakistan has always been what Kashmiris call 'aabi tal shraakh' (a sword underwater); Amanullah Khan suggested that Hizbul assassinated 5,000 JKLF members. Hizbul even ordered the killing of soft supporters like Mirwaiz Farooq, Qazi Nissar, Dr Guru and Ghulam Qadir Wani when their support faltered or paused. In retaliation, the JKLF kidnapped Syed Ali Shah Geelani in the winter of 1993, but his release three days later did not create lasting peace, and the Hizbul soon began targeting JKLF members again. National Conference workers had an early dislike for Jamaat rukuns (workers) and emirs (leaders), and angry mobs targeted the Jamaat-e-Islami by burning the bridge connecting the pro-Jamaat Arwani village to the national highway and cutting down the apple orchard of Jamaat ex-MLA Abdul Razak Bachru when Zia hanged Bhutto. The hanging surprised us as we expected Bhutto to be acquitted. Jamaat supporters distributed sheeri on the announcement of the death sentence, and moves like these did not help their case in the later years. Pakistan's use-and-throw mentality doesn't value loyalty; an ISI proxy murdered Bachru after dragging him in handcuffs through the market in Kulgam in 1996. I remember a local correspondent telling me Pakistan would fight for Kashmir till the last Kashmiri as they were not interested in the people but the land.

Pakistan's declining geopolitical importance after the end of the Cold War was replaced by its partnership with America after the 9/11 attacks (though many Americans now recognize the duplicity of this partnership). Though Pakistan supposedly had small nuclear weapons by the 1980s, the actual test in the late 1990s raised its confidence in using terrorists as a tool of foreign policy. They believe nuclear weapons will prevent India from escalating the consequences of terrorism into a conventional war and force the international community to raise the pressure on India. As academic Sumit Ganguly suggests, 'In the Cold War, NATO used nuclear weapons to compensate for their perceived conventional inferiority, but the US was not interested in using military force to upset the status quo in Europe. In South Asia, however, nuclear weapons have helped Pakistan compensate for the conventional superiority of India, and Pakistan has been interested in using military force to upset the status quo.'

Conclusion

Ghalib warned us the most dangerous lies are the lies we tell ourselves: 'Dhool chehre pe thi, mein aiyna saaf karta raha.' (The dirt was on my face, but I kept cleaning the mirror.) Pakistan is democratically, economically and geopolitically in trouble. The only solution is that Pakistan's awaam (public) reigns in its army, and the government accepts the Simla Agreement and delivers prosperity for its people through economic development. Unfortunately, the identity and power of Pakistan's military comes from suggesting its problems arise from India, other religions and democracy rather than from itself.

Pakistan has no legitimate claims on Kashmir any more than it has on Hyderabad or Bhopal. But the Valley became the vessel for Pakistan's anger at itself after the idea of Pakistan faltered at birth when most Muslims stayed back in India, and it was buried with the creation of Bangladesh. The lens through which the world viewed the vanguard revolutionary tactics of terrorism has changed, with major countries across the globe, including the US, facing now the brunt of terrorism.

Christine Fair in her book *Fighting to the End* suggests the Pakistani military constructs security competition with India in ideological and civilizational terms and insists 'Hindu India' is an existential threat to Pakistan. The army's insistence on the two-nation theory is the fundamental basis of its claims to Kashmir; to forsake the two-nation theory and Kashmir is to accept the permanence of Pakistan's incompleteness.

Stephen Cohen has described Pakistan as the only country that negotiates with a gun to its head; this is exhausting for India and the world, but Pakistan's garrison state is ignorant and incompetent. Yet, it endures because of its partnership with religion. Its support of the US's covert war against Russia using Mujahideen and the ISI was a necessary calculation; General Zia responded to Maulana Bari's hesitations with, 'But how can the Americans stop us from waging jihad in Kashmir when they are waging jihad in Afghanistan?' He also suggested he would massively overinflate the costs of war in Afghanistan – reimbursed by the CIA and Saudis – and divert the surplus to Kashmir.

The US is now rethinking its relationship with Pakistan; Pakistan has been an ally but not a friend, while India has been a friend but may not have been an ally. Unfortunately, China is moving closer and describes its relationship with Pakistan as 'higher than the Himalayas, deeper than the Arabian Sea, sweeter than honey, and stronger than steel'. I hope Pakistan sees China's real agenda and the changing geopolitical situation before they become a vassal state.

The first stage of recovery for an alcoholic in Alcoholics Anonymous is acceptance; Pakistan's military refuses to accept that the global view on terrorism, fundamental Islam and China has shifted against Pakistan. However, there is no doubt that the people of Pakistan deserve better.

6

Terrorism: Origins and Evolution

We will deliver Kashmir to Pakistan in two instalments. The first, freedom from India. Then, annexation by Pakistan.

– Pakistan-Occupied Kashmir president 'Mujahid-e-Awwal' Qayyum Khan to General Zia-ul-Haq in 1985

Bayee sindhi athi seet punnini kaangri wokhool karoon
(Stirring your kangri [firepot] with somebody else's hands)

– Kashmiri proverb

Pakistan's most successful and shameful export – terrorism – is built on the totalitarian mindset of radical Islam that recognizes no limits to power and freely uses words like kafir and jihad. The *Tafseer Surah at-Taubah,* published in English and Urdu by Pakistan-based terrorist Hafiz Saeed, suggests, 'Remember, parents who impede the wish of their youngsters to join jihad sin. Jihad is incumbent on all Muslims.'

I disagree with my friend Sati Sahni, who suggests 'J&K's troubles were neither rebellion nor revolt, neither militancy nor terrorism, neither protest nor alienation, neither insurgency nor insurrection, neither a rising nor an uprising but an unprecedented mix of all of them.' I also disagree with the fatalism inherent to the 'born to be hanged' theory of the circumstances of J&K's birthing in India that condemned it to future terrorism, however delayed. My disagreement dances dangerously close to taking sides in this debate (which is above my pay grade) about whether history is a social science (the circumstances school of Tolstoy) or literature (the great leaders school of Carlyle). There would be no terrorism in J&K without Pakistan's terror factory. There were hardly any gunshot deaths in J&K before 1987, and many Kashmiris participated in the aaba (the Bakri Eid goat sacrifice) by touching the knives to their foreheads before turning their backs to the actual slaughter by a professional kasab (butcher). The two-nation theory that gave birth to Pakistan did not prevent them from prohibiting Ahmadiyaa Muslims from practising, preaching and joining politics, while on the Indian side Abdul Salam Deva was MLA from Anantnag for a decade.

Pakistan did not give up on terrorism in the decades following its first action in 1947 but what caused the phase-by-phase transformation of terrorism in J&K starting in 1988? There are two schools of thought: history and the 1980s. The history school has many suspects. Was it Kashmir defying the two-nation theory? The dithering maharaja taking Ramchandra Kak's poor advice in 1947? Major General Akbar Khan of the Pakistani army and his marauders attacking India and crucifying Maqbool Salim Sherwani in Baramulla in 1947? Arresting Prime Minister Sheikh Abdullah in 1953? Returning the Haji Pir Pass to Pakistan in the Tashkent Agreement of 1965? Supporting the Mukti Bahini in 1971? Returning land and prisoners without freezing borders in the Simla Agreement of 1972? The 1980s school also has its own roll of suspects. Was it General Zia partnering with Jamaat-e-Islami Emir Mian Tufail – his mamu (maternal uncle) – to Islamicize his military? America abandoning its Afghan Mujahideen armed with jihad and weapons? Rajiv Gandhi's adamant call to Farooq Abdullah that the Muslim United Front candidates should not win their elections? Or entitled J&K politicians to weaponize soft separatism via Article 370, religion and Pakistan, to grow their power, wealth and dynasty?

The reasons don't really matter; Pakistan's terror factory pumped in money, arms and personnel to anybody. But the ISI soon realized early terrorist groups like the JKLF wanted independence more than integration with Pakistan. This divergence spooked the ISI and caused it to revitalize its relationship with Jamaat-e-Islami cadres, especially its Askari wing, the Hizb-ul-Mujahideen. Ghulam Qadir Bhat and Khursheed Ahmad Wani's paper 'Rise of Jamaat-e-Islami Jammu and Kashmir: Resurgence of Muslim Political Identity in Kashmir' says that their ideology was similar to other Islamist movements that 'considered armed struggle in the state as religious' and the increasing influence as a reaction to the 'threat to the Muslim identity'. The movement of young people and weapons across borders was problematic, but the rugged terrain through mountains and rivers made sealing it hard, if not impossible. I remember a meeting with the Chinar Corps commander, General D.S.R. Sahani, in 1988, carrying a message from Farooq Abdullah after the police seized their first Kalashnikov, requesting the army's diligence and efforts in stopping infiltration. His response was understanding but highlighted resource constraints. The situation on our border has now changed; the army has plugged many routes, and infiltration is much lower.

Pakistan has hosted radical Islamic terrorists like Osama Bin Laden for decades. Three terrorists – Maulana Masood, Omar Sheikh and Mushtaq Ahmed Zargar – painfully released at Kandahar after the well-planned Christmas Day hijacking of an Indian Airlines flight from Kathmandu to New Delhi by five armed men from Harkat-ul-Mujahideen soon made Pakistan their home. Omar Sheikh went on to finance one of the hijackers of the 9/11 attacks and was involved in the deadly attack on the J&K assembly and Indian parliament. There was a short leap from the terror in Kashmir to everywhere else; radical Islam knows no boundaries and rotates enemies.

The absence of repercussions for attacks on the J&K assembly and Indian parliament emboldened the Lashkar-e-Taiba to orchestrate the 2008 Mumbai attacks, killing 175 people. If there was ever direct proof of Pakistan's terror factory, this was it. We should have responded but didn't. India's terrorism playbook would only change after a new government suffered the pain of Uri and Pulwama and decided Pakistan's terror factory would not back down unless India changed their calculations. Terrorism in J&K did not appear overnight, so let's understand how it evolved.

1947–87

In 1947, despite signing a standstill agreement with the maharaja of Kashmir, Pakistan's first act of terrorism was to send a militia to invade Kashmir. This invasion – fronted by militia but fully backed and provisioned by the army – backfired and ensured the princely state of J&K became a part of India. I often heard stories of how Brigadier Rajinder Singh Jamwal of the J&K state forces, Major Somnath Sharma of the Indian army and National Conference workers like Maqbool Sherwani fought Kashmir's first terrorists. Pakistan lost their first gamble – and every one since – but did not give up and kept things on a slow burn till 1988.

In his autobiography, JKLF chairman Amanullah Khan mentions many pro-Pakistan groups in the northwestern part of Kashmir and in the region's educational institutions. I had heard some of these sympathizers planted a bomb at the Palladium Cinema in Lal Chowk in June 1957, but there was no impact. In 1965, Pakistan tried again; they trained 1.5 lakh Razakar to infiltrate Kashmir and prepare the ground for an uprising, but this escalated to a full-scale war.

One of the first incidents of terrorism involved Maqbool Bhat, a student leader from Kashmir who made his way to Pakistan and formed the Jammu Kashmir National Liberation Front (JKNLF) in 1965. The group recruited young men and trained them to use explosives and small arms and crossed back into J&K in 1966. Major Amanullah (not Khan) and Maqbool Bhat returned to Kashmir, accompanied by youths including Kala Khan and Aurangzeb alias Tariq from Gilgit. Maqbool was arrested for the murder of Criminal Investigation Department (CID) inspector Amar Chand and was given the death sentence. However, he escaped from Srinagar Central Jail in 1968. He was later hanged in Tihar jail many years later for murdering Chand when India reinstated the death penalty. JKNLF members successfully hijacked an Indian Airlines Fokker Friendship plane from Srinagar in January 1971, diverted it to Lahore and blew it up on the tarmac. This hijacking inspired the formation of the Al-Fateh group by some youngsters, but most of them were arrested. In 1974, the Lok Sabha was told ninety-six Pakistani spies had been arrested in the last two years.

The first act of international terrorism by the JKLF took place in 1984 with the kidnapping of Ravindra Hareshwar Mhatre, a forty-eight-year-old Indian diplomat based in Birmingham in the UK. They sent a letter to the Reuters office in London claiming responsibility and demanding 1 million pounds along with the release of Maqbool Bhat and seven Kashmiris arrested during the one-day cricket match in Srinagar against the West Indies. The Indian government refused to negotiate, and the JKLF murdered Mhatre three days later, with the terrorists abandoning his body on a farm in Birmingham. Mhatre died for his country on 11 February 1984.

Across the globe, terrorists hijacked more than 200 planes between 1967 and 1972, one of which was in Kashmir. A second hijack from Nepal, unfortunately, diverted the plane to Afghanistan and forced the release of Maulana Masood Azhar and other terrorists. Plane hijackings are mass kidnappings, but hijacking planes fell out of fashion with terrorists after those first five years because of low negotiating leverage arising from the complexities of controlling and feeding large numbers of hostages, the imperative of aircraft refuelling, few chances to change strategy and no escape routes. By the 1990s, terrorists across the world had realized kidnapping influential individuals or people close to them created high negotiating leverage, continuous press coverage, many chances to change strategy and good odds of escape.

When I returned from my three-year posting at the Indian embassy in Washington in 1977, the state had stopped inducting new All India Service officers and actively discriminated against existing ones. I received a nondescript posting as the commandant of the 5th battalion of the J&K Armed Police. I was considering an opportunity to join the Information Bureau in New Delhi when I received a summons to reach Chief Minister Sheikh Abdullah's office immediately. I thought the meeting was about my central deputation, but Sheikh Sahib had posted me as district police chief of Anantnag and wanted me to join immediately. He had removed M.A. Beg, his deputy CM, and wanted me to reach Beg's hometown within a few hours to handle the fallout (most politicians recognize the power of a non-local when needed). Omar Jan, a state administrative officer related to Abdullah, was also sent with me as the new district magistrate, and this was most likely to keep an eye on me.

Anantnag, also called Islamabad locally, was the largest of the three districts in the Valley and had always been a problematic mixture of political, separatist and muscle-power leaders. The town was the district headquarters and the second-most populated city in the Kashmir region after Srinagar. It had already produced many political stalwarts including Mirza Afzal Beg, Shamas Deen (ex-prime minister of J&K for ninety days), the Kochak brothers and also other names like Mir Qasim, Mufti Mohammad Sayeed, M.L. Fotedar, P.L. Handu, etc., from mufasil (rural) towns. It was also the home of separatist leaders like Shabir Shah and had the widest politico-religious set-up of the Jamaat-e-Islami. Though Beg's supporters had disrupted law and order in Srinagar, we did not allow any disturbances in Anantnag.

Our 1979 arrest of Shabir Shah in Anantnag for rowdyism and his group's links with Pakistan was probably my earliest encounter with a terrorist. He had been first arrested in the late 1960s, but they had established themselves in the area and the local administration was apprehensive about conducting raids or arresting the group. We conducted night patrols in the area, especially around Shah and his associates' houses. Within two weeks, we had enough intelligence to arrest them in pending cases. Any notions of Shabir not being a criminal are at best ignorance and at worst fraud. An unanticipated upside of my posting in Anantnag was the allocation of two probationers, Farooq Ahmad and M.A. Shah. Farooq Ahmad was in the special branch of the CID when I was the police chief and provided excellent intelligence support. Women don't accompany baraats to Kashmiri weddings – or at least they didn't in 1980 – but my wife Vina insisted on attending Farooq's.

The curious relationship between Kashmir and Pakistan was symbolized by the violence after Zulfikar Bhutto's hanging in 1979. Bhutto's long murder trial had been closely but silently engaging the attention of the divided Kashmir society through the BBC, the Valley's most credible news source, in its various stages, from lower courts to the Supreme Court to the final clemency petition. They believed that General Zia-ul-Haq would ultimately grant Bhutto political clemency because of his political popularity. But the confirmation of Bhutto's hanging on 4 April 1979 by the BBC led to massive riots. Before the mob began targeting Jamaat-e-Islami followers, rumours that the Indian state was behind Bhutto's hanging meant they came to burn my house, and my family had to be evacuated by Major Rekhi to the Anantnag army cantonment. Strange are the ways of Kashmir where India being behind the hanging of a Pakistani prime minister was a believable event.

Mobs damaged government offices while police stations tried to control the crowds. However, we could not meet their requests for additional forces. Kashmir had never witnessed such violent attacks by Muslims on Muslims, including attacking police stations with sticks and stones, burning houses and attacking government property. Followers of Sheikh – the Jamaat had always been political rivals of the National Conference, but the intensity and anger increased after they formally stood for elections in 1972 – were blamed for the violence. The district magistrate and I decided to personally deal with the dangerous situation of the abandoned Qazigund Police Station after an attack by a large mob from neighbouring areas like Kulgam, Dooru, etc. Since the mob ignored our repeated warnings and firing in the air, we ordered firing three rounds into the crowd; a mob leader died, and two others received bullet injuries on their legs. Thankfully, policemen rarely have to make choices that hurt civilians. We soon set up a control room at the police lines premises in Khannabal – next to the district wireless headquarters unit – to guide deployments and organized two large, consolidated convoys as quick response teams. Our repeated requests for reinforcements to Srinagar remained unfulfilled till the central government airlifted two battalions of the CRPF to Kashmir and allocated one to Anantnag. We distributed these reinforcements quickly to police stations and then created a loudspeaker-fitted convoy of vehicles announcing and enforcing curfew.

From all this violence, only one good thing emerged. Before this, the police had no detailed records of Jamaat-e-Islami followers. The tragic violence provided us with a crowdsourced database of their identity across police stations in Kulgam, Shopian, Pulwama, Tral, Awantipora and Pampore. Most Jamaat-e-Islami victims had run away during the violent incidents which had involved burning and destroying properties. After tempers cooled down, many returned to their homes and lodged individual cases against some identified mob leaders in the mobs. Although the Kashmiri Pandits remained unharmed in these riots, they met me to express apprehensions about their safety when communal mobs took charge. I didn't know it then, but their intuition was correct. These incidents were a bad omen for the Pandits over the next few decades.

1987–1993

It's hard to date a movement like terrorism, but a rough approximation is the two midnight explosions on 31 July 1988 outside the Srinagar Club and telegraph office. No lives were lost, but the bombs did extensive damage to the two buildings and created a vast and deep crevasse on the road. The police reached quickly, but the scene did not reveal much, so the CID took over the investigations.

As CID chief, I deputed Mirza Hamid Iqbal, a seasoned officer who headed counter-intelligence for the department, to investigate. Iqbal had risen through the ranks with solid investigation credentials, and his father had served as a senior police inspector in the maharaja's regime in the 1940s. His family had connections on both sides of the border, with Jinnah visiting Kashmir in the pre-Independence era to successfully defend a case for Iqbal's father.

Hamid Iqbal's preliminary report suggested local Kashmiris could not have undertaken the explosion without outside help. I briefed Dr Farooq Abdullah; we suspected the technology and training came from Pakistan and conducted a detailed investigation after registering a case in the special police station under the counter-intelligence wing of the CID. We provided Iqbal's team with extra personnel, transport and finances to investigate further.

A breakthrough came in the third week of September 1988 when this team arrested a young science graduate, Manzoor-ul-Islam, in a remote village in the border district of Kupwara. We recovered a Kalashnikov rifle – our first – hidden inside Manzoor's mother's kitchen, and the interrogation revealed that he'd undertaken a six-week trip to Pakistan-Occupied Kashmir for training. The book *What Terrorists Want: Understanding the Enemy, Containing the Threat* by Louise Richardson suggests that three Rs inspire terrorists: revenge for real or perceived wrongs, renown that might give meaning to terrorists' lives and the desire to provoke a reaction from enemies, thus energizing their allies. Kashmir has a fourth: religion. Some combination of these four Rs combined with money to lure many young people into crossing the border and getting weapons training. Their first target was the assassination of police and intelligence officers. Terrorism competes with the state, and the Pakistani deep state had learnt demoralizing and eliminating the enforcers of law and order was high leverage.

The first terrorist assassination of a police officer was Inspector Amar Chand in the late 1960s, but in this wave, it was probably Station House Officer (SHO) Said-Ullah Lone on 1 December 1989 in his own jurisdiction. Over the next year, they also killed four Intelligence Bureau officials: Tej Krishen Razdan, R.P. Singh, Moti Lal Bhan and Kishen Gopal Chauhan. My friend Ashok Bhan, then Anantnag district police chief, was soon shot in the stomach outside his office and saved only by the brave actions of his Muslim driver and personal security officer, who drove him for two hours in the back of a jeep to the army cantonment hospital in Srinagar. Eyewitnesses later recalled the bullets came from the neighbouring but empty court complex and bus stand; the terrorists had shielded the public with advance intimation. The CID gave advance input on a proposed attack on Kashmir Zone police chief A.M. Watali's house, but political and police leaders were still in denial. Thankfully, the attack failed, and Watali was unharmed. Our specific input from the intelligence department meant that I was appointed to chair a committee to investigate the incident. My report detailed the long view of cross-border support and also listed the locals trained and arms supplied. The physical report was flung across the table in a meeting by then J&K police chief Ghulam Jhelani Pandit as 'jhoot' (lies). Later, shockingly, he woke me up in the middle of the night to ask me to visit Watali's house in Rajbagh to take stock of the situation.

But the same message soon came from other sources. Dr Farooq mentioned that his political opponent friend Mir Mustafa, the MLA from the Chadoora constituency, had recently described a curious early morning visit to his house a few days ago from Raja Muzaffar, provincial chief of the JKLF in Pakistan-Occupied Kashmir. Mustafa asked Farooq how such free movement was possible. I wondered what Mustafa was trying to convey since we knew he was sympathetic to the JKLF, and thought that perhaps Mustafa was trying to move away from terrorism. But Pakistan's partnership is a one-way street: terrorists kidnapped him in March 1990, and the police found Mustafa's body two days later near Batmaloo. The politics of soft separatism had deep terrorist connectivity, and Syed Ali Shah Geelani's son-in-law, nicknamed Funtoos, was one of the first leaders trained in the 'armed revolution' to establish Nizam-e-Mustafa in Kashmir.

A police force does not have the training or mindset to handle terrorism. Since terrorists had targeted many officers and their families for kidnappings, militancy had made the police force into passive spectators. There were also suspicions of some of them working with terrorists. While every police officer in J&K would soon be acquainted with the Kalashnikov rifle, when we recovered the first one, we had to go through a small arms dictionary to identify the particular weapon. The Kalashnikov was the preferred weapon of terrorists worldwide because it was practically weatherproof, required little maintenance and was deadly if not accurate. The title of Mikhail Kalashnikov's autobiography *The Gun that Changed the World* is hardly hyperbole. But, as anybody involved in fighting terrorists can attest, it hardly changed the world for the better.

In a meeting with Chief Minister Farooq Abdullah and the counter-intelligence officers, including S.P. Hamid Iqbal, we pointed out the traditional pheran and kangri used to keep people warm was now being used by terrorists to carry weapons. The Dukhtaran-e-Millat (Daughters of the Islamist Nation), Asiya

Andrabi and their ilk used it effectively in downtown and other neighbouring areas of Srinagar. Abdullah then directed his chief secretary to hold a meeting with all the state and central security forces since this could not be a matter for the police alone.

Terrorists inspired by radical Islam are often encouraged to target non-believers. Kashmir was mostly Hindu until around 1200 CE, when the Sufis arrived from Iran and converted the Valley to Islam. Early assassinations and interrogations suggested a strategy of targeting high-profile Kashmiri Pandits to create panic. Kashmiri Muslim and Pandit fissures had long existed but were mostly about economic and educational opportunities, as Sheikh Sahib's submission to the Glancy Commission in 1932 suggested, 'The successful Muslim student rots and vegetates on a meagre salary while the misbehaved Pandit returns home a qualified hand, thanks to his Hindu patrons.' There had also been tensions in 1967 when Parmeshwari Handoo, a sales representative at the government-run Apna Bazar in Srinagar, married her Muslim co-worker Ghulam Rasool Kanth. Eight days earlier, the Kashmiri Pandit woman had converted to Islam and taken a new name, Parveen Akhtar. The love marriage set off a storm in the state, with her mother registering a case of kidnapping, Jan Sangh leader Pandit Prem Nath Dogra condemning the police and the national president of the Jan Sangh Balraj Madok holding public meetings. The police intervened, but nothing came of it because both the conversion and marriage were voluntary.

It is unfair to suggest what happened with Kashmiri Pandits in the Valley in the late 1980s was long coming or due; it was ethnic cleansing. The debate about the number of Pandit deaths being low is not helpful; a UN commission defined ethnic cleansing as '. . . a purposeful policy designed by one ethnic or religious group to remove by violent and terror-inspiring means the civilian population of another ethnic or religious group from certain geographic areas.' The first Pandit assassination was probably of Justice Neelkanth

Ganjoo, and terrorists killed him near Srinagar High Court for sentencing Maqbool Bhat to death. This list soon grew to include the mild-mannered and well-liked forty-five-year-old director of Doordarshan in Srinagar, Lassa Kaul, who had continuously received threats from the JKLF for pro-Indian reporting. Other assassinations included Jan Sangh/RSS member Tikka Lal Taploo, businessmen like Puneet Sahni and Vrinder Suri, and intelligence officers like Tej Krishan Razdan, R.M.P Singh, Kishan Kumar Chauhan and Moti Lal Bhan. Most Intelligence Bureau officers before terrorism escalated were Kashmiri Pandits, and this lack of diversity was a problem. It has since been fixed.

The exodus of Kashmiri Pandits from the Valley began after Pakistan ordered the targeting of Kashmiri Pandit teachers and poets in Srinagar and Anantnag. Islamic terrorism, a political vacuum and the lack of a forceful state response created an atmosphere of fear or dehshat in the Valley. Posters appeared around Pandit houses, tin roofs were banged all night and calls for their murder were made from mosques. The Kashmiri Pandits had lived with Muslim neighbours in peace for a long time, but Pakistan's strategy of division using the JKLF, religion and militancy created a mass movement. The administration was banking on central forces, but with last-minute deployment, a considerable language barrier appeared among the troops. Pakistan saw this exodus as an opportunity to 'liberate' Kashmir, and the closure of liquor stores and cinema halls added to the feeling of fear. The ISI also increased their terrorist inflow into the large and mountainous Doda, Rajouri and Poonch districts in the Jammu division to selectively kill Hindus at night in far-flung villages where there was yet no protection or deployment of security forces. Like the Pandit exodus, these early cells were mandated to create a communal divide and breed fear.

Farooq Ahmed Dar, popularly known as Bitta Karate, was one of the enforcers of this fear and headed the JKLF's charge to drive Pandits out of the Valley. He received the nickname for his karate skills and was known to ruthlessly murder people using his 9 mm pistol. Rumours, no doubt encouraged by him, suggested his aim was so flawless that he operated alone. His first murder, local businessman Satish Kumar Tickoo, started the madness in the Valley, and soon Pandits heard chants of 'Raliv, galiv ya chaliv' (convert, die or leave) everywhere. The Pandits had been forced out of their home for centuries, but I know many relate to the Kashmiri proverb 'Garah wandai gara sasah, garah nerahah ne zah.' (O Home, for you I sacrifice a thousand houses, I can never leave you behind.) I believe though that they will be back someday.

But these assassinations were not limited to Kashmiri Pandits or Hindus. Local Muslims suspected of being associated with or assisting the Indian state were also violently targeted. Most baffling was the terrorism which seemed the equivalent of an auto-immune disease: Pakistan constantly ordered the killing of its soft supporters like Mirwaiz, Abdul Ghani Lone, Mir Mustafa, Abdul Razak Bachroo, Afzal Guru and many others. Unlike terrorism in Punjab, in the early days, the ISI did not adopt mass but conducted targeted killings.

By October, the Pakistani conspiracy raised the stakes with a series of bombings across the state with a concentration in Srinagar. The attempt to blow up Budshah Bridge in central Srinagar failed, but a nearby house was fully gutted. The next day, a blast occurred behind the Khanyar Police Station in downtown Srinagar. Later that night, an explosion occurred in a bus parked near the exhibition ground and another near the Doordarshan office. The bombs weren't limited to Srinagar; many reports of bombings in bus stands came from neighbouring districts like Anantnag, and in the first eight months of 1989, there were 142 explosion incidents in the state.

It is impossible to identify the specific act of terrorism that catalysed violence, but the kidnapping of Rubaiya Sayeed would qualify as a contender. In 1989, a group of armed men from the JKLF stopped the minibus that Rubaiya, a twenty-three-year-old medical intern, was travelling in and pushed her into a Maruti car at gunpoint. Her father had been union home minister only for a week, and the kidnapping was a message to locals. The state machinery under Chief Minister Farooq Abdullah promised to swing into action, but the undercurrents of a bitter political rivalry didn't help. After five days of back-channel negotiations and the official release of five jailed militants, she was set free. In 2022, Sayeed identified Yasin Malik of the JKLF as one of the perpetrators. I was out of the loop with the negotiations and security operations as vigilance commissioner, but my sources confirmed the official number of militants released from jails was understated, with half a dozen additional people being released from police custody in Bijbehara and Anantnag. I can only imagine how difficult it must have been as a father and home minister for Mufti Sahib during this period. But this kidnapping is symbolic of how nobody – including India's home minister – had connected the dots about militancy and its ambitions. If they had connected the dots about terrorism and Pakistan's plans, would the daughter of India's home minister be travelling alone and in public transport?

In March 1990, I returned to mainstream police operations. Militancy had taken a quantum jump after Rubaiya Sayeed's kidnapping, and locals were also providing full support after the appointment of Jagmohan as governor and the sudden resignation of Dr Farooq Abdullah as chief minister. I didn't understand why Farooq resigned with the appointment of a new governor – he had the people's mandate after all. Why didn't he stay and fight? Of course, the environment had changed; people had become less guarded and more vocal about pro-freedom sentiments, and the kidnappings and murders of Hindus – mostly Kashmiri Pandits and Punjabi business people – were rampant.

On 6 April 1990, JKLF members kidnapped Kashmir University's vice-chancellor, Professor Mushir-ul-Haq and his Kashmiri secretary Abdul Ghani. Three days later, speaking in

Pakistan, the JKLF party chairman Amanullah Khan announced the two were dead, and the police later recovered their bodies on the outskirts of Srinagar. The general public criticized the murder of a respected Arabic scholar even – it was discovered he had been shot while offering prayers – though he was from outside the state (Jhansi). Twenty days after the kidnapping, the JKLF released a detailed press release on the series of events, showing the gaps between the two teams across the border. The militants had no allegiance; they killed outsiders and Kashmiris equally and quickly.

Kidnapping was a tool that was frequently used by militants to get information. In 1990, my batman, Ramesh Kumar, stepped out of our house, Rose Mount on Gupkar Road, to shop for vegetables and was kidnapped. Militants grilled him over the next four days to understand my routine, the layout of the house, and details of where everybody slept. The intervention of my police colleague Hafeez Akhtar was critical in convincing the kidnappers to release him. Kumar was one of the fortunate police personnel to have escaped, but they did break his front tooth during the interrogation.

In Srinagar, 21 May 1990 dawned as a dark day for local Kashmiri Muslims – terrorists shot religious leader and soft separatist Mirwaiz Farooq Shah. Separatist and communal movements had already killed many Kashmiri Pandits and Hindus settled in Srinagar, but the mirwaiz was always seen as pro-Pakistan. It is impossible to know for sure, but intelligence reports later suggested the highest levels of the ISI had ordered Mirwaiz's murder after he repeatedly met with George Fernandes, who was the face of peace talks.

Muslim religious politics had always dominated the scene in Kashmir but it had now morphed into fundamentalist Islamic ideas from Pakistan peddling violence and extremism. There were two crucial religio-political centres of power; one was Sheikh Abdullah's large religious following emanating through the pulpits of the moderately Islamic tenets, along with his simultaneous politically powerful National Conference legacy, with its historical headquarters at Mujahid Manzil on the edge of downtown Srinagar. The other was Mirwaiz Maulvi Farooq, with his somewhat fundamentalist-leaning Islamic religious powerbase at the historic Jamia Masjid in the Nowhatta area of downtown Srinagar. Mirwaiz Farooq Shah tilted towards Pakistan and was considered a supporter of the insurgency movement in Islam's name. There were many local Islamic terror groups in Kashmir under Pakistan's comprehensive control. The mirwaiz supposedly patronized a militant group called Tanzeem, named 'Al-Umar' (after his son Umar Farooq), and this now had Pakistan's open support and control. Therefore, no Kashmiri Muslims in Srinagar ever imagined the mirwaiz would himself be a victim or a target of the Pakistan-sponsored terrorism in his downtown stronghold.

In February 1991, Kashmiri leader Saifuddin Soz's daughter Nahida was kidnapped by the J&K Students Liberation Front (JKSLF). At the time, Soz was a prominent member of the National Conference and a member of the Lok Sabha. There was public pressure to have her released, but the kidnappers demanded the release of five militants. Security forces had recently rescued Srinagar deputy commissioner's son Ghulam Abbas from the same front without acceding to their demands. The police had got hold of the JKSLF chief Javed Shalla and had Abbas released in exchange. Applying the same strategy for Nahida, the security forces captured one of the kidnappers, Mukhtar, but did not hold him for long. With pressure from the public and other organizations like the Hizbul and the JKLF for kidnapping a woman, the JKLSF released Nahida after ten days. I heard rumours that Prime Minister Chandra Shekhar spoke to Nawaz Sharif in Pakistan to push for Nahida's release. If this is true, I understand the human instinct to protect Nahida, but this conversation reinforced the ISI's view of the upsides in financing and expanding terror.

Kidnappings were not limited to political families but also targeted media personnel and business people. In August 1991, K. Doraiswamy, the executive director of the Indian Oil Corporation, was held for fifty-five days by the Ikhwan-ul-Muslimeen and the following month, former J&K tourism minister Khemlata Wakhloo and her husband were kidnapped by militants and later rescued by security forces.

A few years later, in 1992, our daily security review meeting in the secretariat with General Zaki, the security adviser to the governor, was interrupted by news about a large crowd of 7,000 people carrying the four dead bodies of militant commanders killed by the BSF in an exchange of fire the previous night in Batmaloo. The procession was shouting religious and separatist slogans. It was determined that the bodies would be presented to the United Nations Military Observer Group in India and Pakistan (UNMOGIP) on Gupkar Road, passing through the main business area about two kilometres away through the main Maulana Azad Road. General Zaki ordered me to deal with the issue. We had no problems letting the procession reach the burial ground but felt the public march to the UN office by such a large and emotional crowd could create problems and had to be stopped. This was an open defiance of the law, even as BBC correspondents were calling the encounter a human rights violation. We were also curious since the BSF had told us they had only killed three militants the night before.

The procession soon swelled to 10,000 people , but disturbingly, it was accompanied by armed militants carrying automatic weapons, forcing civilians to join the procession. The slogan-shouting crowd carrying dead bodies soon attracted press attention. After consulting with my colleagues, the police chief of the Kashmir Range Hafiz Akhtar and Srinagar district police chief K. Rajendra, we immediately passed a message to the control room, ordering small paramilitary forces' contingents on the route of the procession to not engage the crowds since we had planned a surprise interception at the North Polo View Junction on Maulana Azad Road. Rajendra later became J&K police chief and was gravely injured when he bravely fought the Lashkar-e-Taiba terrorists preparing to storm the then chief minister Ghulam Nabi Azad's public rally in Srinagar.

On the day of the procession, along with the Kashmir Range police chief, Hafiz Akhtar, and our security entourages backed by one CRPF company, we blocked the front of this procession. At the same time, Rajendra and his team fired tear-gas shells and barricaded the rear exit points near the Badshah Chowk at Maisuma locality. My decision to let the procession proceed till we were ready drew on my experience in dealing with Kashmiri mobs, my understanding of the physical topography of the area and my determination to ensure that the J&K Police was at the forefront of enforcing order. In full view of the media and in the public glare, these complex operations in civil areas could not be dealt with by the demoralized junior police officers who feared significant casualties if the situation escalated to a violent clash and required police firing. So when we stopped the procession, explaining it violated the legally enforceable prohibitory orders in force in Srinagar, they were surprised by the aggressiveness of the J&K Police. They heard our loudspeaker calls to disperse, but their leaders broke the police cordon. Our response of a simultaneous lathi charge from the front and tear gas firing in the air saw people disappear into the neighbouring bylanes. The mob started throwing stones, and the militants accompanying the mob fired their AK-47s into the air. They escalated by throwing a Chinese hand grenade at us, but the fast, firm and sudden action of the police left the mob bewildered and dispersed. Army experts later defused the hand grenade; the turning of a primed explosive blind was a miraculous escape without which I would not be writing this book.

We finally resolved the mystery of the procession carrying four biers on their shoulders. Since I had ordered the arrest of the people forcefully carrying the dead bodies on their shoulders, many of them had run away, leaving the militants' biers on the ground. To our surprise, as we were collecting the biers, one of the bodies on a bier looked up, realized the mob had abandoned him and tried to run away. Of course, arresting a dead boy covered in a white shroud was a first for the J&K Police! The thousands of footwear pieces left by the panicked mob retreating was a sight to behold and a source of satisfaction.

The police took the biers into custody and later allowed them to be buried at night without any fanfare, after immediate family members gave us an undertaking that they would do a quiet religious burial. This open defiance of militants was made possible by the police pushback of the procession with no loss of lives on either side. This successful operation not only encouraged mocking comments against the terrorists and their cause but also received appreciation from many civilians who suffered unfair and illegal demands by terrorists for donations, and their presence at funerals. But funeral processions have continued to be venues for clashes between the public and security forces.

Small blasts continued, but in January 1992, terrorists audaciously made the police headquarters a target. A bomb was placed in the office by a compromised police constable in the office of J.N. Saksena, the DGP of J&K Police, during a meeting with senior security officers to discuss security arrangements for Republic Day. The blast caused severe injuries to Mr Saxena and my colleagues Veeranna Aivalli, Rajan Bakshi, M.K. Singh and Ashok Patel, and the central government airlifted the injured officers to AIIMS in Delhi. I was posted in Delhi on deputation to the Ministry of Railways, and upon hearing of the incident, I took special permission from the Railway Board Chief to help with the arrangements at the hospital. Over the next few months, Vina and

I regularly visited the hospital with soup, a long-time favourite of Veerana's. Later, many militant outfits, including the JKLF and the Hizb-ul-Mujahideen, claimed responsibility for the blast.

The funerals of terrorists killed by security forces always led to clashes as local supporters came out in large numbers. Some of this crowd was voluntary, some forced and some fearful. In April 1996, the United Nations Human Rights Commission described a mercenary as neither a hero nor a consummate romantic guerilla but a criminal whose acts are associated with violent crimes against life. It further encouraged states and society to become aware of, prevent, punish and morally condemn mercenary activities. The citizens of J&K have not always followed this advice at the funerals of murderers.

The BBC was a preferred media source for the Kashmiris since, like most Western media, it was biased towards Pakistan. However, when the BBC began asking questions about the cross-border dimensions and Pakistan's role in Kashmir, they received a warning through the kidnapping of their local correspondent, Zafar Miraj, from Aru near Pahalgam. Militants were already upset with a mountaineering institute being under construction at Aru as they felt this institute and tourists would interfere with their operations and free movement. Four days after Miraj's release, my announcement of the happy event was received with great relief. But Miraj came back a changed man. He had been an independent correspondent with the BBC who spoke his mind and reported on Pakistani militants' adverse activities in Kashmir. I have often been intrigued by talk of the Stockholm Syndrome, where the victim begins to identify with their captor and goals. This phenomenon is rarer than terrorists think, and an FBI study suggested it only occurs in 8 per cent of hostage victims. I am not sure whether it was out of fear or sympathy, but after his release, Zaffar refused to take up any investigative reporting against militants, did not help with our investigation and returned his reporting to the BBC's traditional bias against India. This kidnapping deprived Kashmir of an independent media voice, and the mountaineering camp shifted from Aru to Auli in Uttarakhand.

This period also saw a shift in Pakistani strategy. After the withdrawal of USSR combat forces from Afghanistan in 1989, Pakistan manoeuvred the battle-hardened militants to the Kashmir Valley to create a new theatre of conflict and terrorism. The prevalent political environment in the Valley and the anger amongst the people at the rigging of the 1987 legislative assembly elections provided an ideal ground for Pakistan to exploit the situation. Pakistan manipulated the disgruntled Kashmiri youth, favouring armed insurgency, to sponsor a 'proxy war' against India through an open Line of Control with the overt or covert involvement of the ISI and other international Islamic organizations. Having repeatedly failed to settle scores with India militarily, Pakistan camouflaged its tactics as a 'fight for Islam'. It organized a wobbly amorphous crusade into a coherent and organized movement by including the Kashmiri youth to challenge the Indian state in Kashmir.

There was a systematic shift from Pakistan's strategy to move from the JKLF to the Hizb-ul-Mujahideen, especially after the second Hazratbal operation, with the Hizb-ul-Mujahideen becoming more prominent as they needed to create new intelligence centres. This period saw the introduction of fresh militants from Pakistan and Afghanistan into J&K. Key arrests including those of Nasrullah Mansur Langaryal, chief of the former Harkat-ul Mujahideen in November 1993; Maulana Masood Azhar, general secretary of the Hizbul Mujahideen in February 1994; and Sajjad Afghani (Sajjad Sajid) took place in Srinagar during my time as chief.

The bait to take up the job of a terrorist was a combination of money and indoctrination. 'You will get houris if you are a martyr.' Some of the terrorists we caught told us they were given money for jobs like throwing grenades and bombs, and more money for bigger jobs. When we questioned Sajjad, who was an Afghani and whose son also operated in Kashmir, after his arrest, he revealed the money being offered and referred to the job as a posting. He told us, 'Hamari yahan pe tainati hui hain.' (We are just posted here.)

Attempts were made to get these terrorists, especially Masood Azhar, out of jail by kidnapping foreign tourists to capture global attention. Azhar, who hailed from Bahawalpur, became a prominent anchor in the growing militancy in the state after his release. The Balakot strike was undertaken in his heartland, and Bawalpur became a hotbed for militants where they would be provided safe passage. Though clashes between factions were rare, Azhar had travelled to Kashmir under an alias to ease tensions between two factions of the Harkat-ul-Ansar when he was arrested from Khanabal near Anantnag. On being arrested, he said, 'Soldiers of Islam have come from twelve countries to liberate Kashmir. We will answer your carbines with rocket launchers.'

I cover the period from 1993 to 1997, my police chief years, in the next chapter.

1997–2019

I left the state in 1997 but kept a close eye on the state, especially as the chief of the CRPF. Relations between Pakistan and India became strained after the nuclear tests and the Kargil War. But Pakistan's terror factory continued to deploy both human and financial capital and continued recruiting within Kashmiri society. In 2001, Jaish-e-Mohammed militants rammed into the gate of the Legislative Assembly building in Srinagar in a Tata Sumo loaded with explosives and killed thirty-eight people. One terrorist rammed the vehicle into the building while the other two scaled the wall and attacked people inside the building before security forces killed them. I heard Farooq Abdullah, the chief minister, was playing golf and continued his game until the security operation was over. However, later in the day, he compensated with his call for

Indian army action against militant training camps across the border. This attack, remaining unpunished, gave five Pakistani terrorists belonging to Lashkar-e-Taiba (LeT) and Jaish-e-Mohammed the confidence to attack the Parliament building in New Delhi a few months later, where eight policemen and one civilian died. The attack on Mumbai in 2008 should have received a strong response but did not. The terrorism situation somewhat worsened with the adoption of mass stone-throwing and killing of Burhan Wani. The situation continued to simmer till the abrogation of Article 370 in 2019 and has seen a marked improvement since.

Conclusion

The influential political scientist Samuel Huntington believed that in poor, resource-deficient societies lacking a small middle class and entrepreneurial skills, the men in uniform could become agents of economic and social development as well as political stability and institution building. Huntington compared Ayub Khan to the Greek lawgiver Solon, but this is not how things have worked out in Pakistan. Prolonged military participation in politics has meant that the military reflects the divisions, stresses and weaknesses of politics without its ability to listen, compromise and represent.

Countries like India who had suffered at the hands of terrorists and terror-exporting countries decades before Osama Bin Laden, find it patronizing when Western countries suggest terrorism began in 2001. Pakistan believed its importance in the Cold War and its nuclear weapons inoculated it against a conventional military response from India, but we have now exercised our right for cross-border strikes twice. I hope we don't have to use that tool again, but if we need to, we must. In J&K, we must dry the funding swamp, create monetary and criminal consequences for terror supporters and make heavy investments in sealing our borders.

Pakistan now deals with what Jacob Shapiro calls the terrorist's dilemma: as they delegate work like collecting funds, recruiting and planning to operatives, collaborators, etc., they need everybody to be perfectly committed to the cause, share the same understanding and have access to the same information. But this is impossible no matter how coherent the organization is or how obedient the agents are. These fissures were first visible as Hizbul agents murdered members of the JKLF. The growing splintering, criminality and discrediting – as demonstrated by the support of local Hazratbal residents during the second siege – of Pakistan's proxies is our opportunity against Islamic terrorism.

The words 'jihad' and 'kafir' are barbaric and unnecessary in the modern world. Their use is slowing but must stop.

7

The Police Chief Years: Fighting Back

Sweat saves blood, blood saves lives, but brains save both.

– Field Marshal Erwin Rommel

Kshma shobti us bhujang ko jis ke paas garal ho.
(Only the powerful can afford to be kind, benevolent or generous.)

– Ramdhari Singh Dinkar

A little after midnight on 17 June 1994, six months after the terrorists' surrender in the first siege of Hazratbal and twenty-four hours after they were officially formed, the SOG of the J&K Police carried out their first mission. The targets were three terrorists of the Al Farhan group in Malagam village located about 100 kilometres from Srinagar. The SOG requested the Army's 26th Punjab regiment to help with the outer cordon and sniper support but tackled the terrorist safe house themselves. The terrorists responded to the SOG's repeated announcements to surrender with indiscriminate AK-47 fire, but despite some losses, the SOG killed all three before sunrise. This operation synthesized everything I had hoped for in the J&K Police's terrorism response: specific intelligence, detailed scenario planning, no civilian casualties, no collateral damage and teamwork with the army and paramilitary forces but with the actual operation being carried out by police officers equipped with the latest gear, weaponry, tactics and training.

My career was defined by Pakistan, terrorism and militancy, but I don't want to leave you with the impression the J&K Police never had a 'normal' role. We handled what every other state police did before 1988 – crime, riots, security, disputes, etc. – and I remember the Kashmiri saying 'zan, zar aur zameen' (woman, money and land) ignited a person's instincts to commit a crime. The J&K Police was formally born in 1873 with one police officer (kotwal) and fourteen thanedars (station-in-charges) for Srinagar. In 1895, British civil servant Walter Lawrence described the J&K Police as 1,000 village chowkidars (guards), usually from the Dom caste. The strength of the J&K Police in 1890 was 1,040 personnel. In 1944, it was 3,179, and today, it is more than a lakh.

I was the first J&K police chief to straddle two worlds as the first UPSC-recruited IPS officer who had spent decades in the state. I set myself three priorities. The first was resolving the Hazratbal sieges without violence or arms entering the mosque. The second was restoring the strength and will of the J&K Police to fight militancy. I believed that the army and paramilitary forces were powerful tools and allies, but sustainably controlling terrorism required ground intelligence, community connections and the local recruits that only a police force can provide. The third was taking the security situation to the point where the government could hold elections without security concerns. I was pleased with the progress on all three priorities when I left my post in 1997. The first Hazratbal siege ended peacefully and the J&K Police's response was spearheaded by a specially trained and armed SOG, and the state's longest stint of Governor's Rule ended in 1996 with Farooq Abdullah being sworn in as chief minister.

Of course I have some nadaamat (regret) from my police chief years that include not being able to prevent the burning of Charar-e-Sharief shrine, not bring the Pandits back to the Valley after they were driven out, not finding the four foreigners or their bodies that were abducted by terrorists I directly negotiated with, not convincing the world that Kashmir was merely the first phase of global Islamic terror and my inability to do anything or convince the central government to take radical action against Pakistan's terror factory across the border.

I can't know for sure, but I've heard I was almost not appointed police chief; Governor Rao received leaked information about internal security minister Rajesh Pilot initiating approval from the Cabinet Appointments Committee for K.P.S. Gill from Punjab to head the J&K Police. The governor, however, decided that he was not the right choice and held an urgent administrative council meeting to finalize my appointment. General Rao told me he was happy with his choice, but I don't underestimate the power of destiny and chance in providing opportunities.

Revitalizing the J&K Police

Soon after the events at Hazratbal in 1993, I asked for a one-on-one meeting with Governor Rao. I was tired of the J&K Police's role being reduced to writing panchnamas (records of observation by five people) for bodies and FIRs for terrorist strikes, and I made the case for the J&K Police to return as the face of anti-militancy operations. Of course, without the unflinching courage, rigorous training and superior firepower of the army and central paramilitary forces, we could never have stood up to the terrorists, the ISI and Pakistan.

I told the governor my plan for revitalizing J&K Police would start with a specially chosen elite unit whose language skills, tactics, weapons, terrain knowledge and intelligence sources would be complemented by the army and paramilitary forces. I found sound counter-terrorism advice in the words of Kabir, 'Jahaan kaam aave sui, kaha kare tarvari.' (A sword is useless when you need a needle.) General Rao was understandably sceptical; in recent memory, a compromised policeman had placed a bomb in the police chief's office, clashes between the army and police had led to a strike and some high-profile terrorists had turned out to be former policemen. But Rao was a strategic thinker and risk-taker – he gave me a broad go-ahead but asked me to keep him posted as I moved forward.

The backbone of my revitalization plan was involving and building local leadership. My predecessors had all been competent, but they were from outside the state. My career until even that point had taught me that effective policing requires blending intimacy with history, culture and local networks. It was unsurprising that recent police leadership from out of the state had been overly suspicious of locals; the top four police officers – Police Chief J.S. Saxena, the advisor on home affairs J.M. Qureshi, J&K CRPF chief D.D. Gupta and the Srinagar BSF chief Ashok Patel were from the Madhya Pradesh Police cadre. This was not my first time making such a case; I remembered an incident where in the 1966 university student agitation in Jammu the Punjab Armed Police personnel on deputation overreacted. The army was needed to restore civil order for the next fifteen days. As a rookie officer, the quiet return of the Punjab Police to their state left a deep impression.

In 1993, after nearly three decades in Kashmir, my confidence in repairing the trust gap was anchored in my insider/outsider status, relationships across the state and experience in Valley policing. One of my first decisions was to symbolically shift my office, home and car security cordon back to the J&K Police. My old Kashmiri driver, Ghulam Nabi, was soon responsible for my staff cars. My security and support staff at home also came from the local police despite warnings from my friends and intelligence officials. But I was sure I could trust the locals; people notice what you do more than what you say, and I wanted my choices to reflect my hopes, not my fears.

These changes I made to the J&K Police drew inspiration from an early boss. As a rookie officer in Jammu, I set up a control room under the direct guidance of Sheikh Ghulam Qadir 'Ganderbali'. Kashmiris referred to him being 'paadher saeh aasoon' (like a lion); he was more than six feet tall, feared by rowdies and had been promoted to the IPS from the rank of head constable. He would often destroy the radio sets of people listening to Pakistan radio. He aggressively suppressed pro-Pakistan and secessionist elements by organizing a group of 'khuftan fakirs' (wandering informants) who would travel incognito throughout the Valley to collect intelligence for him. He also organized the 'Rice Brigade', consisting of informants and musclemen temporarily employed in the food and supplies department across the Valley. Both gave me an early appreciation of the power of local intelligence networks. His legacy is controversial – most people in the Valley believe he had an anti-National Conference agenda, compounded by the fact that he was one of the officers who arrested Sheikh Abdullah in 1953. He was later shunned in Kashmir, and an informal ban was enforced on anybody buying his land in Ganderbal till the government purchased this land for the Armed Police Training Centre in 1990.

We needed a different approach for the sparsely populated but largest mountain district of Doda. Militants from Pakistan would use the Pir Panjal Pass to cross over and target Hindu Rajputs and ex-servicemen to create a communal divide. Village defence societies using Home Guards from the Jammu region, including Udhampur and Doda, were deputed in the field as special police officers to collect intelligence and provide assistance to the police. These special police officers were issued .303 rifles from police armouries, given a fixed stipend and supported by the army deployed there. Almost a third of the names of the police martyrs at the end of this book belong to special police officers (SPOs). A special Rashtriya Rifles division was set up to bring some ground control. My talented colleague Kuldeep Khoda headed the Udhampur–Doda region when the village defence group scheme was implemented. Khoda had studied nuclear physics at IIT and later greatly raised the tech game for the J&K Police in his tenure as chief.

Before renewing the police force and re-engaging locals, I needed to weed out some bad apples. This problem was real but small compared to my experience as superintendent of police in Jammu where 20 per cent of the constables were political appointees who were used to slothful absenteeism from their duties. Transparent and merit-based promotions, postings and recruitment were a priority. The civil administration had collapsed but I recognized that big changes needed everybody's support. As police chief, I served with four chief secretaries: Sheikh Ghulam Rasool, Hindal Tyabji, Ashok Kumar and finally, my batchmate Ashok Jaitly, and all of them supported our strategy.

Many competent local officers were frustrated with the militant violence and were also tired of the suspicion with which previous administrations had viewed them. Many came forward to join the fight back. The police provided personal security to VIPs, officers and locals, and this had sapped our numbers in the field. It became vital to recruit and train additional units quickly. Some armed police battalions were merged and renamed the India Reserve Battalions, funded by the union home ministry but within the J&K Police setup. With these additions, the overall strength of the J&K armed police range doubled during my tenure. My colleague S.P. Vaid, who later became J&K police chief, was posted in the police headquarters with me during my tenure as chief. With his quick decision-making and intelligence, he efficiently found the needed resources and later handled militancy with courage as police chief.

After my tenure in J&K, I became the director general of the CRPF in Delhi. I greatly respected the CRPF throughout my term in J&K and appreciated its importance as the firefighting force that always moved quickly to affected areas. With such rapid movement, its associated officers sometimes jokingly refer to it as 'Chalte Raho Pyare Force' (Keep Moving Beloved Force). Given my experience with the effective partnership between the J&K Police's SOG and CRPF, I recognized how the BSF, ITBP and SSB were not the right units to deal with civilian situations – as a matter of fact, they were never even issued lathis, the first tool for crowd control. When I hosted the Vohra Committee appointed by the home ministry to deal with internal security, I presented the case forcefully, stating that the CRPF should be the primary central force for internal security, and the BSF should work on border security. These roles has since been formalized.

Fighting Back: The Special Operation Group

Like life, fighting terrorism is not like solving a sum but more like painting a picture. The primary tool is the battle for hearts and minds, or building a narrative, but four other tools are guns, financing, logistics and politics. In recent years, the National Investigation Agency (NIA) has been a powerful tool in shutting down terror financing by tracking money and seizing militant properties but this was not an arrow in my quiver. Cross-border military strikes required efficient logistics, but despite my repeated requests, I was told this decision was beyond my pay grade. The road to politics ran along terrorism, so I decided the best place to start fighting back was to create a small, elite unit called the Special Task Force (STF) in Srinagar.

I invoked the Kashmiri proverb 'Shistarah chhuh shishtaras tchataan' (Iron is cut by iron) in early discussions with my colleagues about a small unit carrying out targeted operations acting on specific intelligence. We needed strong partnerships between the police, army and other paramilitary forces, but partnerships usually work well between equals. The J&K Police had suffered years of deserved and undeserved suspicion, and we needed some early wins to restore their confidence, capability and courage.

My years at the Indian embassy in the US during the 1970s was useful because everybody in Washington was then marinating in much public and private reflection about the humiliating Vietnam War. Henry Kissinger feared 'We were being lured into the role of a bull in a bullfight, who always forces the other side to give way, but in the process slowly has his strength drained.' The fantastic book *Learning to Eat Soup with a Knife: Counterinsurgency Lessons from Malaya and Vietnam* by John Nagl suggests that the US army entered Vietnam with plans well suited to fighting a conventional war in Europe but which were worse than useless for the insurgency it was about to face. The US forces implemented 'search and destroy' operations rather than 'clear, hold and build' ones, resulting in huge civilian losses. They also used napalm, Agent Orange and artillery. The Indian army has long been provoked by insurgents but almost never fought in Kashmir like they would fight a war with Pakistan.

I remember my neighbour in Washington, a Marine veteran, being frustrated with the heavy use of helicopters, artillery and large army operations. He showed me a Marine doctrinal manual from the Second World War that suggested 'In small wars, the goal is to gain decisive results with the least application of force and the consequent minimum loss of life. The end aim is the social, economic and political development of the people subsequent to the military defeat of the enemy insurgent. In small wars, tolerance, sympathy, and kindness should be the keynote of our relationship with the mass of the population.' Every counterinsurgency campaign is unique but is best designed after understanding the enemy, politics, politicians, terrain and culture. The most important terrain is always the human terrain.

I personally made a list of potential leaders, conducted interviews with a small group of my colleagues and selected Farooq Khan to lead the STF. I knew his family; his grandfather Sardar Pir Mohammad had migrated from Peshawar to serve as a colonel in the maharaja's army and later served in the Rajya Sabha while his father Sardar Mohammad Sarwar Khan served honourably in J&K Police. I took him to meet the governor and Khan was given a one-rank promotion. Farooq was perfect for the role – he had the skills, experience, courage and temperament to build this team.

In June 1994, I asked Farooq to start picking his team while we made arrangements for a base for them to operate from at an abandoned Indian Airlines cargo terminal. Farooq picked his team: the first were two deputy superintendents R.K. Jalla and Joginder Kumar followed by sub-inspectors Sewa Singh, Gulbadhar Singh, Kulwant Singh, Tajinder Pal Singh, Prithpal Singh and Shiv Kumar Chauhan. We needed officers who could hit the ground running and selected them for their experience. A few lines from George Bernard Shaw's *Arms and the Man* have stayed with me since my English literature days, when the veteran soldier Bluntschli says, 'You can know a soldier by what he carries on the war front – the young ones carry cartridges, and the old ones carry grub.' Farooq's picks were old enough to be veterans but young enough to be in the field. We soon requisitioned two CRPF companies and added personnel from the police counter-intelligence wing. I remember Farooq even requisitioning a guard commander from Sheikh Sahib's youngest son's house in Tangmarg!

In the second half of 1995, we renamed the STF as SOG and replicated it in other districts. The SOG received the legal status of a general police station and set up their interrogation centres and lock-ups. They were encouraged to be bold and knew all their operations within the law had my support. My talented colleague Gopal Sharma, who later became J&K police chief and headed our intelligence/CID wing at Hari Niwas, played an essential role in ensuring the success of the SOG. He had earlier succeeded me as the Anantnag police chief and has had the career-long advantage of people underestimating his mettle and will because of his superior listening skills.

The SOG carried out hundreds of operations, and speed, teamwork, weapons, training, fitness, tactics and information were vital to their success. Farooq drastically reduced our response time by allocating shifts to fully kitted officers who sat on wooden planks in specially modified Tata 407 vehicles which were ready to go. I remember BBC correspondent Nayeema Mehjoor calling the governor for help when militants were surrounding her house, and he instructed the army and BSF to help. Nobody reached her house, and so she called him again. This time, he reached out to me, and I asked Farooq to send out an SOG team. The team reached immediately, rescued Mehjoor and captured two militants. I later heard that the governor, a former army man, gave a dressing down to some of his former colleagues. Our transformation was small but working very well.

The flow of information was crucial to the SOG's success. Local sources soon felt confident they would be anonymous and safe, and after a year, information started flowing rapidly. In late 1995, Farooq received information about Sher Khan, the leader of Al Umar Mujahideen, who operated around the Dal Lake. The informant was a distraught father whose daughters had been serial-raped by these terrorists. Farooq and I were in a meeting with Governor General Rao when Farooq got news from the informant about Sher Khan spending the night at the Dal Lake. He passed me a note asking to be excused from the meeting, but the governor noticed and, with slight irritation asked what was going on. But when he heard about the possibility of Sher Khan's arrest – he was among the terrorists released in exchange for the release of Rubaiya Sayeed – the governor let Farooq go and asked him to call him whenever the operation ended.

Close to midnight, two groups from the SOG made their way to a house in the middle of Dal Lake in shikaras and as they approached, they stopped using oars and paddled by hand. Only two guards were awake; one was killed by a sniper and the other ran away. A bigger round of firing followed, and the SOG killed four terrorists including Sher Khan. One terrorist, Badshah Khan, escaped and was killed later. I have heard our informant kicked – some say danced on – the body of the terrorist/rapist and let out a cry of anguished relief at his family's ordeal coming to an end. Farooq called the governor at 2 a.m. with the good news, who finally retired for the night. Thousands of innocent young women have suffered humiliation after the gun culture infected Kashmir. The SOG hunted down terrorists, but it was often too little, too late. A wistful Kashmiri once called me to describe the SOG success as 'Haalav maran magar daaness dith daah.' (Locusts will die but destroy the crop.) I could only assure him one day India would go upstream and destroy the source of the pestilence.

The role of reliable information to the success of the SOG cannot be overstated. For example, a young petty criminal from Bagati Kanipora in Budgam district would often visit Farooq, claiming militants were visiting his relatives and he would give specific information in return for a cycle. Khan gave him the cycle, and the young man kept his word. The SOG reached the house, and firing began but the terrorists had entrenched themselves well. Sadly, three members of the SOG – one from the police, army and CRPF each – lost their lives early in this mission. The SOG withdrew tactically but successfully regrouped and killed five militants. We later realized these terrorists were from what was then an unknown organization, Lashkar-e-Taiba. I can only wish we'd then had access to C. Christine Fair's excellent book *In Their Own Words: Understanding Lashkar-e-Taiba*. We would have been so much more careful and aggressive in hunting this cancer down.

I remember that information about foreign terrorists from locals started flowing in first. Residents living ahead of the Soura Medical College were tired of Afghani militants ordering all houses to have 12 foot-high walls, keeping back doors unlocked and enforcing a ban on dogs. The SOG soon killed seven militants on this information. Another operation in Bandipore was planned based on information from a retired sub-inspector about ISI Major Umar and cordoned off the house on Diwali. After neutralizing the guards outside, R.K. Jalla crossed the boundary with a colleague who peeped into a window; his colleague saw a gun behind the window and selflessly jumped in front of Jalla, taking the brunt of the gunfire. Even though all the militants were neutralized after heavy firing, the SOG officer lost his life.

The SOG's successes resulted in reduced militant recruiting, many terrorist surrenders and better coordination amongst security forces. The surrendered militants not involved in serious offences were integrated within our security se-tup, and our intelligence capacities got a huge boost. We also learnt from the army; their regular road opening parties (ROPs) with anti-sabotage equipment on highways were replicated and gave the locals confidence. The central government soon recognized the SOG's work, and more funding enabled us to get better communication equipment, sophisticated weaponry and independent interrogation centres across various districts in Kashmir and Doda. However, the biggest success of the SOG was the boost to civilian confidence.

The Response to Revitalization

Governor General K.V. Krishna Rao and I worked well during my entire time as police chief between 1993 and 1997. The governor knew Prime Minister Narasimha Rao well, and the army trusted him – and I had extensive local networks and knew J&K Police well. Militancy was waning, and there was hope for elections. These efforts did not go well with the controllers of terrorism in Pakistan, and RAW officials let us know that militants were planning operations targeting the governor and civilian and police leadership.

The first indication was multiple bomb blasts at the Republic Day function in 1995 at the Maulana Azad Stadium in Jammu when Governor Rao was taking the salute. The governor escaped unharmed, but the blasts killed eight people and injured fifty others. Terrorists from Hizb-ul-Mujahideen used a remote control to set off the three explosions – two on the stadium's outer periphery and one near the salute podium – by burying RDX deep into the ground. Governor Rao called it a 'plot by Pakistan which claims Kashmir as its own to assassinate me'. It was the first attack to get so close to the governor, and it signalled a shift in militancy from the JKLF to the Hizb-ul-Mujahideen.

At the time, I was in Srinagar for the Republic Day celebrations at Bakshi Stadium and reached Jammu by helicopter to supervise the aftermath of the explosions. Security agencies, including sniffer dogs, had failed to detect anything in their anti-sabotage checks because the terrorists had not only updated their technology but had buried the bombs long before the event. However, the blasts raised questions about the competence of the security set-up and administration. Some even demanded the governor's resignation for this 'monumental' security lapse and for me to be transferred or suspended. The CBI was asked to investigate, and a team led by their special director, Arun Bhagat, arrived in Jammu. While the J&K Police, RAW, Intelligence Bureau and the BSF supported the group in different ways, the CBI announced a reward of Rs 10 lakh to those providing information to crack the case and get the accused arrested.

Investigations suggested terrorists from Pakistan had infiltrated India through the nearby RS Pura border area in the Jammu district. While this was a popular infiltration route in the 1960s, we assumed that the BSF had sealed it. The police worked overtime with the BSF to close unfenced and porous spots on the border and increased patrolling in coordination with local informers. The police also formed a second line of control for additional interception, especially along the internal village roads linking the border to Jammu. Security matters and investigations require a lot of luck, and this time, we had some. A local village informant told the police about the suspicious movement of two heavily clad persons near Bishnah town. A police party immediately left and intercepted the bus. They questioned the two men who tried to give fake credentials, but the gaps in their story and strange accents suggested we interrogate them further. After questioning, they admitted they were first-time infiltrators and revealed their identity as Mohammed Irfan and Wasim Ahmed Malik from Sialkot, and they had been sent by ISI operatives to arrange the blast. When the investigations concluded, I returned to Jammu for a press conference along with the arrested suspects. The CBI had acknowledged the arrest of the real culprits in the bomb blast by the police and sent the reward money to be distributed among the officers and civilian informants.

The next issue was the threat of assassination, which struck very close to home. A United News of India (UNI) report of 31 January 1995, quoting defence sources, said 'they had intercepted a message from the ISI to the Hizb-ul-Mujahideen stating 5 crore rupees had been placed at the service of the suicide squads to eliminate the Director General of Police, Mr M.N. Sabharwal and Advisor to the Governor (Home), Lt General M.A. Zaki'. This was not the first time I had been threatened, and many of my colleagues in the state had also faced similar situations. Vina, however, had a much bigger burden; she did not leave our Sonawar house for a year when I was police chief and bore the isolation with a smile. She only faltered once; I remember there was panic in my office when they realized a bad toothache had forced her to go the police hospital. Plain-clothes officers at the hospital heard rumours about 'people' soon arriving to 'deal' with her and they whisked her back home. Later, terrorist posters announcing a reward for killing General Rao, Zaki and me appeared in Srinagar. My faith in locals had never faltered, and this quick action was a testament to their reciprocity. I had signed up for a life in uniform and knew the challenges I would face, but public targeting of this kind is always hard for our families.

News of Kidnappings

In 1995, the presence of security arrangements for the Amarnath Yatra in Pahalgam attracted foreign trekkers. On 4 July, terrorists kidnapped four tourists, demanding their commander's release in exchange. The high mountain ranges complicated information gathering from the abductees' wives, slowing down our search. Meanwhile, the terrorists assured the local media that the abductees were safe and were awaiting their release. The Pakistan-based Al-Faran group claimed responsibility and at noon, many central agencies and foreign countries began appealing to the terrorists to release the hostages.

Police and security forces continued their search without success. On 13 August, we found the beheaded body of the Norwegian tourist Hans Christian Ostro near Pahalgam. Ostro had served in the army special forces of Norway and had spent a month travelling through India and had arrived in Kashmir for a trek after Kathakali training sessions in Kerala. We later realized the terrorists moved the abductees every night, and during one transition, Ostro challenged his kidnappers and tried to escape but failed. His captors brutally beheaded him in an Islamic zaba style (the slow style of slaughter) and slit his throat.

Ostro's remains were brought to the Srinagar helipad. We had the heartbreaking experience of seeing his mutilated body, with 'Al-Faran' inscribed on his chest. Representatives from the Norwegian embassy travelled to Srinagar so we could hand over the body to them. This kidnapping case was now a murder as the post-mortem conducted at AIIMS in Delhi established beheading as the cause of the death. Shortly after Ostro's murder, two more foreigners, Dirk Hasert from Germany and Keith Mangan from Britain, were kidnapped. Given the upcoming yatra and this escalation, Governor General Rao directed his security advisor Lieutenant General Saklani and me to visit Pahalgam.

We took an armed security officer, Inspector M.L. Mehra, in the chopper piloted by retired Wing Commander Kahlon. Before landing in Pahalgam, we decided to conduct an aerial survey of the security forces deployed on the Amarnath Yatra route. After fifteen minutes of flying low, we spotted somebody desperately raising a white cloth flag from a tiny meadow between the forest. As we circled closer, we realized a foreigner was waving his white jacket to grab our attention. Since the weather was clear, Kahlon, a competent and daring pilot, who tragically lost his life in a helicopter accident in Ganderbal a few years later, suggested the helicopter could land. Despite security concerns, we decided to take a chance to land in the area and rescue the stranded individual. When we landed, the individual ran back into the forest and came towards the chopper only after he saw the khaki uniforms on me and my Kalashnikov-wielding security officer. We swiftly sat the individual in the helicopter between us in the rear seats and took off. He soon identified himself as John Childs, the American engineer kidnapped by the terrorists, and we immediately returned to Srinagar.

Expectedly shaken, Childs first began praying and thanking the Lord for sending us to save him from the terrorists. He soon started sharing details of what had taken place; a large group of militants roaming the high regions of Pahalgam checked his identification since they were only interested in kidnapping those from Western countries. He said the heavily armed abductors, who had beards and long hair, used big satellite phones to take instructions from Pakistan in a language not spoken in Kashmir and sounded like heavily accented Pashto. Childs had also heard Ostro's shrieks as he was beheaded and had decided to escape, feigning a stomach upset that needed him to ease himself far away. The terrorists agreed, and he used this opportunity to run for three days and nights before we saw him.

Back in Srinagar, we took Childs to a state guest house for medical treatment and recorded a detailed statement the next day. The US embassy immediately sent their political counsellor and two FBI agents who questioned him separately about the kidnapping and the rescue mission. Two days later, Childs, on his insistence, was taken to the US embassy in New Delhi and sent back to the US. The FBI agents stayed in Kashmir for over a month to assist in the investigations to help rescue the remaining US citizens.

The miracle of Childs' rescue notwithstanding, we had four more hostages to worry about. John Childs' debriefing helped us change our strategy. Intelligence agencies began monitoring the use and exchange of satellite phones, which allowed us to establish contact with the terrorists. R.K. Tikoo, the police chief of Kashmir Range, began negotiating, and the terrorists' demand was to release twenty of their associates for the four foreigners. Tikoo had a narrow mandate: continue negotiations and buy the security forces searching the area more time. The terrorists were often frustrated with the prolonged negotiations and threatened to kill the remaining tourists unless 'Sabharwal' agreed to the final terms.

Exasperated by the lengthy negotiations, Tikoo took short leave, and Governor General Rao ordered that I take over. I had three long satellite phone calls with the abductors to shrink their demands. On two of these calls, representatives from the FBI and Scotland Yard joined me. The kidnappers finally brought down their demands to release three terrorists, including Maulana Masood Azhar, and Rs 6 crore within forty-eight hours before they killed the hostages. We wanted to buy more time and keep talking, but the terrorists seemed determined there would be no contact after these final demands. And so, I made an appeal for patience and kindness during the prime-time news in the evening on Doordarshan. I reminded Al-Faran the world was watching and 'the hostage's welfare was their sole responsibility'. There was, however, no direct contact with the kidnappers after they made their final demands.

In October, I announced to the press at Baramulla 'the hostages were alive and well.' A few weeks later, in November, I held a short press conference in response to an Al-Faran message dropped off at the Press Enclave that the hostages were sick and that their families should 'rush to Srinagar' immediately so they could collect their bodies. The ordeal had already lasted 134 days, and the pressure of security forces was raising the terrorists' tempers. My message in the press conference was that this blackmail of the hostages' families only exposed the terrorists as savages. Extended hostage situations are difficult for terrorists; I have heard Qadir Dar, the Muslim Janbaz League's field commander who kidnapped two Swedish engineers in 1992 for ninety-four days, confessed, 'It was one of our most stressful operations. They ate more than we could afford. They wanted to drink things we could never find in a Muslim country. We could never communicate with each other, as poor English, theirs and ours, got in the way.'

Security forces continued to diligently monitor satellite communications and conducted ground searches in the mountainous terrains. While this persistent surveillance didn't directly lead to resolving the primary situation, it proved instrumental in apprehending other terrorist factions active in the region. Information filtered through informal channels about the exhausted terrorists considering surrender and to meet them some part of the way. We continued the search in winter despite the challenging nature of operations because till early December, we continued to receive tips about the beleaguered kidnappers. Yet disappointingly, we never found the remaining tourists or their bodies.

The book *The Meadow: Kashmir 1995 – Where the Terror Began* by Adrian Levy and Cathy Scott-Clark, which was about this kidnapping, got one hypothesis wrong and one right (even while I disagree with their description of me as plump and my smile as a rictus). Their belief about Indian and Kashmir security authorities extending negotiations for 'PR value' is inaccurate and unfair. We deployed massive ground intelligence, security forces and technology in the hostage search and tried many informal and diplomatic channels to negotiate their release. I even held my nose during satellite phone calls to offer favourable exit terms for the terrorists if they released the hostages. I'm unsure if it was orders or ideology, but it felt like they had decided to kill the hostages, irrespective of our conversations.

The book's primary thesis, however, is absolutely accurate. These kidnappings were an early sign of Islamic terrorism expanding their targets beyond India to include Western countries and their citizens. They suggest a short leap from the kidnappings of Kashmir to the suicidal assaults in New Delhi, Srinagar, New York, Washington, London and Mumbai that killed and injured thousands. Over the previous decade, the Americans had ignored our specific intelligence inputs about terrorist plans to target Westerners; we had even shown them a note by kidnappers promising Western powers, led by America, of consequences for their anti-Islamic stance. But the Americans ignored us, implying we had a self-interest in making Pakistan or Islam look bad.

In 1998, Osama Bin Laden and six others (two of whom were Pakistanis) issued a fatwa in the name of an International Islamic Front for jihad, according to which every Muslim was obliged to kill Americans and their allies, both those in uniform and civilians. The militants' endeavours to secure Masood Azhar's release didn't work with this kidnapping, but they were successful in 1999 when he was released after Indian Airlines flight 814 was hijacked to Kandahar. In 2002, Masood's bodyguard and one of his British recruits adopted tactics honed during the Kashmir kidnapping to abduct a *Wall Street Journal* reporter, Daniel Pearl, and film his horrific beheading. Unfortunately, Masood's murderous ways continue unchecked from Pakistan.

The Attack on Charar-E-Sharief

Pakistan made religion an important fault line with the ethnic cleansing of Kashmiri Pandits from the Valley. They later expanded this mandate to include Sikhs (the Chattisinghpora massacre was particularly tragic), Shias, migrants, temples and pilgrims. It was only a matter of time before the Wahhabis and Pakistan began targeting Kashmir's ziarats and shrines.

The Charar-e-Sharief was one of Kashmir's most respected Muslim shrines, located on the hilly road to Yusmarg about 35 kilometres from Srinagar in the Budgam district. Built in 1460 and dedicated to Kashmiri Sufi saint Noor-din-Wali (Nund Rishi), it symbolized liberal Sufi Muslim religious thoughts and allowed visits by Hindus and people of all other faiths. I have often visited the shrine with my family before my children's exams or upcoming promotions! The shrine's structure, with its wooden architecture embellished with the most exquisite Khatamband ceiling – thousands of small parts of carved deodar wooden pieces joined together without any nails like a puzzle – was an architectural marvel. After Sheikh Abdullah's arrest in 1953, it was briefly used by Bakshi Ghulam Mohammad as a base for his mass-contact programmes.

In 1990 a JKLF call, 'Chalo Charar', saw over 3 lakh people assembled in the holy and otherwise peaceful town, and the JKLF vowed a jihad till azadi was achieved. Its proximity to the Pakistan border made it a transit point for transporting weapons from across the border, and it became the base for Haroon Khan, alias Mast Gul, one of the most wanted terrorists on our list. He operated from the shrine, set up living quarters in a school and used an abandoned Food Corporation of India warehouse to store arms, including rocket launchers. Originally from Khyber Pakhtunkhwa, he lived in Khawaja town of Peshawar when the ISI chose him to be a Hizb-ul-Mujahideen commander because of his brutality and his fluency in Urdu. An Afghan war veteran, he was known among locals as Maut (death) Gul due to the ruthlessness of the operations he had ran for the Hizb-ul-Mujahideen since his arrival in Anantnag in 1994. His agenda was to launch a 'holy war against Indian state terrorism and [win] the right for Muslims to live their life their way'.

In 1995, there were intelligence and ground reports of hundreds of Pakistani militants and Hizb-ul-Mujahideen supporters roaming around in the hilly neighbourhood of the shrine. The J&K Police only had one small post adjacent to the shrine, and we requested the Indian army to set up camp to patrol the town. We had intercepted wireless signals from Pakistan instructing these terrorists to 'go back to Allah's protection'. Burned by our experience at Hazratbal, we evacuated citizens living close to the shrine to neighbouring villages.

Before Mast Gul burned down the Charar-e-Sharief, there was a long stand-off between the terrorists and security forces. The army saw some terrorists on the lawn and used a light machine gun (LMG) to kill four terrorists. With both sides getting restless with the wait, the security forces decided to comb the town to take the terrorists down. Meanwhile on 11 May around 8 p.m., inside the shrine, Gul changed strategy and broke his team into smaller groups to fan out and burn the town. By 2 a.m., almost two-thirds of the town was on fire. But the terrorists lost control of the fire; it soon spread to the shrine, and the security forces had no option but to attack.

The fire brigade trucks arrived soon after but could not help because of the pitched gun battle. The Charar-e-Sharief shrine burnt down in one hour, causing widespread resentment and anger among the civilians of the town, who had already suffered heavy damage to their property. The loss of their beloved shrine, which had been associated with their town's identity, during the army operations was also widely condemned and marked with utter sorrow in Kashmir and the rest of the country. The All Party Hurriyat

Conference's Mirwaiz Umar Farooq said: 'The Indian government is destroying our religious places to suppress our political struggle.'

The cover of darkness, confusion of guns firing and raging fire offered Mast Gul the perfect opportunity to escape. On Eid, it was a tragedy to see the holy town of Charar gutted and many residents dead. The mastermind's escape caused further resentment; Gul had breached the army cordon and reached Pakistani territory 100 kilometres from the site. His appearance at a public gathering in Lahore greatly embarrassed me. A few days later, the Hizb-ul-Mujahideen giving him a cash award, a gold medal and the bravery award of Hilal–i-Jurat rubbed salt on my wounds, or as they say in Kashmir, 'Akis chhe' dazzan dae'r byaak chhus wushanaawan atha.' (One person's beard is on fire and the other person is warming his hands with it.)

The loss of the shrine is one of the most painful episodes of my tenure as police chief; even if we hadn't caught Mast Gul, we should have ensured the shrine did not burn. This pain grew with personal attacks made by ex-governor Jagmohan in an article in the *Tribune* the next day, blaming me for Mast Gul's escape. Of course, the buck did indeed stop with me as police chief. I immediately left for the scene to re-establish contact with the already dispersed shrine board management of Charar-e-Sharief and local leaders of the town to communicate our profound sympathy and participate in their grief. The J&K Police post was re-established as part of an immediate confidence-building measure. Prime Minister Narasimha Rao announced the central government would not only re-build the shrine to its original form but also committed to providing resources to rebuild surrounding areas of the shrine. An all-party goodwill parliamentary delegation, led by Lok Sabha speaker Somnath Chatterjee, arrived in Srinagar by special flight and visited the site with prominent political leaders, including Inderjeet Gupta (who later became the home minister of India).

The 1996 Elections

The book *How India Became Democratic: Citizenship* by Ornit Shani wonderfully details the mechanics of our first national voter list and how the almost pathological worry of our election officials about missing anybody combined with their determination to ensure everybody voted in 1952. India's election track record is enviable. Our first parliamentary elections in 1952 required a constitution, a list of 17 crore voters (85 per cent of whom could not read or write), and 2.25 lac polling booths. They were highly competitive; 30 parties fielded 1,874 candidates, and the Congress Party got 45 per cent of the votes but 75 per cent of the seats. Since then, half of the seventeen general elections have led to a new central government. Our voter population is about 97 crores, and 370+ political parties campaign vigorously, assuming everybody votes where they live.

Terrorism and democracy marked the start and end of my time as the J&K police chief; my first day involved the Hazratbal siege, and my last year involved ensuring peaceful and safe parliamentary and assembly elections. This is not a coincidence. Terrorists compete with the state and are terrified of the vibrant, competitive, legitimate politics arising from elections. The government's decision to hold elections after nine years meant ensuring the safety of 1,029 candidates in 87 constituencies and 6,324 polling booths became an inspiring challenge for the police. Farooq Abdullah emerged victorious and got a powerful opportunity for what Kashmiris called 'nove zanim heon' (to have a new birth). It is for history to judge, but I don't think he seized the chance.

I served the J&K Police for six elections before overseeing the one in 1996 as chief. Each election came with its own set of challenges and learnings. Many J&K politicians who defended special constitutional status did not share this instinct for inclusiveness and often defied our constitution by insisting voter lists should not include all state residents. In the first state election of 1951, the National Conference won all seventy-five seats, helped by forty-three of their candidates being elected unopposed, the nominations of thirteen candidates from the Praja Parishad being rejected (this party later merged with the Jan Sangh), and two independent candidates opting out a week before voting. Nominal National Conference members won two seats in Ladakh. In 1957 and 1962, the National Conference acquired a majority before polling began since many of their candidates were elected unopposed or the Opposition candidate's nomination papers were rejected.

The 1967 assembly elections brought the Congress-led G.M. Sadiq government to power in the backdrop of the 1965 war, and refugees became the focal point. In the 1972 elections, women candidates contested for the first time, and the Congress similarly adopted the unopposed or rejection technology for their candidates to win. Indira Gandhi fought the 1983 elections ferociously – she hadn't forgotten Sheikh Abdullah's betrayal of 1977 and was irritated by Farooq's recent belligerence. She campaigned for a few weeks as a sitting prime minister, but Farooq Abdullah led National Conference to victory in partnership with his rival Maulvi Farooq. This victory was soon sabotaged by Farooq's sister's husband, G.M. Shah, in partnership with Indira Gandhi. Mufti Sayeed's leaving the Congress in 1987 influenced consequent state elections and created opportunities for Ghulam Nabi Azad to become chief minister.

Many politicians till 1977 were elected by what was known locally as the 'Khaliq formula', named after Abdul Khaliq, the sly district magistrate of Anantnag who pioneered arranging 'unopposed' elections by rejecting candidates on technicalities. Changing your mind about elections and politics in J&K used to be fatal. The assassination of Mirwaiz Maulvi Farooq of the Awami Action Committee baffled all of us in 1990 because the hardliner leader consistently supported Pakistan. But his tentative suggestion that peace needed political dialogue led to his murder by the Hizb-ul-Mujahideen. But the restoration of democracy in J&K with parliamentary and assembly elections in 1996 was a defeat for Pakistan and terrorism. Prime Minister Benazir Bhutto declared she would not allow them to happen, and before Friday prayers from Jama Masjid, the secessionist Abdul Ghani Lone said, 'The Hurriyat considers the election process a gamble which will shed the blood of the people of Jammu and Kashmir' and 'it was a game plan aimed at dividing the people of Kashmir with the ulterior motive to break us since the government has not been able to kill us with bullets directly or break our nerve.'

But elections are exercises in hope. In 1996, militants who had surrendered and former militant commanders like Kuka Parray, Naba Azad and Javed Ahmed Shah, with their overground supporters, joined the constitutional path and electoral race with the newly formed Awami League. The general law-and-order situation in J&K was improving, and we seized a window and held an election. Elections are invisible threads tying Sheikh Abdullah's frequent distinction between siyasat (politics), riyasat (government) and awaam (citizens).

The Parliament elections were held first and laid the ground for the state assembly elections. Of six parliamentary seats, the Congress won four seats while the BJP and Janata Dal won one seat each. The Indian parliamentary elections of 1996 saw 591 million people exercise their right to vote, of which 4.4 million were from J&K. The highest registered voters were from Jammu (7.44 lakh), followed by Srinagar (5.42 lakh) and Anantnag (4.81 lakh), and the smallest constituencies included Leh (63,105 voters) and Kargil (64,624 voters). Over 700 paramilitary companies protected 6,170 polling stations. Our security challenges meant the number of phases in state elections was usually close to the number of parliamentary constituencies.

Terrorists had planned another attack on the Hazratbal shrine in March, but a swift operation led by our SOG ensured the state was ready to hold parliamentary elections. Phased parliamentary elections involved Jammu and Ladakh constituencies voting on 7 May 1996, Anantnag and Baramulla on 23 May and the remaining constituencies of Srinagar and Udhampur on 30 May. Interestingly, two phases of elections took place after Atal Bihari Vajpayee formed a government and lost power after less than a fortnight. People said the elections had no national impact, but a successful election was a giant leap for us in J&K.

The Election Commission began holding rounds of discussions and assessing the situation to conduct polls in early 1996. During their visit to the state, the three-member Election Commission team, each with independent ideas about the election, held discussions at the Nehru Guest House in Chashme Shahi. T.N. Seshan, the chairman, wanted to assert his final authority. But the other two members, M.S. Gill and V. Krishnamurthy, had recently been empowered with equal voting rights by the Supreme Court and challenged his authority. Mr Seshan had called a media briefing on the commission's assessment, but Mr Krishnamurthy decided to visit Lal Chowk to talk with locals at the last minute. Thus, the media briefing started in his absence. Mr Seshan and Mr Gill briefed the media, and the question–answer session ended when Mr Krishnamurthy returned from Lal Chowk, and so we restarted the press conference. Amidst serious discussion of law and order, this incident provided some comic relief.

Members of the Election Commission went on to meet Governor General Rao. I had already briefed the governor about the developments and my assessment; even though the National Conference led by Farooq Abdullah had decided not to contest the parliamentary elections, it was important for the state to go ahead and assure the public that we could conduct elections. The governor was on board and assured the members of the Election Commission that his administration would maintain law and order.

The Election Commission members left for Delhi and soon announced a three-phase parliamentary election in J&K. Staggered elections were recommended by the police to ensure the rotation of the security force across constituencies, especially the susceptible ones in Kashmir. Preliminary groundwork started as soon as the election officers left. The first task was integrating the central security forces with the local police to tackle the Hurriyat aiming to disrupt the elections. The second was to manage state employees, especially in the sensitive constituencies of south Kashmir, who had expressed their widespread apprehensions. We finally had to bring central government employees to work the polling booths in these constituencies.

As expected, the National Conference boycotted the parliamentary elections but the participation of all the other major recognized political parties and many independents enabled us to achieve our objective of holding elections with significant media presence and some international observers. The wide-ranging threats of disruption from the militants to disturb this election failed.

Governor General Rao and Prime Minister Narasimha Rao were both keen on conducting elections in the state. The prime minister even held a large public meeting in Maulana Azad Stadium in Jammu, which went smoothly. In his address, he announced, 'Give me stability, and I will give you prosperity.' But the results were something else as Narasimha Rao and the Congress couldn't form a government. Atal Bihari Vajpayee took over as prime minister for thirteen days before passing the baton to H.D. Deve Gowda, the Janta Dal leader from Karnataka, who led a weak coalition government.

The election saw a voter turnout of 48 per cent despite militant threats, higher than what we see in many Indian metropolitan cities today. Though critics like the Hurriyat called it a 'sham election' and some media said people were 'coerced to vote'. The Election Commission was pleased and, in a letter to Governor General Rao, complimented the J&K Police for its 'extraordinary contributions and high leadership abilities displayed in organizing the successful conduct of the elections'.

We were now determined to hold assembly elections in J&K, with 1,029 candidates vying for the votes of 4.76 million people. As the Kashmiris say, 'Yus karie harkaeith taeis daeiy barkeith' (God helps those that help themselves), and so we acquired over 200 bulletproof Ambassador cars, 250 bulletproof Gypsy jeeps, 4,000 vehicles, 25,000 bullet-proof jackets, fibre-reinforced huts, communications equipment, weapons, RDX-detection equipment, bomb-disposal equipment and jammers. Until the Parliament elections in 1995, the J&K Police only had twenty-five bulletproof cars. But we knew the combination of mobility and protection meant bulletproof cars were vital. We worked with the Punjab Ex-Servicemen Association in Mohali to provide us with five cars every day. They were paid for using central funding and were spread between the Lok Sabha and assembly elections. Successful parliamentary polls had made the Election Commission confident, and the central government continued to provide additional manpower and financial resources to prepare for the assembly elections.

On 7 August, the election commission announced four separate polling dates spread across September for the eighty-seven-member assembly. The first phase covered twenty-six seats, including Baramulla, Leh and Rajouri. The second phase had thirty-four seats, including Anantnag, Pulwama and Jammu. The third phase had twenty-one seats, including Srinagar and Badgam. The fourth phase was for six seats in Doda. The assembly elections were being held after a decade, and the Election Commission conducted a drive to refresh the voter list. The state administration also devised a plan to tackle the three main challenges: cross-border terrorism, internal protests by the likes of the Hurriyat and people's participation.

In an interview with *India Today*, Dr Farooq Abdullah emphasized, 'If Jammu and Kashmir has to remain a part of India, autonomy has to be given . . . this has to happen to win the people's hearts. They can dismantle me, but the issue will not disappear.' He articulated his demands in a letter to the prime minister, advocating for the permanency of Article 370, the restoration of the title of Sadr-e-Riyasat, and the exemption of the state from Article 356 (authorizing central intervention if a state fails to run as per the constitution) and Article 249 (permitting Parliament to legislate on matters within the state list in national interest). Dr Farooq did not contest the parliamentary elections, believing that securing a popular mandate would be challenging without addressing the autonomy issue. Nonetheless, the National Conference had been actively re-establishing its grassroots presence and ultimately decided to participate in the state elections.

Military history teaches us the importance of logistics – an army marches on fuel and food – and this is no different for holding an election confronted by terrorists determined to stop it. The J&K Police were the most visible face of the civil administration, coordinating and controlling security during the entire exercise. My colleague Ashok Bhan, who later headed intelligence in the state and even joined the National Security Board, was crucial in organizing security and logistical arrangements for these elections. He also supervised the upgradation and organization of the security control room, which helped bring greater transparency to police operations. The police gave bulletproof vehicles and armed escorts to candidates in selected constituencies, but soon, we had all the candidates reach out to us. Another significant partner was the state CRPF inspector general Amarjot Gill – he later deservedly became chief of the CRPF and Rajasthan Police – he had a disciplined mind and was computer savvy. His spreadsheets keeping track of the many logistics, resources and vehicles, and ensured we didn't lose a single candidate or have a single booth overrun.

Our SOG played an important role as well. The surrender of many militants with arms at Baramulla, Srinagar, Awantipora, Pulwama and Anantnagar created confidence, momentum and morale. Many became part of our security apparatus and helped us improve our intelligence and counter-insurgency grid. This momentum was also helped by the setting up of a dedicated counter-intelligence centre and state security effort at Hari Niwas overlooking Dal Lake. All the tactical intelligence and operational requirements for the security of political leaders at home and while campaigning were provided by this nerve centre of state police.

Governor General Rao's leadership also stood out during this time. He often reminded us, 'If one has to serve the people, you have to take some risks.' To not scare public perception, he advised the army to avoid polling stations and instead provide support in specific sensitive constituencies. We planned the election exercise extensively, and militants hurt none of the candidates or those involved in managing the election, nor were there any noticeable disturbances anywhere in the state. There were some disruptions by militants in south Kashmir, who used grenades at a rally of Dr Farooq's in Pulwama and fired at a rally of A.R. Takroo of the Communist Party of India (CPI). The police managed both situations efficiently, but we constantly had to be on our toes.

Campaigning saw the expenditure of a colossal amount of energy. Party workers were reaching out to people on the ground, and they responded. A famous slogan from 1947, 'Hamlawar, khabardar, hum Kashmiri hain taiyyar' (Aggressors beware, we Kashmiris are ready), was once again heard on the streets across the state. Electors were hopeful, and the assembly election saw a turnout of 54 per cent, which was higher than the parliamentary elections held a few months earlier. Ahead of the polls, then prime minister Deve Gowda even visited the state, which included a visit to the Valley, the first by a prime minister after nine years.

The National Conference emerged victorious with a two-thirds majority and won fifty-seven seats. The party had a clean sweep in the Valley, with one seat going to Kuka Parray, who had ditched militancy and joined electoral politics. The National Conference also won seats in the Muslim-dominated areas of Jammu. The BJP consolidated Hindu votes and, for the first time, emerged as the second-largest party with eight seats. However, the previously more assertive Congress only won seven of the eighty-four seats it contested and was in third position.

Farooq Abdullah, who took charge as chief minister on 9 October 1996, ended the political vacuum and long President's Rule in the state. He took charge with twelve cabinet ministers, twelve ministers of state and two deputy ministers. Attendees at his swearing-in ceremony included the former prime minister V.P. Singh, Congress president Sitaram Kesari and the general secretary of the Communist Party of India (Marxist) [CPI (M)] Harkishen Singh Surjeet.

Academic David Shulman wrote, 'All the great civilizations, and probably all human societies, have known human beings are capable of imagining; India merely cultivated this art, or faculty, more boldly than most.' The difference between India and Pakistan is India defies the odds of being a vibrant democracy despite being big, poor and diverse. Unlike our neighbours, democracy is now at the core of India's identity; our constitution is written by good forebears who have ensured India counts our citizens and doesn't weigh them. China forces its citizens to choose between freedom and their wallets, and Pakistan frames it as a choice between religion and citizenship.

A confluence of many of India's civilizations and societies, J&K must build a representative state government populated by a new breed of politicians who listen, heal and rebuild rather than oppress, exploit and destroy. Politics in J&K were dynastic, uncompetitive and corrupt. The state now holds assembly elections under the Indian constitution, but the last eleven were held under the JK state Representation of the People Act, 1950, with six-year government tenures and residents excluded from voting based on their birthplace, birthdate or ancestors. As the 1996 elections demonstrated, elections are not magical solutions to terrorism, but they do offer soothing representation, recognition and voices.

Farooq assured all of us and his voters that J&K remains an integral part of India and that he was striving for a clean and responsive government. I left the state three months after Farooq's election but sensed he had a unique chance since this was his first clear majority to conclude its full term. Yet, Farooq didn't live up to expectations. He announced 60,000 government jobs but chose the route of nepotism and corruption to fill those seats with party workers. He reneged on his pledge to rehabilitate victims of militancy and the families of Kashmiri Pandits. He weakened the highly effective SOG of the J&K Police. He prioritized the construction of a golf course over hospitals and schools, and the state remained entirely dependent on grants from the centre. It is easy to be disappointed, but as Oscar Wilde wrote, 'We are all in the gutter together, but some of us are looking at the stars.' I am in Wilde's camp and believe free and fair elections can help find solutions to many of J&K's problems.

Conclusion

There are five ways to fight terrorism: security forces, elected representatives, drying up financing, destroying terrorists' logistics and supply chains, and breaking down their narratives (the battle for hearts and minds). And until recently, India did not deploy all these tools in our fight against Pakistan's terror factory.

Security forces are of all kinds: army, paramilitary, intelligence and police. But the army cannot substitute for the police, as being embedded in the community, intelligence networks and language familiarity are key to sustained peace. A border state like J&K will always need the army and without them, we would not have been able to reduce terrorism to the level it has been today. And the early years of terrorism were devastating for police forces; they didn't have the weapons or tactics, their families were easy targets and some of them were compromised. Terrorism is an asymmetric game as recognized in the Kashmiri proverb 'Rachhis doh te' tshooras gaer.' (The watchman gets the whole day but a thief only gets a few moments.)

I look back upon my time as J&K police chief as most people do about their career, with a mix of pride about what got done, regret for what went wrong and wistfulness for risks not taken. I am reminded of a wonderful passage in Tolstoy's *War and Peace* in which Prince Andrei, waiting for the Battle of Borodino, reflects on the difference between war and chess. In chess, a bishop is always more powerful than a pawn, while in battle, a platoon can sometimes overpower a company. In other words, war has no rules, just strategies to handle unpredictability. This feels true of my career in the J&K Police, which was an encounter between skill and willpower and the forces of fortune and chance.

The reinvigoration of the J&K Police that begun with the establishment of the SOG in 1994 has been steadily and competently taken to the next level by talented cadre police chief successors like Ashok Suri, Gopal Sharma, Kuldeep Khoda, K. Rajendra Kumar, Shesh Vaid, Dilbagh Singh and R.R. Swain. The abrogation of Article 370 is an opportunity for J&K Police to emerge as an essential stakeholder of peace, the face of security and intelligence-led operations and bring justice to terrorists. The J&K Police are the tip of the spear that is necessary in Kashmir. It was an honour to lead it and has been a joy to watch it rise to even greater heights after I left.

Epilogue: Naya Kashmir

In peace, sons bury their fathers. In war, fathers bury their sons.
– Herodotus

If we want everything to remain the same, everything must change.
– *The Leopard* by Giuseppe di Lampedusa

I believe every book should end by answering the question: 'Whose mind do you expect to change about what?'

I hope the people in J&K recognize the sectarianism, factionalism, Islamism, regionalism and nepotism prevalent in their state since 1947 was not God's will and that things are changing. I hope J&K's politicians recognize the days of soft separatism are over, and they participate in generating alternatives to the 'elite bargain' that made J&K a 'closed access society'. I hope every young person in J&K recognizes the economic opportunities India offers. I hope Pakistan's awaam recognizes that they confront a stronger India, and that the world has changed its view about their state-sponsored terrorism fuelled by radical Islam, so that they reconsider their occupation of Indian land. I hope policymakers and security forces recognize the long road ahead in peace and prosperity and don't confuse the commendable current momentum with victory. I hope poet Allama Iqbal, wherever he is, now agrees he was wrong in suggesting that 'Jis khaak ki zameen mein hain aatish chinar, mumkin nahin hain ki sarad ho woh khaaki arjumand.' (The earth that has within its bosom the embers of the chinar, this exalted earth can never cool down.)

My case for changing minds is built on history. Sheikh Abdullah returned to power in 1975 with little to show for twenty-two years of detention, because, as he told me, 'Siyasat suleh hain, suleh siyasat hain' (Politics is compromise, compromise is politics.) He mischievously, but wisely, added 'Zindagi bhi suleh hain.' Politicians in J&K must recognize their demands for autonomy have always been delusional at best and poisonous at worst. The most thoughtful advice for politicians is to campaign in poetry but govern in prose. The era of soft separatism in campaigning and governing is over and is never coming back. I am 'khoash fahmi munz rozoon' (optimistic for good results) about Naya Kashmir because of five changes since I retired.

The Abrogation of Article 370: Special constitutional status allowed J&K's politicians to practise what Kashmiris call 'moolan droth ta patran sag' (watering the leaves while cutting the roots). The abrogation of Article 370 answers the 1950s call in Parliament by Syama Prasad Mookerjee of 'Ek desh me do vidhan, do pradhan, do nishan nahin chalenge.' (One nation cannot accept two constitutions, two heads of state and two flags.) Sheikh Abdullah was the first Kashmiri in 358 years to rule J&K. However, circumstances kept J&K politics oligopolistic, dynastic and stale. I remember the hopes that filled our hearts with the election victories of 1996, 2002, 2008 and 2014, but we were left disappointed. Harvard Professor Pippa Norris suggests electoral thresholds influence whether parties adopt bridging or bonding strategies, ballot structures shape how far parties adopt diverse or homogeneous candidates, and context affects the emphasis on programmatic or particularistic campaigning. Future J&K elections will be held under the Indian Constitution and will have exciting new electoral thresholds, ballot structures and context. This abrogation helps new politicians and parties who will use the 'civilized civil war' of democracy to convert conflicts into trade-offs through a new slate of ideas that blunt passions, create interests and forge compromise. This new breed must remember the Mahabharata's advice of 'dharmo rakshati rakshitah' (the system protects those who protect the system).

Cross-border military strikes: The Pakistan military never expected the cross-border military strikes from India after testing nuclear weapons, but the Uri and Pulwama responses answered the decades-old prayers of the security leadership in J&K for the hot and cold pursuit of terrorists. Those prayers weren't bloodlust but an intuition that Pakistan's terror factory wouldn't back down without new calculations. Facing no consequences for their attack on the J&K assembly in 2001 led to more significant attacks on the Indian parliament in 2001 and Mumbai in 2008. These strikes undermine Pakistan's military promise of a gravity-free world. I wasn't familiar with Nobel Laureate Thomas Schelling's book *The Strategy of Conflict* before retiring, but his framing of deterrence as the promise of future pain resonates with me. India's surgical strikes signal new rules from a more decisive, prosperous and less passive India and strengthen the hands of Pakistani people who want defence forces that defend and not rule.

Global acceptance that radical Islam is fuelling terrorism: The false narrative of jihad was useful to the US in drafting Mujahideen to fight the USSR in Afghanistan. But clearly, the CIA hadn't heard of the myth of Bhasmasur, the demon you create that turns on you. It was only a matter of time before radical Islam and the Wahhabis turned their attention to the West. There were early signs; a 1990s US National Intelligence Council report about Islamic terrorism lamented that decisive action against them felt unviable till a 'domestic Pearl Harbour' took place. India's warnings were dismissed as self-interest, and I remember being amazed at how ignorant the FBI agents sent to Srinagar to liaise during kidnapping negotiations were about the terror infrastructure and

Pakistan's intentions. Sadly, it took the 9/11 attacks for the US to recognize the dangers of radical Islam and galvanize action on global financing, training, propaganda and the weapons trade fuelling terrorism. India's position on cross-border terrorism is no longer lonely or unique. Hopefully, this will make Pakistan's position and actions untenable.

Pakistan's rising weaknesses: Pakistan's geopolitical importance was greatly diminished by the 9/11 terrorist attacks, Osama Bin Laden's role in them and US–China rivalry. Internal anger is also rising against Pakistan's economically incompetent garrison state weaponizing Islam and sabotaging mass prosperity. The country's per capita GDP is lower than Bangladesh, the total GDP is lower than Maharashtra, and they have had twenty-three bailouts by the International Monetary Fund since 1947. The garrison state's political and social control tools are formidable, but the abrogation of Article 370 strengthens the case for Pakistan's awaam choosing ittihad (friendship) over military-sponsored jihad. The path to a more normal democracy in Pakistan is unclear, but its rising internal and external weakness diminish its ability to get away with murder. Every country is what in Sanskrit is called an 'antarlaapika' or a riddle in which the answer lies within the riddle – only Pakistan's awaam can send its military back to the barracks.

India's rising strengths: India created the world's largest democracy after 1947 but failed to create mass prosperity. But this is changing; a massive renovation of India's intellectual, security, financial, diplomatic, investment, welfare and economic infrastructure is underway. India is now the fifth-largest economy in the world and will soon be third after China and the US. In recent years, we have exported more software than Saudi Arabia did oil. This gives our military a massive edge in a digital world where the distinction between military and civilian technology is eroding. The most significant change is a new policy tone from the top; we don't have to be Western to be modern. We have zero tolerance for terrorism, and we must be a developed country by 2047 with India@100. India's soft and hard power must change Pakistan's calculations, options and niyat (intentions).

Many people in J&K will understandably be unnerved by these five changes. But decades of blood, pain and misunderstanding meant risk-taking was necessary because as Ghalib said, 'Manzil to milegi bhatak ke hi sahi, ghumrah to wo hain jo ghar se hi nahin nikle.' (We will find out destinations even if we are wandering but lost are those who did not leave home.) American philosopher Martha Nussbaum reminds us that risk-taking is 'more like a plant than a jewel, something rather fragile, but whose very particular beauty is inseparable from its fragility'. But the job in J&K is far from finished, and change must continue to cement gains and end terrorism forever. I suggest we spend the next few years pursuing five things: the police piloting law and order, rebooting India's UN engagement, establishing new political parties, restoring statehood, and reasserting Kashmiri moderate Islam.

The case for restoring J&K Police to the driver's seat for law and order will sound like a plug for my profession. It has been my privilege and honour to work with all forces but my case is made within the context of very different capabilities, roles and fitrat of the civil police, paramilitary and military forces. Every democracy gives its police a monopoly on internal violence. The military has a different thought world than any civil administration; their battalions regularly rotate with a clear mission for every operation, their huge cordon-and-search operations involve thousands of officers, and they are trained for war, not insurgency. They often don't speak the language and have limited intelligence networks. The lessons from Vietnam, Afghanistan and Iraq for the US army are many but as David H. Petraeus's paper 'Lessons of History and Lessons of Vietnam' suggested 'We will have to conduct military operations, peacekeeping operations and provide humanitarian operations all on the same day and all within a few miles.' Besides versatility, military power will have to work in tandem with political, economic, humanitarian and informational warfare because their role in achieving strategic goals has increased and sometimes exceeds the power of force. I salute the professionalism and performance of our army and paramilitary forces. However, community-embedded organizations with deep networks, context awareness, political accountability, local recruitment and language fluency are best suited for monopolies on violence. Within the paramilitary forces, it has been a wonderful decision to dedicate CRPF for internal security across India. Using the SSB, ITBP, BSF and military for internal security has greatly declined in the last two decades and must be avoided.

I cannot imagine J&K's security situation coming under control without our military and paramilitary forces. But it's time for a rejigging of roles; making local police staffed by local officers the first line of defence and offence in law and order is logical, emotional and powerful. The many new tools in our terrorism toolkit demonstrate the power of the military, paramilitary and police working together while performing different roles. The wars in Gaza and Ukraine also suggest a radical revamp of information, technology and organization architecture, and flattening of hierarchies and of the culture of steep authority gradients in our military and paramilitary forces. We should also implement the police commissioner system in Jammu and Srinagar cities; the current structure diminishes accountability, efficiency and effectiveness. Dr Farooq Abdullah had accepted my recommendation and publicly announced adopting this when he was chief minister. But it still hasn't happened. We must continue the impressive transformation of the reach, resilience, lethality, collaboration, speed and intelligence of our police, paramilitary and military in J&K because while Pakistan's military is losing, it is not defeated.

The United Nations office in Srinagar must be closed – it became redundant after the 1972 agreement when Pakistan accepted Kashmir as a bilateral issue – and we must now shift our UN engagement to executing UN Resolution 1373, which obliges all states to undertake actions to prevent and undermine the ability of terrorists to use their soil to organize, recruit and train, and raise funds. This resolution considers terrorist events a threat to international security and carries the possibility of a forceful response by the UN and member states. If any country deserves this response from the international community, it is Pakistan. So replicating the UNSC 1267 Committee (the Al-Qaeda sanctions committee) for Pakistan's deep state actors involved in terrorism will help their gasping democracy.

Kashmiri Islam must reassert itself against alien strains. We would do well to think about a genre in literature called Dialogues of the Dead that brings together thinkers who lived in different places and eras and would never have met in life. In the afterlife of heaven and hell, everyone is everyone else's contemporary, and the world's greatest minds, and most powerful leaders defend their beliefs from scrutiny more pointedly than they encountered in this world. What better way could there be to reveal fallacies, expose pretence or progress closer to the truth? Imagine such a dialogue between syncretic Kashmiris like Kalhana, Shah Hamdan, Nooruddin Noorani, Lal Ded, Habba Khatun, Sheikh Abdullah, and Islamic fundamentalists like Muhammad ibn Abd al-Wahhab (the founder of Wahhabism), and Maulana Syed Maududi (the founder of Jamaat-e-Islami). The history of Kashmir makes it easy to see the victory of 'open-minded dialogue over dogmatism, tiny alterations to consciousness over unquestionable overarching theory, and wonder over certainty'.

Finally, statehood must be restored, but I agree with sceptics who suggest that full statehood for J&K is a destination best travelled through a hybrid model like Delhi, where the state and central government share power. Democracy separates India from Pakistan, but Kashmir has not always benefited because separatism became a viable political strategy to grow wealth and dynasty. Former National Conference leader Professor Balraj Puri believed that Kashmiri regionalist, Islamic fundamentalist, Muslim communalist, pro-Pakistan, anti-centre and anti-Congress sentiments overlapped. These overlaps must now end.

As the Kashmiri mystic Nund Rishi wrote, 'I broke my sword and made it into a sickle,' and the only viable strategy is cadre-based parties quarrelling with Delhi without peddling separatism. Does anybody think Tamil Nadu falls in line with everything the central government wants? Sheikh Abdullah made a speech at Hazoori Bagh in 1972 in which he said, ' Some people believe Pakistan is a party to the issue. I don't know of anybody who has a letter of attorney from Pakistan. If Pakistan has the might, it should prove its credentials. I appeal to you not to turn to Pakistan or China for the solution to your problems. We have to solve them ourselves. This land belongs to us, and only we can decide its future.' His rival Mirwaiz Farooq suggested, 'One person and one party is not the entire Valley. The Sheikh is not the sole representative of the people here . . . Gain the confidence of the youth and don't rely on the old guard.' This kind of brutally competitive state politics without separatism has been missing in J&K. But it is our best hope for peace and prosperity.

The Kashmiri expression 'Saadi saet lughin ya laetmitch' (the start of seven-and-a-half-year period) is rooted in the myth of budhshervaar (a lousy period lasting seven and half years) occurring a maximum of three times in one life. The last few decades have seen many bad periods in J&K, but changes now improve the odds of 'Saadi saet nairin' (the end of seven and a half). Better days, I believe, lie ahead.

Notes

Preface

xiv **'We [the princely states] are the real India'** John Zubrzycki, *Dethroned: Patel, Menon and The Integration of Princely India*, Juggernaut, 2023.

1. Hazratbal: A Tale of Two Sieges

8 **'To kill a rat, you don't have to bring down the house'** Khushwant Singh, *Truth, Love and a Little Malice*, Penguin India, 2002.

14 **'Hazratbal was a god-sent opportunity for the Hurriyat leadership . . .'** Sati Sahni, *Kashmir Underground*, Har-Anand Publications, 1999.

15 **'damaged the Azadi Movement at the behest of the Indian government . . .'** Ibid.

15 **'he has been indulging in an opportunist, undemocratic, and dictatorial style . . .'** Ibid.

15 **'The emergence of Malik as the JKLF supremo . . .'** Ibid.

15 **'We are soldiers of Allah . . .'** R.C. Ganjoo, *Operation Khatma*, Locksley Hall Publishing LLP, 2022.

2. J&K Is Not the Valley

23 **'To write about the character of Kashmiris is not easy . . .'** C.E. Tyndale Biscoe, *Kashmir in Sunlight and Shade*, Seeley, Service and Co., 1922.

24 **Nobel laureate Douglass North described as a 'limited access' society** Douglass C. North, John Joseph Wallis, Steven B. Webb and Barry R. Weingast, 'Limited Access Orders in the Developing World: A New Approach to the Problems of Development', Policy Research working paper, no. WPS 4359, World Bank Group, 2007.

25 **'Indecisive by nature, he [Hari Singh] played for time . . .'** Sandeep Bamzai, *Gilded Cage: Years That Made And Unmade Kashmir*, Rupa Publications, 2023.

32 **'. . . the state was a wholly artificial creation . . .'** Jawaid Alam (ed.), *Jammu and Kashmir 1949–1964: Select Correspondence Between Jawaharlal Nehru and Karan Singh*, Penguin, 2006.

3. Delhi in J&K: Fraught Federalism

41 **'There was an innocence of a child in his demeanour which made one love him'** Sheikh Mohammad Abdullah, Khushwant Singh (trans.), *Flames of the Chinar* [*Aatish-i-Chinar*], Viking, 1993.

41 **'There is no doubt Sheikh Abdullah is by far the most outstanding leader in Kashmir'** John Zubrzycki, *Dethroned: Patel, Menon and the Integration of Princely India*, Juggernaut, 2023.

63 **But most of all, I disagree with his writing a book with a Pakistani deep-state player (ISI chief)** A.S. Dulat, Asad Durrani and Aditya Sinha, *The Spy Chronicles: RAW, ISI and the Illusion of Peace*, HarperCollins, 2018.

4. Politics in J&K: Separatism as Strategy

77 **'Bakshi frequently saved Abdullah from the consequences of his naivete . . .'** Chitralekha Zutshi, *Sheikh Abdullah: The Caged Lion of Kashmir*, Fourth Estate, 2023.

78 **'the most efficient person is Bakshi Ghulam Mohammad, who gets gets . . .'** *Selected Works of Jawaharlal Nehru: 7 April 1948 to 21 June 1948*, Jawaharlal Nehru Memorial Fund, 1987.

78 **'unambiguous, predictable, stable and pro-India'** Chitralekha Zutshi, *Sheikh Abdullah: The Caged Lion of Kashmir*, Fourth Estate, 2023.

81 **'It is not your motherland cannot provide you with roti . . .'** Ibid.

81 **'communal politics doesn't suit the temperament of the people of this state'** Sheikh Mohammad Abdullah, Khushwant Singh (trans.), *Flames of the Chinar [Aatish-i-Chinar]*, Viking, 1993.

82 **Jinnah described the National Conference as a 'band of gangsters'** *Khemlata Wakhlu, A Kashmiri Century: Portrait of a Society in Flux*, HarperCollins, 2021.

83 **'he was secular in so far as he did not believe . . .'** B.K. Nehru, *Nice Guys Finish Last: Memoirs*, Penguin, 2012.

83 **'whose conscience was Muslim, his heart was Kashmiri and his brain**

was secular' Chitralekha Zutshi, *Sheikh Abdullah: The Caged Lion of Kashmir*, Fourth Estate, 2023.

85 **'the discharge of his duty to his people'** Sheikh Mohammad Abdullah, Khushwant Singh (trans.), *Flames of the Chinar [Aatish-i-Chinar]*, Viking, 1993.

85 **'Whenever Sheikh Sahib wishes to back out . . .'** A.G. Noorani (ed.), *Article 370: A Constitutional History of Jammu and Kashmir*, Oxford University Press, 2011.

85 **'I fear Sheikh Sahib's mind is so utterly confused he doesn't know what to do'** Chitralekha Zutshi, *Sheikh Abdullah: The Caged Lion of Kashmir*, Fourth Estate, 2023.

87 **'Pakistan has ultimately got its saviour after its share of trials and tribulations'** Praveen Swami, *India, Pakistan and the Secret Jihad: The Covert War in Kashmir, 1947–2004*, Routledge, 2006.

103 **'If that were true, then large parts of India would have been disturbed'** M.N. Sabharwal, Manish Sabharwal, 'With Bharat Jodo Yatra Ending in Kashmir, a Reason to Remember Sheikh Abdullah', *The Indian Express*, 6 March 2023.

112 **'Being hooted at after a defeat is understandable, but this was incredible'** Suni Gavaskar, *Runs 'n Ruin*, Rupa Publications, 1984.

118 **'corrupt, lecherous, arrogant, ill-mannered, unpleasant, pro-Pakistan, anti-India and anti-Hindu'** B.K. Nehru, *Nice Guys Finish Last: Memoirs*, Penguin, 2012.

126 **'More Muslim youth are seen in the mosques . . .'** Surinder Singh Oberoi, 'Ethnic Separatism and Insurgency in Kashmir', Asia-Pacific Centre for Security Studies, 2011. Retrieved from http://www.apcss.org/Publications/Edited%20Volumes/ReligiousRadicalism/PagesfromReligiousRadicalismandSecurityinSouthAsiach8.pdf.

129 **Journalist M.J. Akbar had once asked, though the Kashmir nose** M.J. Akbar, *Kashmir: Behind the Vale*, Roli Books, 2017.

5. Pakistan in Kashmir: The Terror Factory

136 **'Since there is no other institution to rival our military . . .'** Aqil Shah, *The Army and Democracy: Military Politics in Pakistan*, Harvard University Press, 2014.

139 **'Musalmans should realize Hindus can never . . .'** Yashee, '44 Years of Zulfikar Ali Bhutto's Hanging: The Man Who Would "Wage a War for 1,000 Years" with India', *The Indian Express*, 4 May 2023.

151 **'a hawk that flies high in the sky, out of danger . . .'** Akbar Khan, *Raiders in Kashmir*, National Book Foundation, 1975.

152 **'As a Muslim, I believe in the kalima . . .'** Praveen Swami, *India, Pakistan and the Secret Jihad: The Covert War in Kashmir, 1947–2004*, Routledge, 2006.

153 **'In the Cold War, NATO used nuclear weapons . . .'** Sumit Ganguly, R. Harrison Wagner, 'India and Pakistan: Bargaining in the Shadow of Nuclear War', *Journal of Strategic Studies*, Vol. 27, Issue 3, 8 September 2003.

155 **'But how can the Americans stop us from waging Jihad in Kashmir when they are waging Jihad in Afghanistan?'** Praveen Swami, *India, Pakistan and the Secret Jihad: The Covert War in Kashmir, 1947–2004*, Routledge, 2006.

7. The Police Chief Years: Fighting Back

188 **'We were being lured into the role of a bull in a bullfight . . .'** Niall Ferguson, *Kissinger 1923–1968: The Idealist*, Penguin, 2015.

208 **'If Jammu and Kashmir has to remain . . .'** Ramesh Vinayak, 'Dogged by Unkept Promises, CM Farooq Abdullah Bargains for Greater Autonomy for J&K', *India Today*, 14 January 2014.

211 **'All the great civilizations, and probably all human societies . . .'** David Shulman, *More than Real: A History of the Imagination in South India*, Harvard University Press, 2012.

Bibliography

This book stands on the shoulders of giants. The exciting and painful history of J&K has inspired many interesting books we tasted, savoured or digested. We benefited greatly from the detailed indexes and sources in these books and think it would be helpful to give you a broad sense of what we read. We owe these authors a debt of gratitude that will remain unpaid; this book would have remained unwritten without your ideas, scholarship and hard work. Only when one wants to express something more profoundly or keenly felt does one realize the inadequacy of language. Thank you.

History: While this book is mostly about my time in Kashmir, reading up on the earlier periods helped us understand many things about the situation today. The anthology *Kashmir; History; Politics, Representation*, edited by Chitralekha Zutshi, had many diverse perspectives. *Kashmir in Sunlight & Shade: A Description of the Beauties of the Country* by C.E. Tyndale Biscoe, a missionary and school teacher who arrived in 1891, gives an interesting view of the early Kashmir. Other interesting books were *Kashmir and Jammu: Imperial Gazetteer* by Walter Lawrence, *Looking Within: Lesson from Lal Ded* edited by Shonaleeka Kaul, *The History of Struggle for Freedom in Kashmir* by Prem Nath Bazaz, the three volumes of *Kashmir: From Ancient to Present; A Socio-Cultural and Political History* by M.J. Aslam, *Kashmir: Being a History of Kashmir from the*

Earliest Times to Our Own by G.M.D. Sufi, *Kashmir's Transition to Islam: The Role of Muslim Rishis (15th to 18th Centuries)* by M. Ishaq Khan, *Nund Rishi: Poetry and Politics in Medieval Kashmir* by Abir Bazaz, the three-volume *A Modern History of Jammu and Kashmir* by Harbans Singh contains a lot of research. We got a peek into the royalty years through Dr Karan Singh's *Autobiography*, *Dethroned: The Downfall of India's Princely States* by John Zubrzycki, *Gilded Cage: Years that Made and Unmade Kashmir* by Sandeep Bamzai and *Integration of the Indian States* by V.P. Menon. We gained insight into the perspective of the UN from *Danger in Kashmir:1931* by Joseph Korbel.

Pakistan: No book about Kashmir can be whole without thinking and understanding Pakistan. Two books by my professional colleague Tilak Devasher, *Pakistan: Courting the Abyss* and *Pakistan at the Helm*, were a great place to start. *The Army and Democracy: Military Politics in Pakistan* by Aqil Shah, *Military Inc.: Inside Pakistan's Military Economy* by Ayesha Siddiqa, *A History of the Pakistan Army: Wars and Insurrections* by Brian Cloughley, *Pakistan: Between Mosque and Military* by Hussain Haqqani, *Faith, Unity, Discipline: The ISI of Pakistan* by Hein G. Kiessling, and *The Pakistan Military in Politics: Origins, Evolution, Consequences* by Ishtiaq Ahmed helped us understand why no Pakistani prime minister has completed their entire term and how the armed forces maintain a firm grip on the nation's politics. *The Blood Telegram: India's Secret War in East Pakistan* by Gary Bass and *1971: A Global History of the Creation of Bangladesh* by Srinath Raghavan should be mandatory reading for anybody in J&K who believes Pakistan runs a fair government where the citizens have a voice. The divergent destiny of J&K and Pakistan-Occupied Kashmir became real for us in the pages of *Forgotten Kashmir: The Other Side of the Line of Control* by Dinkar Srivastava and *The Two Kashmirs: A Comparative Analysis* by Sheikh Khalid Jahangir. Other exciting books we read were *Anger*

Management: The Troubled Diplomatic Relationship between India and Pakistan by Ajay Bisaria, *Pakistan Adrift: Navigating Troubled Waters* by Asad Durrani, *Born to be Hanged* by Syeda Hameed, *The People Next Door: The Curious Case of India's Relations with Pakistan* by T.C.A. Raghavan, *Crossed Swords: Pakistan, Its Army, and the Wars Within* by Shuja Nawaz, *The Struggle for Pakistan: A Muslim Homeland and Global Politics* by Ayesha Jalal, *The Idea of Pakistan* by Stephen Cohen, *Jinnah of Pakistan* by Stanley Wolpert, *The Military in Pakistan: Image and Reality* by Brigadier A.R. Siddiqi, and *What's Wrong with Pakistan* by Babar Ayaz.

Politics: Sheikh Abdullah's autobiography *Aatish-e-Chinar* is valuable reading despite the controversy about its authenticity or originality. Gaps about him and the post-Delhi Accord period came from *Sheikh Mohammad Abdullah: Tragic Hero of Kashmir* by Ajit Bhattacharjea, *The Making of Modern Kashmir*

Sheikh Abdullah and the Politics of the State by Altaf Hussain Para, *Nice Guys Finish Second: Memoirs* by B.K. Nehru, *My Life: Years at the Bar, Bench and in Kashmir Politics* by D.D. Thakur, *Kashmir: Behind the Vale* by M.J. Akbar, *Kashmir in the Aftermath of Partition* by Shahla Hussain, *Kashmir and Beyond 1966–84: Select Correspondence between Indira Gandhi and Karan Singh* edited by Jawaid Alam, *Kashmir: The Untold Story* by Huma Quraishi, and *The Lost Rebellion: Kashmir in the Nineties* by Manoj Joshi. Recent books with diverse perspectives include *Azaad* by Ghulam Nabi Azad, *Kashmir: The Vajpayee Years* by A.S. Daulat and Aditya Sinha, *Our Moon Has Blood Clots* by Rahul Pandita, *Paradise at War: A Political History of Kashmir* by Radha Kumar, *A Kashmiri Century: Portrait of a Society in Flux* by Khem Lata Wakhlu, *Kashmir Rage and Reason* by Gowhar Geelani. A fantastic new biography, *Sheikh Abdullah: The Caged Lion of Kashmir* by Chitralekha Zutshi, brought everything together and we have learnt much from her. Former Governor General K.V. Krishna Rao's autobiography *In the Service of the Nation: Reminiscences* gave us the perspective of the governor's perch during those years.

Terrorism: My talented friend, the late Sati Sahni, wrote the most detailed book on terrorism in J&K, *Kashmir Underground*. The Pakistani side is best captured in *Shadow War: The Untold Story of Jihad in Kashmir* by Arif Jamal, *India, Pakistan and the Secret Jihad: The covert war in Kashmir, 1947–2004* by Praveen Swami, *Fighting to the End: The Pakistan Army's Way of War* by C. Christine Fair and *Sleepwalking to Surrender: Dealing with Terrorism in Pakistan* by Khaled Ahmed. *Operation Khatma* by R.C. Ganjoo and Ashwini Bhatnagar is a sound reconstruction and chronicle of J&K's Special Operations Group. An excellent history of India's home ministry called *Governance by Stealth* by Subrata Mitra provided insights into Delhi's thinking and work, which is not always visible from the state. Other exciting books that help better understand the violence include *Kashmir's Untold Story: Declassified* by Iqbal Malhotra and Maroof Raza and *Kashmir at the Crossroads: Inside a 21st-Century Conflict* by Sumantra Bose.

Other Sources: This book benefited from many short research papers, newspapers and online platforms. Columns written with my son that published in the *Indian Express* nudged us to put together our thoughts on Article 370, terrorism and politics in J&K. The Nehru Memorial Museum and Library in New Delhi helped by providing their microfilm collection, including the *Daily Excelsior* and other newspapers from the 1990s. News organizations, including *Greater Kashmir*, the *Tribune*, *Print*, *Frontline*, *Outlook*, *Mint*, the *Indian Express*, the *Hindustan Times*, the *Times of India*, and News 18 have continuously covered the state. *India Today*'s reportage on the critical events in my career, including the Hazratbal siege, militancy and the burning of Charar-e-Sharief, was comprehensive and fair. Overseas platforms like the *Daily Times*, *New York Times*,

Quartz, *LA Times* and *Irish Times* were also helpful for their reportage on Kashmir and its history. The websites of the Election Commission of India, union home ministry, J&K finance ministry, J&K department revenue and the J&K Police provided a repository of statistical information. Academic papers, including the work of the United Nations and Observer Research Foundation, helped us understand some of the nuances of the plebiscite and patterns of conflict.

In Memory and Honour

The 1608 J&K Police & 511 CRPF Officers Martyred Fighting Terrorists 1989–2023

'Qatal gahon se chun kar hamare alam
Aur niklenge ushaak ke quafile'
(The caravan of patriots will march after collecting the flags from the hands of martyrs on the battlefield)
– Faiz Ahmad Faiz, quoted in *Aatish-i-Chinar*, Sheikh Abdullah's autobiography

J&K Police

1 Said-Ullah Lone	19 Makhan Lal Wangno	37 Qadeer Ahmad Shah
2 Mumtaz Ahmad Shah	20 Ghulam Rasool Ganai	38 Muzaffar Hussain Khan
3 Ghulam Qadir Qasab	21 Shiban Lal Kaloo	39 Omkar Nath
4 Ghulam Mustafa	22 Sher Singh	40 Abdul Majeed Masoodi
5 Abdul Hamid	23 Isher Das	41 Naseeb Singh
6 Abdul Karim Ganie	24 Noor Mohammad Khan	42 Abdul Aziz
7 Chuni Lal Shala	25 Shuban Lal Koul	43 Mohammad Yamin
8 Abdul Hamid Khan	26 Ghulam Mohi-Ud-Din	44 Mohammad Ramzan Gori
9 Dilshad Abdul Gani	27 Farooq Ahmad Bhat	45 Sher Mohammad Khan
10 Abdul Rehman Rahi	28 Ram Nath	46 Abdul Rashid
11 Ghulam Hassan Mir	29 Mahesh Chander	47 Amir-Ud-Din
12 Jaggar Nath	30 Hari Singh	48 Mudasir Sajad Dar
13 Ghulam Hassan Shawl	31 Mulkh Raj	49 Tara Chand
14 Mohammad Yousuf Bhat	32 Shabir Ahmad Lone	50 Mehar Singh
15 Dalip Singh	33 Ali Mohammad Lone	51 Farid Ahmad Sheikh
16 Abdul Rehman Bhat	34 Balwan Singh	52 Ghulam Hassan Mir
17 Dawarka Nath	35 Madan Lal	53 Abdul Gani Ganie
18 Prem Nath	36 Suresh Kumar	54 Abdul Ahad Bhat

55 Mohammad Maqbool	97 Nazir Ahmad	139 Romesh Lal
56 Mohammad Yaseen Mir	98 Chain Singh	140 Ali Mohammad
57 Mohammad Raza Beig	99 Abdul Samad Lone	141 Mohammad Akram Ganie
58 Ghulam Nabi Shah	100 Ahmadullah	142 Mushtaq Ahmad Sheikh
59 Ravail Singh	101 Abdul Gani	143 Shah Hussain
60 Mohammad Hamza	102 Reyaz Ahmad	144 Abdul Rashid
61 Amarjeet Singh	103 Ghulam Nabi	145 Abdul Rashid Khan
62 Bashir Ahmad	104 Habib-Ullah Wani	146 Mohammad Iqbal Wani
63 Mohammad Subhan	105 Mohammad Sadiq Waza	147 Ishfaq Ahmed
64 Mohammad Sharief Sheikh	106 Ghulam Qadir Mir	148 Abdul Rashid
65 Mohammad Maqbool	107 Aijaz Ahmad Malik	149 Abdul Gaffar
66 Abdul Rehman Khan	108 Hoshyar Singh	150 Abdul Majeed Teeli
67 Ghulam Jeelani	109 Ashok Kumar	151 Dost Mohammad
68 Ghulam Rasool Bhat	110 Mohammad Maqbool Ganie	152 Abdul Rashid Sheikh
69 Shiv Dev Singh	111 Mohammad Sikander	153 Mushtaq Ahmad Mongriyal
70 Mohammad Yousuf	112 Balwan Singh	154 Abdul Rehman Najar
71 Dewan Singh	113 Vinod Kumar	155 Gulzar Ahmad Mir
72 Surrinder Kumar	114 Udhaibir Singh	156 Abdul Hamid Ganai
73 Ravi Singh	115 Romesh Lal	157 Krishan Dutt
74 Hamid Hussain	116 Ghulam Mohi-Ud-Din	158 Abdul Salam Kuchay
75 Mohammad Shafi	117 Ganesh Dass	159 Bashir Ahmad Wani
76 Abdul Rehman Bhat	118 Nazir Ahmad	160 Dilshada Akhter
77 Tilak Raj	119 Syed Shabir Hussain	161 Ghulam Ahmad
78 Jodh Ram	120 Ali Mohammad Bhat	162 Amanullah Khan
79 Raghu Nath	121 Sham Lal	163 Fayaz Ahmad Thoker
80 Mohammad Yaqoob	122 Mohammad Ismail Khan	164 Habib-Ullah
81 Ali Mohammad Gojjar	123 Mushtaq Ahmad Khan	165 Mohammad Akram
82 Nazir Hussain Shah	124 Sona-Ullah Sheikh	166 Mohammad Yousuf
83 Ali Mohammad Yatoo	125 Ghulam Mohammad Shah	167 Abdul Gaffar
84 Vijay Singh	126 Mohammad Yasin Khan	168 Nazir Ahmad Dar
85 S. Sheetal Singh	127 Mohammad Abdullah	169 Abdul Rehman Lone
86 Abdul Rashid Khan	128 Abdul Rashid	170 Nazir Ahmad
87 Mohinder Singh	129 Skinder Kumar	171 Abdul Rashid
88 Noor Mohammad Khan	130 Ghulam Mohi-Ud-Din	172 Nazir Ahmad Wani
89 Rattan Singh	131 Abdul Rashid Mir	173 Abdul Ali
90 Ashok Kumar	132 Triloki Nath	174 Abdul Khaliq
91 Chain Singh	133 Jatinder Singh	175 Abdul Rashid Nadaf
92 Abdul Rehman	134 Mohammad Yousuf Kochay	176 Mohammad Aslam
93 Laxman Dass	135 Abdul Aziz Lone	177 Mohammad Ayoub Khan
94 Sansar Chand	136 Mohammad Yousuf	178 Abdul Gani
95 Abdul Gani	137 Ghulam Mohi-Ud-Din	179 Ghulam Ahmad Rather
96 Prithipal Singh	138 Abdul Rashid Lone	180 Bashir Ahmad Shahbaz

181 Mohammad Yousuf Mir
182 Ghulam Mohi-Ud-Din Dar
183 Saif Din
184 Abdul Karim
185 Mushtaq Ahmad
186 Abdul Aziz
187 Mohammad Sultan
188 Farooq Ahmad Wani
189 Mohammad Rafiq Bhat
190 Bashir Ahmad
191 Bashir Ahmad Bhat
192 Mohammad Suliman
193 Shabir Ahmad Rather
194 Bashir Ahmad
195 Dewan Chand
196 Abdul Hamid Bhat
197 Manohar Lal
198 Mohammad Ishaq
199 Abdul Ahad Dar
200 Ghulam Rasool
201 Mohammad Yousuf Naik
202 Shamim Ahmad Wani
203 Mohammad Ramzan
204 Mohammad Ismail
205 Mohammad Azad Shah
206 Daljit Singh
207 Mohammad Ashraf Sheikh
208 Mohammad Ramzan Shah
209 Ghulam Qadir Ganie
210 Muneer Ahmad Thoker
211 Abdul Rehman
212 Mohammad Farooq Khan
213 Mohammad Sidiq Pandit
214 Abdul Rashid Sheikh
215 Bashir Ahmad Sheikh
216 Nazir Ahmad Dagga
217 Bashir Ahmad
218 Jagdish Raj
219 Sindh Raj
220 Shabir Ahmad
221 Mushtaq Ahmad Baba
222 Bashir Ahmad Malik
223 Fateh Mohammad Mir
224 Ravinder Kumar
225 Ghulam Nabi Wagay
226 Majoor Ahmad
227 Shadi Lal
228 Abdul Rashid Ganie
229 Khurshid Ahmad Ganie
230 Lal Hussain
231 Abdul Rashid Mainya
232 Satish Kumar
233 Mehfooz Ahmad
234 Mukhtar Ahmad
235 Mohammad Bashir
236 Mohammad Ramzan Wagay
237 Ashiq Hussain
238 Abdul Qayoom Reshi
239 Jai Kumar
240 Noor Mohammad
241 Habibullah Wani
242 Mohammad Hanief
243 Ghulam Mohammad
244 Mohammad Farooq
245 Tariq Ahmad Paul
246 Qayoom Hussain
247 Zakir Hussain
248 Chain Singh
249 Iftikhar Hussain
250 Gulbadan Singh
251 Bashir Ahmad Deedad
252 Mohammad Amin Paddar
253 Khurshid Ahmad
254 Abdul Hamid
255 Khurshid Ahmad Lone
256 Mohammad Amin Shah
257 Gulzar Ahmad
258 Abdul Rashid Wani
259 Mohammad Ramzan
260 Girdhari Lal
261 Ghulam Mustafa Mir
262 Tasadaq Hussain Khan
263 Nizam-Ul-Huq
264 Shabir Ahmad Naikoo
265 Ghulam Rasool Malik
266 Ghulam Mohammad
267 Mustaq Ahmad
268 Afroz Ahmad Shah
269 Mohammad Qasim
270 Mohammad Zubee
271 Bashir Ahmad Rather
272 Peer Mohamad Yaqoob
273 Nizam Din
274 Ali Mohammad Lone
275 Ghulam Mohi-Ud-Din
276 Ajay Gupta
277 Mohammad Sageer
278 Mohammad Bashir
279 Ghulam Mohammad
280 Hari Chand
281 Ghulam Nabi Rather
282 Mohammad Yassin Peer
283 Saif-Ullah Khan
284 Bashir Ahmad Hajam
285 Mohammad Hussain
286 Mohammad Ishaq Najar
287 Gull Mohammad Wagey
288 Roop Lal
289 Roshan Lal
290 Naresh Kumar Kapai
291 Hakim Din
292 Mohammad Jamal
293 Ali Mohammad Chopan
294 Mohammad Hussain Kada
295 Girdhari Lal
296 Wahid Hussain
297 Mohammad Ashraf Lone
298 Sarfaraz Ahmed
299 Mohamamd Rajab Bhat
300 Ashiq Hussain Shah
301 Ghulam Mohi-Ud-Din Wani
302 Mohammad Hussain
303 Nazir Ahmad Bhat
304 Ghulam Mohammad Lone
305 Ghulam Mohammad Mir
306 Abdul Rehman Lone

307 Reyaz Ahmad	349 Mustaq Ahmad	391 Mohammad Hanief
308 Shabir Ahmad Sofi	350 Mustaq Ahmad	392 Ghulam Mohammad Mir
309 Ram Lal	351 Fayaz Ahmad Malik	393 Ravinder Singh
310 Rattan Lal	352 Shamim Ahmad Wani	394 Abdul Latief
311 Suraj Bhan	353 Satish Kumar	395 Mohammad Dayim Mir
312 Paramvir Singh	354 Dewan Singh	396 Fida Hussain
313 Madan Lal	355 Inam Ahmad Mughal	397 Nissar Ahmed
314 Ghulam Mohanmmad Sheikh	356 Rafiq Ahmad	398 Abdul Rashid
315 Farooq Ahmad War	357 Fayaz Naikoo	399 Nazir Ahmed Wani
316 Abdul Latief Malla	358 Krishan Chand	400 Abdul Rashid
317 Ghulam Mohi-ud-Din	359 Pardeep Kumar	401 Pritam Singh
318 Ghulam Hassan Ahanger	360 Ravi Chand	402 Ghulam Hassan Shah
319 Azmat Ali Mughal	361 Bashir Ahmad	403 Naser Ahmed
320 Mohammad Ashraf Shah	362 Ghulam Mohammad Wagay	404 Abdul Qayoom
321 Faqir Hussain	363 Tariq Ahmed	405 Abdul Hamid
322 Mohammad Yousuf Shah	364 Nisar Ahmad	406 Sonam Durjay
323 Nazir Ahmad Malla	365 Altaf Hussain	407 Reyaz Hussain
324 Showkat Ahmad Mir	366 Khurshid Ahmed	408 Kuldeep Singh
325 Mohammad Jaffar Mir	367 Ghulam Mohammad Ganie	409 Jeevan Lal
326 Abdul Ahad Magray	368 Jagdish Raj	410 Harbans Lal
327 Gulzar Ahmad Mir	369 Mehraj-Ud-Din Rather	411 Khushi Ram
328 Mohammad Iqbal Gojar	370 Manzoor Malik	412 Shiv Nath
329 Ashok Kumar	371 Bharat Bushan	413 Mohammad Abass
330 Ashok Kumar	372 Ajit Singh	414 Nazir Hussain
331 Essa Lohar	373 Asgar Ali	415 Sanjivan Kumar
332 Sarwar Hussain	374 Abdul Rashid So	416 Ghani Sham
333 Rakesh Kumar	375 Bashir Ahmed	417 Liyaqat Ali
334 Gulzar Hussain	376 Nazir Ahmad Bhat	418 Javid Ahmad Bhat
335 Ghulam Hassan Mir	377 Muzamil Ahmed Shah	419 Rajinder Singh
336 Managat Mir	378 Ali Mohammad Mir	420 Mehraj-Ud-Din Sofi
337 Latief Khan	379 Bashir Ahmad Bhat	421 Liyakat Ali
338 Abdul Rehman Lone	380 Abdul Gaffar Ganie	422 Abdul Ahad Khanday
339 Mohammad Hussain	381 Mahesh Kumar	423 Mohammad Yousuf Khan
340 Mohammad Ismail	382 Jhangir Ahmed Pandit	424 Ali Mohammad Lone
341 Sabzar Ahmad Shah	383 Mohammad Ahsan	425 Bashir Ahmed
342 Ishpaul Singh	384 Mohammad Rafiq	426 Zahoor Ahmad
343 Ghulam Nabi Kar	385 Qawam-Ud-Din	427 Bashir Ahmed Sheikh
344 Ghulam Ahmed Rather	386 Abdul Jabar Malla	428 Mohammad Amin
345 Nazir Ahmad Sofi	387 Mohammad Ishaq Khan	429 Ashok Kumar
346 Janat Hussain	388 Azad Ahmed	430 Assadullah Shah
347 Tarseem Lal	389 Pritam Kumar	431 Hilal Ahmed
348 Gafoor Ahmad	390 Mumtaz Ahmed	432 Mohammad Shaban Lone

433 Mushtaq Ahmed Shah
434 Abdul Rashid
435 Abdul Aziz
436 Nazir Ahmed Shah
437 Safdar Hussain
438 Femu Ram
439 Mushtaq Ahmed Sheikh
440 Santosh Kumar
441 Mohammad Din
442 Rajinder Kumar
443 Mohammad Ashraf Sheikh
444 Farooq Ahmad Lone
445 Pamposh Ahmad Miyan
446 Bodh Raj
447 Altaf Hussain
448 Mohammad Latief
449 Mohammad Arif
450 Mohammad Shair
451 Abdul Rashid Gojari
452 Mohammad Safeer
453 Manzoor Ahmad
454 Om Singh
455 Mohammad Alyas
456 Imtiaz Ahmed
457 Mukesh Kumar
458 Daya Singh
459 Bilal Ahmed Bakshi
460 Showkat Ahmed
461 Ghulam Nabi
462 Zaffar Ahmad Khan
463 Mohammad Shafi Wani
464 Nazir Ahmad Ganie
465 Raj Kumar
466 Ghulam Qadir Bhat
467 Farooq Ahmed Mir
468 Mohammad Shafi Ganie
469 Vijay Kumar
470 Abdul Qayoom
471 Vaid Prakash
472 Bashir Ahmed Gazi
473 Pardeep Kumar
474 Paramjeet Singh
475 Ehtisham-Ul-Haq
476 Abdul Hamid
477 Gurdeep Singh
478 Mohammad Mussa Malik
479 Mohammad Ramzan Mir
480 Shabir Ahmed
481 Nissar Ahmad Malik
482 Mohammad Ashraf
483 Reyaz Ahmed Dar
484 Karanjeet Singh
485 Rattan Singh
486 Ghulam Hassan Wani
487 Mohammad Rafiq Khan
488 Sajad Shafqat
489 Sheikh Aijaz Rashid
490 Bagh Hussain
491 Mohammad Iqbal Gojar
492 Mohammad Ramzan
493 Krishan Chand
494 Bushan Lal
495 Shabir Ahmad Shah
496 Arshad Mehmood
497 Manzoor Ahmad Bhat
498 Ali Mohammad Mir
499 Ghulam Hassan Dar
500 Irshad Ahmed Sheikh
501 Abdul Hamid Rather
502 Suraj Singh
503 Kuldeep Kumar
504 Bodh Raj
505 Ravinder Kumar
506 Mohammad Yaqoub Lone
507 Naseer Ahmed
508 Imtiaz Ahmed
509 Nissar Ahmed Wani
510 Jan Mohammad
511 Abdul Rashid
512 Mohammad Altaf Bakshi
513 Ghulam Nabi
514 Mushtaq Hussain
515 Chadiaya Khan
516 Mohammad Shafi Reshi
517 Zahoor Ahmad
518 Mohammad Yaqoob Chechi
519 Mushtaq Ahmed
520 Anil Kumar
521 Ghulam Mohammad Lone
522 Liyaqat Ali
523 Abdul Majid
524 Abdul Majid
525 Raja Saleem
526 Latief Ahmad Khan
527 Manzoor Ahmad Wani
528 Abdul Hameed Lone
529 Mohammad Farooq
530 Javid Iqbal Sheikh
531 Zakir Hussain
532 Abdul Majid
533 Abdul Rashid Dar
534 Ghulam Mohammad
535 Mohammad Altaf Keena
536 Chandail Singh
537 Ghulam Mohi-ud-Din
538 Ghulam Mohammad
539 Ashaq Hussain Ganie
540 Farooq Ahmad Kuttay
541 Showkat Hussain Rather
542 Ghulam Mohi-Ud-Din Mir
543 Zahir Ahmad
544 Sultan Ahmad
545 Mohammad Naseem
546 Mohammad Afzal
547 Mahinder Singh
548 Abdul Qayoom
549 Yashpal Singh
550 Vinod Kumar
551 Liyaqat Khan
552 Ghulam Hassan Mir
553 Romesh Kumar
554 Farooq Ahmad Bhat
555 Abdul Qadoos Sheikh
556 Tariq Ahmad Bhat
557 Nazir Ahmad Mir
558 Mehraj-ud-Din Darzi

559 Shahnawaz Ahmad Lone
560 Ghulam Nabi Malik
561 Gulzar Ahmad Bhat
562 Shafqat Hussain
563 Abdul Rahim
564 Bashir Ahmad Dass
565 Abdul Aziz Dar
566 Abdul Rashid Lone
567 Lal Hussain
568 Zahoor Ahmad
569 Ghulam Nabi
570 Satpal Singh
571 Ghulam Hassan Bhat
572 Abdul Majeed Lone
573 Ved Raj
574 Abdul Majeed Ganie
575 Mohan Lal
576 Raj Singh
577 Abdul Majid
578 Shamim Ahmad Khan
579 Reyaz Ahmad Bhat
580 Zahoor Ahmad
581 Javid Ahmad
582 Farooq Ahmad Bhat
583 Tariq Ahmad Bhat
584 Gousia Jan
585 Gulfam Bhat
586 Mangat Ram
587 Raj Kumar
588 Nazir Ahmad Hurra
589 Asif Ali Bhat
590 Ghulam Rasool
591 Paramjeet Singh
592 Abdul Majeed Wani
593 Manzoor Ahamd Dar
594 Mohammad Abdulla Wani
595 Ghulam Nabi Wagay
596 Abdul Ahad Khan
597 Abdul Rashid Malik
598 Manzoor Rather
599 Surinder Singh
600 Jagdish Singh
601 Hari Ram
602 Mohammad Shaban
603 Shabir Ahmad
604 Mohan Singh
605 Rajinder Singh
606 Subash Chander
607 Rishi Kumar
608 Tarlochan Singh
609 Liyaqat Ali
610 Mohammad Razaq
611 Mohammad Fareed
612 Mohammad Afzal
613 Fayaz Ahmad
614 Khrushad Ahmad
615 Farooq Ahmad
616 Mubarak Hussain
617 Ghulam Ahmad Ganie
618 Bashir Ahmad Rather
619 Ghulam Mohammad Jahra
620 Mohammad Shaban
621 Mohammad Sultan
622 Kamal Singh
623 Mohammad Amin Shah
624 Sunil Kumar
625 Kamal Singh
626 Ghulam Mohammad Wani
627 Mohammad Yousuf Hajam
628 Mohammad Sadiq Khan
629 Ghulam Ahmad Sultan
630 Habibullah
631 Manzoor Ahmad Bhat
632 Nisar Ahmad Shah
633 Abdul Majid Bhat
634 Mehbooba
635 Abdull Rashid Bhat
636 Showkat Ahmad Khan
637 Shafiqa
638 Reyaz Ahmad Bhat
639 Nazir Ahmad
640 Sulinder Singh
641 Ghulam Hassan
642 Sethi Ram
643 Shamim Ahmad
644 Janak Raj
645 Mohammad Rafiq
646 Vipan Singh
647 Mohammad Rafiq
648 Ashok Kumar
649 Suresh Kumar
650 Mohammad Asadullah Mir
651 Ali Mohammad
652 Ghulam Rasool
653 Gulab Chand
654 Baldev Raj
655 Showkat Ahmad Shah
656 Abdul Rehim Ganie
657 Ghulam Nabi Bhat
658 Mohammad Mushtaq Badana
659 Abdul Qayoom
660 Jungbahadur Singh
661 Ramesh Krishan Raina
662 Niyaz Ahmad
663 Parveen Kumar
664 Sakhi Akbar
665 Sham Parshad
666 Ranjeet Singh
667 Ramesh Kumar
668 Jamal-Din
669 Mohammad Shabir
670 Bawa Ram
671 Mohammad Ashraf Wani
672 Syed Mohammad Athar
673 Bashir Ahmad Bithi
674 Ishfaq Ahmad Parray
675 Gharu Ram
676 Mohammad Bashir
677 Farhad Ahmad
678 Mohammad Shafiq
679 Mohammad Rashid
680 Ghulam Mohammad Chopan
681 Mohi-ud-Din
682 Mohammad Fazal
683 Gian Chand
684 Bilal Ahmed Sheikh

685 Vipan Kumar
686 Hans Raj
687 Jahangir Akhtar
688 Mohan Lal
689 Kulwant Raj
690 Mohammad Rafiq Khan
691 Daleep Kumar
692 Sarfaraz Hussain
693 Shabir Ahmad Mir
694 Shabir Ahmad Bhat
695 Farooq Ahmad
696 Mohammad Iqbal
697 Maqsood Ahmad
698 Bhagu Teedwa
699 Mohammad Iqbal
700 Ashok Kumar
701 Subash Chander
702 Khurshid Ahmad Parray
703 Rohit Sadhu
704 Bashir Ahmad Hajam
705 Mohammad Ashraf War
706 Abdul Gaffar Bhat
707 Manzoor Ahmad
708 Ashaq Hussan
709 Nazir Ahmad Tantray
710 Bashir Ahmad
711 Bashir Ahmad
712 Javid Ahmad Ganai
713 Banori Lal
714 Mohammad Younus Lone
715 Kalyan Singh
716 Jagdish Singh
717 Nazir Ahmad Dar
718 Abdul Ahad
719 Mohammad Sharief
720 Davinder Kumar Sharma
721 Gurbachan Singh
722 Krishan Lal Khajouria
723 Imtiyaz Ahmed Shah
724 Ghulam Mohammad Hajam
725 Bansi Lal
726 Faqeer Ahmad Gojjar
727 Mohammad Iqbal
728 Mohammad Yousuf Sheikh
729 Assadullah Mir
730 Mohammad Maqbool
731 Kulbushan Kumar
732 Kamal Singh
733 Prem Parkash
734 Ghulam Nabi Ganie
735 Firdous Ahmad
736 Mohammad Ibrahim
737 Bashir Ahmad Lone
738 Manzoor Ahmad Thoker
739 Mohammad Akbar Shah
740 Ravinder Singh
741 Mohammad Bashir
742 Abdul Qayoom
743 Abdul Rashid
744 Mohammad Ashraf Kaloo
745 Hans Raj
746 Nazir Hussain
747 Ali Jan Khan
748 Amir Chand
749 Muneer Hussain
750 Imtiyaz Ahmad
751 Manzoor Ahmad
752 Manzoor Ahmad
753 Papu Singh
754 Zaffer Iqbal
755 Govind Singh
756 Maqsood Hussain
757 Mushtaq Ahmed Yatoo
758 Jalal-U-Din
759 Ghulam Nabi Bawani
760 Saraj-ud-Din
761 Gulzar Ahmad
762 Jagdev Singh
763 Bhikam Singh
764 Mohammad Qasim
765 Alam Singh
766 Kamal Singh
767 Churan Chand
768 Ghulam Hassan Jangu
769 Abdul Aziz
770 Mohammad Yousuf
771 Yesh Pal
772 Kamal Singh
773 Salima Khalida Parveen
774 Khurshid Ahmad
775 Deeraj Kohli
776 Arshad Hussain
777 Ravi Kumar
778 Sonaullah Bhat
779 Bashir Ahmad
780 Parkash Singh
781 Ghulam Rasool Khan
782 Bashir Ahmad Dar
783 Sanjay Kumar
784 Mohammad Ishaq Malik
785 Surinder Singh
786 Masood Ahmad
787 Girdhari Lal
788 Muneer Ahmad
789 Shabir Ahmad
790 Mohammad Abass
791 Mushtaq Ahmad
792 Mohammad Shakoor
793 Gulzar Ahmad
794 Suresh Kumar
795 Fateh Mohammad
796 Kuldeep Kumar
797 Uttam Singh
798 Sabzar Ahmad
799 Mushtaq Ahmad Wani
800 Nissar Ahmad
801 Mohinder Singh
802 Mohammad Iqbal Sofi
803 Rameez Raza
804 Tanveer Ahmad
805 Abdul Khaliq
806 Fayaz Ahmad
807 Bashir Ahmad Zarger
808 Shamsheer Ahmad
809 Mushtaq Ahmad
810 Ghulam Ahmad Mir

811 Muzaffar Ahmad Shah	853 Mohammad Yaseen Bhat	895 Farooq Ahmad
812 Bilal Ahmad	854 Showkat Hussain	896 Ajaz Ahmad Parray
813 Abdul Hamid Lone	855 Ghulam Ahmad Dar	897 Asif Iqbal Dhobi
814 Raman Singh	856 Likat Hussain	898 Maqsood Ahmad
815 Abdul Latief	857 Jagdev Singh	899 Bashir Ahmad
816 Khadam Hussain	858 Feroz Ahmad	900 Bashir Ahmad Malik
817 Mohammad Yousuf	859 Noor Mohammad Chopan	901 Mushtaq Ahmad
818 Mohammad Ayoub Bhat	860 Mohammad Farooq	902 Ghulam Mohammad Mir
819 Jaswant Singh	861 Ali Mohammad Khan	903 Mohammad Ashraf Sheikh
820 Rajinder Kumar	862 Jagtar Singh	904 Pardeep Singh
821 Ranbir Singh	863 Kali Dass	905 Tashoq Ahmad
822 Hakumat Singh	864 Rajinder Singh	906 Gulzar Ahmad
823 Mohammad Shafi Kumar	865 Hakeem Din	907 Mulakh Hussain
824 Reyaz Ahmad	866 Abdul Lateef	908 Mohammad Ramzan Wani
825 Nayeem Ahmad Shah	867 Mohammad Iqbal	909 Ajaz Ahmad
826 Beer Singh	868 Khurshid Ahmad	910 Mohammad Shabir
827 Mohammad Yousuf	869 Shakti Kumar	911 Shamim Ahmad
828 Mohammad Amin Reshi	870 Reyaz Ahmad	912 Mohammad Yousuf Chopan
829 Prem Nath	871 Fayaz Ahmad	913 Altaf Hussain
830 Nahida Akhter	872 Sharief-ud-Din	914 Manjeet Singh
831 Ravi Jee	873 Abdul Wahid	915 Manohar Lal
832 Mohammad Yousuf	874 Riyaz Ahmad	916 Farid Ahmad
833 Farooq Ahmad Ganie	875 Ghulam Mohammad	917 Showkat Ali
834 Mohammad Ashraff	876 Abdul Rashid Dar	918 Sheer Singh
835 Mohammad Shafi	877 Abdul Khaliq Wani	919 Nissar Ahmed
836 Mehboob Ahmad	878 Mohammad Maqsood	920 Mohammad Akram
837 Abdul Rehman Khan	879 Aftab Iqbal	921 Angrez Singh
838 Mohammad Qasim Khan	880 Mumtaz Ahmed	922 Abdul Lateef
839 Mohammad Ayoub	881 Ishrat Qamir	923 Zaheer Abass
840 Ali Mohammad Mall	882 Mushtaq Ahmad	924 Muktar Ahmad Khan
841 Bashir Ahmad Sheikh	883 Abdul Majid	925 Reyaz Ahmad Parray
842 Gulzar Ahmad	884 Ghulam Rasool	926 Mohammad Ashraf Dar
843 Shabir Ahmad	885 Shankar Dass	927 Rakesh Kumar
844 Ghulam Nabi Bhat	886 Niyaz Ahmad	928 Shakeela Akther
845 Sanjay Kumar	887 Mohammad Akram Bhat	929 Sameer Ahmad
846 Mushtaq Ahmad Ganie	888 Mohammad Ashraf	930 Muzaffar Ahmad
847 Abdul Kabir	889 Balvinder Singh	931 Zubair Ahmad
848 Mohammad Shafi	890 Des Raj	932 Shadi Lal
849 Mushtaq Ahmad Najar	891 Mohammad Saleem	933 Billal Ahmad Allie
850 Bishan Singh	892 Tej Ram	934 Billal Ahmad Wani
851 Mohammad Iqbal	893 Som Raj	935 Ishfaq Hussain
852 Ghulam Mohammad Parray	894 Javid Ahmad Vailoo	936 Mohammad Amin

937 Manzoor Ahmad Shah
938 Girdhari Lal
939 Ashok Kumar
940 Farooq Ahmad Khokhar
941 Abdul Rashid
942 Irshad Ahmad
943 Foja Singh
944 Mohammad Yousuf
945 Mohammad Iqbal
946 Mustaq Ahmad Magray
947 Abdul Kaliq
948 Bahir Ahmad Sofi
949 Abdul Hamid
950 Ghulam Hussain
951 Mushtaq Ahmad Malik
952 Mohammad Ashraf Wagay
953 Ghulam Nabi Dar
954 Karan Singh
955 Jattu Ram
956 Mohammad Sharief
957 Neeraj Charak
958 Aya Singh
959 Ghulam Hassan Reshi
960 Fayaz Ahmad Mir
961 Rajesh Kumar
962 Naseeb Singh
963 Mohammad Amin
964 Mohammad Ayoub Khan
965 Inderjeet Kour
966 Sajad Ahmad
967 Varinder Singh Jaipuria
968 Mohammad Jameel
969 Abdul Rashid Thakur
970 Kam Raj
971 Ram Rattan
972 Hakam Chand
973 Daljeet Singh
974 Manishwar Singh
975 Mohammad Younis Mir
976 Sheer Mohammad
977 Shakeel Ahmed Ganie
978 Inder Singh
979 Bagh Hussain
980 Ghulam Rasool
981 Reyaz Ahmed
982 Sunil Kumar
983 Pershotam Singh
984 Kurshed Ahmed Shah
985 Shakeel Ahmed
986 Rajnish Singh
987 Mohammad Zahoor
988 Mohammad Akram
989 Mohammad Azeem
990 Babu Ram
991 Gulzar Ahmad Najar
992 Mohan Singh
993 Zahoor Ahmad Parrey
994 Abdul Rashid Khan
995 Mohammad Aslam
996 Kuldeep Singh
997 Mansa Ram
998 Muneer Hussain
999 Munawar Hussain
1000 Rajinder Singh
1001 Mohammad Saleem
1002 Brij Lal
1003 Vikramjeet Singh
1004 Sheraz Ahmad Dar
1005 Amin Khan
1006 Jai Lal
1007 Mohammad Yousuf Teli
1008 Mohammad Maqbool
1009 Shamas-u-Din Shah
1010 Rajinder Singh
1011 Javid Iqbal
1012 Bal Krishan
1013 Lal Hussain Mirza
1014 Garwal Singh
1015 Showkat Amin
1016 Hillal Ahmad Ganie
1017 Javid Iqbal
1018 Sabzar Ahmad Mir
1019 Mohammad Hafiz
1020 Mohan Singh
1021 Raj Kumar
1022 Raj Kumar
1023 Abdul Rashid Kumar
1024 Hanse Paul
1025 Mohammad Amin Bhat
1026 Zahoor Ahmad
1027 Shankar Nath
1028 Mohammad Nissar
1029 Maqsood Ahmad
1030 Charanjeet Singh
1031 Ghulam Qadir Chopan
1032 Mohammad Shafi Sheikh
1033 Asgar Ali Joo
1034 Abdul Rashid
1035 Johan Mohammad
1036 Harbans Lal
1037 Sukhwinder Singh
1038 Naresh Kumar
1039 Ashok Kumar
1040 Abdul Hamid
1041 Mushtaq Ahmad
1042 Mohammad Sadiq
1043 Rakesh Kumar
1044 Abdul Rashid Bhat
1045 Bashir Ahmed
1046 Mohammad Akbar Joo
1047 Ghulam Mohi-ud-Din
1048 Surinder Singh
1049 Mohammad Saleem
1050 Abdul Qayoom
1051 Abdul Wahid
1052 Shabir Ahmad
1053 Tanveer Hussain
1054 Puran Singh
1055 Anil Kumar
1056 Mohammad Amin Beigh
1057 Om Parkash
1058 Kuldeep Kumar
1059 Inder Singh
1060 Mushtaq Ahmad
1061 Bashir Ahmad
1062 Khurshid Ahmad Ahanger

1063 Mohammad Aslam	1105 Jan Mohammad	1147 Billal Ahmad Shalbaf
1064 Mohammad Sabir	1106 Abdul Rahim Sofi	1148 Ali Mohammad Rather
1065 Ali Mohammad Najar	1107 Balbir Singh	1149 Surinder Kumar
1066 Irshad Ahmad Khan	1108 Manzoor Ahmad	1150 Zahoor Ahmad
1067 Mushtaq Ahmed	1109 Ram Parshad	1151 Reyaz Ahmad
1068 Raj Kumar	1110 Vijay Paul Singh	1152 Bushan Kumar
1069 Mehboob-Ul-Haq	1111 Ali Mohammad	1153 Reyaz Ahmad
1070 Billal Ahmad	1112 Noor-ul- Amin	1154 Mohammad Altaf
1071 Safiya Bano	1113 Ghulam Mohammad	1155 Abdul Majeed Khan
1072 Sheer Singh	1114 Shakir Ahmad	1156 Mohammad Rafi Lali Gojar
1073 Ghulam Rasool	1115 Mumtaz Ahmad	1157 Ghulam Hassan Qurashi
1074 Mohammad Azam	1116 Manzoor Ahmad Ganie	1158 Javid Iqbal
1075 Mohammad Ramzan	1117 Tahseem Ahmad Malla	1159 Mohammad Zakir
1076 Mohammad Ashraf Shiekh	1118 Farooq Ahmad Mir	1160 Mohammad Shafi
1077 Gulzar Ahmad Naik	1119 Mohammad Rajab Chopan	1161 Juma
1078 Mohammad Kahliq	1120 Shahzad Ahmad	1162 Gulshan Ahmad
1079 Showkat Ali	1121 Imtiyaz Ahmed Rather	1163 Farooq Ahmad
1080 Showkat Ahmed	1122 Rajinder Singh	1164 Mohammad Shabir
1081 Naseeb Singh	1123 Azhar Ahmad	1165 Ghulam Hassan Bhat
1082 Rajin Kesri	1124 Mohammad Mushtaq	1166 Imtiyaz Khan
1083 Haseena Akhther	1125 Dilhair Singh	1167 Ranjeet Singh
1084 Mohammad Amin Mir	1126 Jahangir Ahmad Tramboo	1168 Abdul Rashid Sheikh
1085 Ajaz Ahmad	1127 Mohammad Rafiq	1169 Sunil Kumar
1086 Naseer Ahmad Mir	1128 Parkash Chand	1170 Abdul Qayoom
1087 Rattan Singh	1129 Firdous Ahmad	1171 Mohammad Altaf Ganie
1088 Mushtaq Ahmad	1130 Ramesh Kumar	1172 Sunil Singh
1089 Ghulam Nabi Yazdani	1131 Fahmeeda Bano	1173 Miran Baksh
1090 Kailash Chand	1132 Jagbir Singh	1174 Nissar Ahmad Teeli
1091 Keemat Lal	1133 Ghulam Nabi Khan	1175 Jugal Kishore
1092 Rajinder Singh	1134 Ghulam Mohi-Ud-Din	1176 Mintoo Kumar
1093 Sham Lal	1135 Mohammad Ashraf Paswal	1177 Sanjay Kumar
1094 Mohammad Shafi Khan	1136 Abdul Qayoom	1178 Mohammad Yousuf
1095 Bashir Ahmad	1137 Noor Mohammad Bajad	1179 Zubair Ahmad Mir
1096 Anil Kumar	1138 Mohammad Zaman	1180 Khadim Hussain
1097 Ghulam Mohammad Kataria	1139 Ghulam Nabi	1181 Anar Singh
1098 Pawan Kumar	1140 Ravi Kumar	1182 Madan Lal
1099 Khurshid Ahmad	1141 Muzaffar Ahmad	1183 Javid Ahmad
1100 Faqir-ud-Din	1142 Gowhar Ahmad	1184 Noor Ahmad
1101 Hari Parkash	1143 Mushtaq Ahmed	1185 Liyakat Ali
1102 Altaf Hussain	1144 Mohammad Sharief	1186 Ajay Sharma
1103 Showkat Hussain	1145 Ali Mohammad Shah	1187 Abdul Wahid
1104 Mohammad Ashraf	1146 Mohammad Maqbool Lone	1188 Mushtaq Ahmad

1189 Mehbooba Akther	1231 Dimpal Singh	1273 Showkat Ahmad
1190 Mohammad Iqbal	1232 Billal Ahmad	1274 Mohammad Amin Sheikh
1191 Abdul Rashid Wani	1233 Nazir Ahmad	1275 Bashir Ahmad
1192 Gulzar Ahmad	1234 Mohammad Yasin Najar	1276 Mohammad Dilawar Ganie
1193 Mohammad Irshad	1235 Nazir Ahmad Bhat	1277 Ghulam Mohi-ud-Din Hajam
1194 Abdul Gaffar Rather	1236 Muzaffar Ahmad	1278 Bikram Singh
1195 Nissar Ahmed Dar	1237 Farooq Ahmad	1279 Ghulam Hassan Lone
1196 Mohammad Ashraf	1238 Ghulam Mohi-ud-Din	1280 Mohammad Hanief
1197 Mushtaq Ahmad	1239 Ghulam Nabi Kanjal	1281 Abid Hussain Mir
1198 Kusheed Ahmad	1240 Bilal Ahmad Dar	1282 Farooq Ahmad Dar
1199 Muneer Ahmad	1241 Bashir Ahmad Malik	1283 Manzoor Ahmad Lone
1200 Romesh Kumar	1242 Hillal Ahmad	1284 Chand Mohammad Khan
1201 Jagdish Raj	1243 Mohammad Shafi Bhat	1285 Abdul Rashid Mir
1202 Fayaz Ahmad	1244 Gulzar Ahmad Sheikh	1286 Shanti Seroop
1203 Mohammad Yousuf Lone	1245 Feroz Ahmad	1287 Bishan Dass
1204 Abdul Qayoom	1246 Tazeem Ahmad	1288 Abdul Majid Chouhan
1205 Qayoom Ahmad	1247 Mohammad Yasin	1289 Shally Singh
1206 Gulzar Ahmad Rather	1248 Karan Jeet Singh	1290 Manzoor Ahmad Para
1207 Ghulam Mohammad Lone	1249 Ghulam Rasool Reshi	1291 Khurshid Ahmad
1208 Mohammad Shafi Kataria	1250 Raj Kumar	1292 Farooq Ahmad
1209 Shabir Ahmad	1251 Sazadh Hussain	1293 Rashid Mohammad
1210 Ghulam Nabi	1252 Mohammad Amin Itoo	1294 Shally Singh
1211 Noor Mohammad	1253 Mohammad Jamal	1295 Anchal Singh
1212 Aijaz Ahmad Sah	1254 Dayan Chand	1296 Manzoor Ahmad Para
1213 Wali Mohammad	1255 Jagdish Singh	1297 Khurshid Ahmad
1214 Ishfaq Ahmad	1256 Fared Ahmad Lachi	1298 Farooq Ahmad
1215 Pardeep Kumar	1257 Bashir Ahmad Ganie	1299 Rashid Mohammad
1216 Nissar Hussain	1258 Naresh Kumar	1300 Waheed Ahmad Tantray
1217 Abdul Rashid Kalas	1259 Manhori Lal	1301 Baldev Singh
1218 Mehraj-ud-Din	1260 Abdul Gaffar Mir	1302 Sher Mohammad
1219 Ali Mohammad Malik	1261 Jarman Singh	1303 Manzoor Ahmad Mir
1220 Ghulam Rasool Jan	1262 Ishar Lal	1304 Bilal Ahmad Bhat
1221 Mohammad Muzzafar Khan	1263 Abdul Hamed Khan	1305 Mohammad Sharief
1222 Abdul Ahad Wagay	1264 Noor Alam	1306 Shah Hussain
1223 Nazir Ahmad Ahanger	1265 Gulshand Ara	1307 Shabir Ahmad Wani
1224 Hafiz-Ullah Allie	1266 Ghulam Mohammad Malik	1308 Mushtaq Ahmad
1225 Balwant Singh	1267 Abdul Gani	1309 Imtiyaz Ahmad
1226 Reshi Kumar	1268 Ghulam Mohammad	1310 Shamas Din
1227 Dharminder Kumar	1269 Haseena Begam	1311 Gagandeep Sharma
1228 Nazir Ahmad Mir	1270 Randhir Singh	1312 Mohammad Ashraf
1229 Ghulam Qadir	1271 Gulzar Hussain	1313 Aurangezeb Khan
1230 Wiryam Singh	1272 Nazir Ahmad Khan	1314 Shakeel Ahmad

1315 Mushtaq Hussain
1316 Mohad Kabir
1317 Irshad Ahmad Shah
1318 Bashir Ahmad Mir
1319 Nazir Ahmad Dar
1320 Mohammad Tariq Bhat
1321 Kikar Singh
1322 Manzoor Ahmad
1323 Mohammad Irfan Mughal
1324 Manzoor Ahmad
1325 Abdul Rashid Jungli
1326 Anjeev Rana
1327 Mohammad Maroof
1328 Maqbool Hussain Shah
1329 Ghulam Mohi-ud-Din
1330 Ghulam Hyder Kallan
1331 Naresh Kumar
1332 Mushtaq Hussain Shah
1333 Nissar Hussain
1334 Altaf Ahmad Shah
1335 Phulail Singh
1336 Karan Singh
1337 Ghulam Mustaffa
1338 Fayaz Ahmad
1339 Ghulam Nabi
1340 Mushtaq Ahmad Fafoo
1341 Sethi Ram
1342 Mohammad Shafi
1343 Mohammad Shafi Bhat
1344 Mohammad Ashraf
1345 Manzoor Ahmad
1346 Ajaz Ahmad Mir
1347 Mohammad Khan
1348 Rakesh Kumar
1349 Sagar Singh
1350 Riyaz Ahmad
1351 Abdul Gani
1352 Abdul Kabir Pahloo
1353 Manzoor Ahmad Kana
1354 Farooq Ahmad Koul
1355 Khursheed Ahmed
1356 Romesh Lal
1357 Nazir Ahmed
1358 Mohammad Yousuf Bhat
1359 Mohammad Irshad
1360 Mohammad Yousuf Sofi
1361 Arif Mushtaq
1362 Ashiq Hussain
1363 Bashir Ahmed
1364 Bilal Ahmed Najar
1365 Barkat Ali
1366 Ghulam Hassan
1367 Ruksar Ahmed
1368 Farooq Ahmad Kuchay
1369 Abdul Majid Ganie
1370 Shabir Ahmed lone
1371 Farooq Ahmed Wani
1372 Davinder Singh
1373 Delhar Singh
1374 Mohammad Rafiq
1375 Mohammad Ashraf Shah
1376 Gulab Singh
1377 Stanzin Narbo
1378 Abdul Khaliq Bhat
1379 Farooq Ahmad Dar
1380 Mohammad Shafi
1381 Manzoor Ahmad Najar
1382 Shabir Ahmad Bhat
1383 Marifat Hussain
1384 Sheraz Ahmad
1385 Gulzar Ahmad
1386 Ghulam Mohammad Khuroo
1387 Sajad Ahmad Parray
1388 Bilal Ahmad
1389 Mohammad Hanief
1390 Gulzar Ahmed
1391 Mohammad Shafi
1392 Sukhpaul Singh
1393 Mukhtar Ahmad Bhat
1394 Dalbir Singh
1395 Reyaz-ul-Hassan
1396 Mushtaq Ahmad Malla
1397 Niyaz Ahmad
1398 Santosh Singh
1399 Azad Chand
1400 Abdul Rahim Beigh
1401 Mudasir Ahmed Bhat
1402 Gulshan Ahmad Bhat
1403 Mudasir Ahmad Parray
1404 Farooq Ahmed Sheikh
1405 Nazir Ahmed
1406 Mohammad Maqbool Mir
1407 Mushtaq Ahmad Bhat
1408 Sonaullah Zargar
1409 Parvaiz Ahmed Wani
1410 Tariq Ahmed Bhat
1411 Mudasir Ahmad Dar
1412 Salamat Ullah Khan
1413 Altaf Ahmad
1414 Rattan Singh
1415 Shiv Kumar
1416 Pardeep Singh Jamwal
1417 Mukesh Kumar
1418 Kanwarnain Singh
1419 Syed Shabir Ahmad
1420 Kafil Ahmed Mir
1421 Farooq Ahmad
1422 Mukhtar Ahmad
1423 Reyaz Ahmad Lone
1424 Mohammad Shafi
1425 Abdul Hamid
1426 Vinod Kumar
1427 Altaf Ahmad Ganie
1428 Mohammad Syed Khan
1429 Rajinder Singh
1430 Mohammad Yaqoob Shah
1431 Mehraj-u-Din
1432 Mohammad Rafiq Mir
1433 Sanjay Koul
1434 Mohammad Akbar Mir
1435 Abdul Majeed Wani
1436 Zahoor Ahmad Dar
1437 Sanjeewan Singh
1438 Parshotam Lal
1439 Mohammad Shafi Dar
1440 Shabir Hussain

1441 Mushtaq Ahmad
1442 Nisar Ahmad Wani
1443 Arif Nazir Khan
1444 Abdul Majeed Ganie
1445 Fayaz Ahmad
1446 Mohammad Altaf Dar
1447 Ghulam Mohammad Bhat
1448 Nazir Ahmad Mir
1449 Mohammad Sidiq
1450 Reyaz Ahmad Ganie
1451 Bashir Ahmad Ahanger
1452 Reyaz Ahmad Sheikh
1453 Afroze Ahmad Lone
1454 Mudasir Rasool
1455 Mohammad Manzoor Parray
1456 Prithipaul Singh
1457 Khursheed Ahmad
1458 Rajinder Kumar
1459 Rouf Ahmed
1460 Nazir Ahmad Wani
1461 Mohammad Shafi Dar
1462 Tanveer Ahmad Lone
1463 Jalal Din Khanday
1464 Abdul Karim Sheikh
1465 Manzoor Ahmad Naik
1466 Shams-u-Din Sheikh
1467 Bashir Ahmad Dar
1468 Farooq Ahmad Bhat
1469 Muzafar Ahmad Bhat
1470 Mohammad Qasim
1471 Ishfaq Ahmad Hajam
1472 Mahmood Ahmad Sheikh
1473 Mohammad Younis
1474 Shahzad Dilawar Sofi
1475 Shabir Ahmad Dar
1476 Sheeraz Ahmad Bhat
1477 Feroz Ahmad Dar
1478 Shariq Ahmad Lone
1479 Tasveer Ahmad Dar
1480 Sabzar Ahmad
1481 Mohammad Asif Nazki
1482 Mohamad Ayoub Pandith
1483 Gowhar Ahmad Tantray
1484 Amarjeet Singh
1485 Imtiyaz Ahmad Sheikh
1486 Mohammad Yousuf Hajam
1487 Mohammad Rafiq
1488 Abdul Rashid Shah
1489 Krishan Chand
1490 Imtiyaz Ahmad Mir
1491 Ashiq Hussain Jawhar
1492 Khurshid Ahmad Tak
1493 Abdul Haleem Gojar
1494 Zaheer Abass Khan
1495 Abdul Salam Khan
1496 Imran Hussain Tak
1497 Irshad Ahmad
1498 Parvaiz Ahmad
1499 Mohammad Amin
1500 Ghulam Nabi
1501 Babar Ahmad Khan
1502 Mushtaq Ahmad Awan
1503 Kultair Singh
1504 Farooq Ahmad Itoo
1505 Deepu Thuasoo
1506 Mohammad Yousuf Bajad
1507 Mushtaq Ahmad
1508 Mohammad Ashraf Mir
1509 Mohammad Lateef Gojar
1510 Mohammad Shamim Thoker
1511 Bilal Ahmad shah
1512 Aqib Ahmad Wagay
1513 Ghulam Hassan Wagay
1514 Ghulam Rasool Lone
1515 Abdul Hamid Gujjar
1516 Mumtaz Ahmad Awan
1517 Tanveer Ahmad Lone
1518 Habib-u-llah Lone
1519 Aashiq Hussain Malik
1520 Javaid Ahmad Dar
1521 Mudasir Ahmad Bhat
1522 Saleem Ahmad Shah
1523 Parvaiz Ahmad
1524 Fayaz Ahmad Shah
1525 Mohammad Yaqub Shah
1526 Mohammad Ashraf Dar
1527 Ishfaq Ahmad Mir
1528 Mohammad Iqbal Mir
1529 Javaid Ahmad Bhat
1530 Adil Manzoor Bhat
1531 Nissar Ahmed Dobi
1532 Firdoos Ahmad Kochey
1533 Kulwant Singh
1534 Saqib Mohi-ud-Din Mir
1535 Javid Ahmad Lone
1536 Kamal Kishore
1537 Imtiaz Ahmad Mir
1538 Basharat Ahmad Wagay
1539 Hamid-u-llah Ganie
1540 Mehraj-ud-Din Dar
1541 Abdul Majeed Ganai
1542 Anis Ahmad Mir
1543 Sameer Ahmad Mir
1544 Abdul Rashid Kalas
1545 Aman Kumar Thakur
1546 Ghulam Mustafa Barah
1547 Naseer Ahmad Kolie
1548 Khushboo Jan
1549 Bilal Ahmad Magray
1550 Shahbaz Ahmad
1551 Pashid Iqbal
1552 Manzoor Ahmad Dar
1553 Altaf Hussain
1554 Mohammad Ashraf Bhat
1555 Ranmiz Raja
1556 Sageer Hussain
1557 Javid Ahmad Dar
1558 Wajahat Assadullah
1559 Ashfaq Ahmed
1560 Ghulam Hassan
1561 Nisar Ahmed Wagay
1562 Tawseef Ahmad Wani
1563 Masroor Ali Wani
1564 Rajinder Kumar
1565 Fayaz Ahmad
1566 Mohammad Sultan

1567 Zubair Ahmed	1581 Fayaz Ahmad	1595 Anoop Singh
1568 Rohit Kumar	1582 Ishfaq Ayoub Khanday	1596 Amir Hassan
1569 Showkat Ahmad	1583 Sarfaraz Ahmed	1597 Parvaiz Ahmad Dar
1570 Waseem Ahmad	1584 Manzoor Amad	1598 Abdul Rashid
1571 Fayaz Ahmad	1585 Mohammad Amin	1599 Mohammad Ashraf
1572 Mushtaq Ahmed	1586 Arshad Khan	1600 Saifiullah Qadri
1573 Arshad Ashraf Meer	1587 Javid Ahmad Kambay	1601 Mudasir Ahmad Sheikh
1574 Reyaz Ahmad	1588 Muzaffar Ali Dar	1602 Ishfaq Ahmed
1575 SPO Tahir Khan	1589 Bantoo Ji Sharma	1603 Farooq Ahmad Hajam
1576 Himayun Muzzamil Bhat	1590 Farooq Ahmad Mir	1604 Fayaz Ahmed Bhat
1577 Ghulam Hassan	1591 Mohammad.Altaf Najar	1605 Ali Mohammad Ganaie
1578 Shafeeq Ahmad	1592 Suhail Mushtaq Lohar	1606 Shafat Nazir
1579 Rameez Ahmad	1593 Mohammad Yousuf Bajad	1607 Babu Ram
1580 Riyaz Ahmad	1594 Farooq Ahmad	1608 Ghulam Mohammad Dar

CRPF

1 Mohan Singh	25 Shiv Raman	49 V. Ramesh Chand
2 Bhopal Singh	26 Jag Dev Singh	50 Uday Sharma
3 K. Sankaran	27 R.S. Upadhya	51 Sukhwant Singh
4 Nripender Kumar	28 Sh. R.S. Kuhar	52 Shri Krishan
5 Raspal Singh	29 Silai Kudada	53 B. Manikandan
6 Kameshwar Choudhary	30 Bihari Lal	54 Subhash Upadhya
7 Sayed Abdul Ahuid	31 Satish Kumar	55 Sh. Diwan Singh
8 Hari Singh Bhai	32 G. Srinivasan	56 Abdul Hamid Ansari
9 Kailash Chand	33 R.D. Chaudhary	57 Chander Bhan
10 Bhim Bahadur	34 Dharnidhar Nath	58 Ramesh Chander
11 Bhuneshwar Singh	35 Shamsul Haq	59 Jitender Singh
12 R.K. Pandey	36 Shamsuddin	60 Ishwar Singh
13 Ranjit Kumar Singh	37 Ram Lal	61 K.C. Bora
14 Pratap Giri	38 Bharat Pratap Singh	62 Ram Pravesh Sharma
15 Munshi Lal Verma	39 Devi Dass	63 Abdul Mazeed
16 Puran Ballabh	40 Girdhari Lal	64 Jai Pal Singh
17 Usman Ali	41 Tharsa Mark	65 N.G. Rao
18 Darshan Lal	42 Lal Bahadur	66 Bashir Hussain
19 Mohammad Salim	43 Asha Ram	67 Ganesh Dutt
20 Ranjit Singh	44 B.V. Bhim Rao	68 Roshan Lal
21 Bimal Ram	45 K.D. Sharma	69 Ravi Kumar
22 Prem Singh	46 S. Pathak	70 Rekha Kushwah
23 S. Govind Swamy	47 P. Bariak	71 Girdhari Choubey
24 Virdhi Chand	48 Daulat Ram	72 Amarjit Singh

73 Ravinder Singh
74 C.N.R. Pillai
75 G.C. Pant
76 Sri Krishan
77 Mathura Lal
78 D. Ramulu
79 Badri Prasad
80 Ram Swaroop
81 Hardeo Singh
82 Kalyan Mal
83 L.R. Gaur
84 G. Venu Das
85 N. V. Jiddewar
86 Shyam Lal
87 Narvair Singh
88 Rishiram Pandey
89 Anant Kumar Dass
90 G.C. Nagpure
91 Kailash Chand
92 Kripal Singh
93 Darshan Singh
94 Sohan Singh
95 Joginder Singh
96 Harnath Meena
97 Manoj Kumar
98 Vijay Shankar Rai
99 T. Ravi
100 Anand Prasad
101 Devraj Singh
102 Amrit Bhai
103 Giri Raj Prasad
104 Delip Singh
105 Gulam Mohammad Lon
106 Shiv Karan Singh
107 G. Baba Sahib
108 A. Chinaiyya
109 Shiv Ram Singh
110 S.P. Mukherji
111 Ravinder Nath Singh
112 R. Chiranjivi
113 Shiv Prasad
114 Hawa Singh
115 M.S. Krishna
116 Brahma Prakash
117 Dharam Singh
118 K. L. Tiwari
119 Hussain Beig
120 Uttam Singh Negi
121 Salam Iboyame
122 Mohammad Naushad Ali
123 Jadu Kisku
124 Dahi Ram Bora
125 Shyam Lal
126 P.N. Singh
127 Nand Ram
128 Khushal Singh
129 Udheshwar Das
130 Jagdish Prasad
131 Surtiya
132 Bhoop Narayan Mishra
133 K. Rajender Kumar
134 S.S. Mishra
135 K.P. Ravi Shah
136 Dayal Singh
137 Sat Pal Singh
138 B.S. Rahi
139 Purshottam Chand
140 Rupen Chand Nath
141 B. Venkatarao
142 Jai Bhagwan
143 G.R. Bhai
144 G. Srikumar
145 Hardayal Singh
146 P.K. Behra
147 K.M. Prahraj
148 Sagir Ahmed Khan
149 Ishwar S. Nagpure
150 Ramesh Singh
151 Manpal Singh
152 Sugreev Pandey
153 Mohammad Latif
154 CT/GD Mohammad Rafiq
155 T.S. Anil Kumar
156 Rajendra Babu
157 Virender Ram
158 Adesh Kumar
159 S.M. Karim
160 Kalidas
161 Mohammad Iqbal Khan
162 Mohammad Munshi
163 P.C.H. Pullaiah
164 C.B. Chandrahasa
165 Pawan Kumar
166 R. Laxman Bhai
167 K.S. Munda
168 Kamal Das
169 S. Sahdevan
170 Padam Singh Negi
171 Indrajit Singh
172 Sidha Gouda Patil
173 Gurnam Singh
174 Dayal Singh
175 Maniram
176 Ashok Kumar
177 Smir Kumar Das
178 Ashok Kumar
179 Raj Singh Yadav
180 L.B. Sundresha
181 M. Basker Reddy
182 G. Dhananjay
183 Bharat Bhushan Proliya
184 D.D. Patil
185 Kiran Topno
186 Labh Singh
187 E. Ranjit Singh
188 Ram Murmu
189 A. Abdul Majid
190 Sukhvinder Singh
191 K. Sambaiah
192 Shankar Lal Vaykar
193 Imtiyaz Ahmed
194 Santosh K.R. Pandey
195 Mahipal Singh
196 B.P. Rai
197 Ram Vyas Singh Yadav
198 Om Prakash

199 Praveen Kumar Choubey
200 Rajesh Kumar
201 S.B. Hanvatey
202 Papita Kumar Sharma
203 P.M. Pradhan
204 Abdul Sattar
205 Jagpati Ram
206 Ram Prakash Yadav
207 Shiv Kumar Kushwah
208 Bindu Kumbre
209 Mahabir Prasad Gujjar
210 Abdul Qyum
211 Phool Pati
212 Gulam Hyder
213 Wazir Singh
214 Mahaling Kopad
215 Sushanta Kumar Sinha
216 Montu Pada Halder
217 A.A. Prakash
218 Badri Prasad
219 Chitte Gajendra
220 Chandra Kant Shinde
221 Avtar Singh
222 Shanker Ram
223 A.K. Nath
224 R.P. Sharma
225 Jai Karan
226 H.L. Gupta
227 Anand Solanki
228 Balkar Singh
229 Vijay Panwar
230 P. Bhattachariah
231 Lal Mohan Paswan
232 Dhirendra Singh
233 D.B. Malik
234 Upender Kumar Bhoi
235 Madhukar Hotkar
236 Suraj Bali Rai
237 Satender Prasad Singh
238 S. Prem Kumar Singh
239 Ajay Kumar Singh
240 G. Venkataiah
241 Ved Prakash
242 Ramphal Yadav
243 Sher Singh
244 Sajjal Malakar
245 Gyan Singh
246 Rattan Lal Meena
247 Kishan Singh
248 Girdhari Lal
249 Aphal Singh
250 Ramesh Kumar
251 D.G. Ade
252 Gautam Pradhan
253 Dhaneshwar Das
254 Mhaske Jayhind Dhondiram
255 Virender Singh
256 Ashok Kumar Patel
257 S. Ingle
258 Pradeep Singh
259 Tuntun Kumar
260 Manohar Mandal
261 Mohammad Ishaq Khan
262 Balbir Singh
263 Thirumallaiah
264 Raj Mohammad
265 Abdul Khaliq
266 G.D. Bhai
267 Kishan Bahadur
268 Chet Ram
269 Nandji Singh
270 P.L. Gupta
271 Nimbu Lal
272 Nirmal Das
273 Kalam Singh
274 Vrikodar Singh
275 Krishna Kishore Pandey
276 Prakash Chand
277 Surjit Singh
278 R. Jagdishan
279 A.M. Bhengra
280 Hari Kishan Mani
281 Bayyarapu Prasad
282 B. Khodanda Ramaiah
283 Satyawan
284 Shiv Kumar Rai
285 H.S. Prabhu Swami
286 Rajeshwar Singh
287 G.M. Khan
288 Pritam Chand
289 Raj Bahadur
290 Harpal Singh
291 Hari Chand Rajwar
292 Ravinder Kumar Mishra
293 S.P. Sharma
294 R. Ajay Kumar
295 Uday Singh Tomar
296 Sanjeev Kumar Singh
297 Shiv Charan
298 Ashok Jamwal
299 Sarun Anoth
300 Suresh Babu
301 S.R. Ranga Gowda
302 Subhash Kumar
303 M. Yadaiah
304 Howthinlam
305 Rupesh Kumar Singh
306 Santanu Sarkar
307 Pawan Kumar
308 A. Anandan
309 Chetram Kulhar
310 Ashok Kumar Saha
311 M. Shiva Murgan
312 A. Thulasi
313 Gagan Singh
314 Rampal Sharma
315 K. Shiv Raj
316 Mohammad Sayeed
317 Mane Kumar
318 Ajmeen Ansari
319 Ved Pal
320 Raksha Ram Pathak
321 Mohinder Singh
322 Syed Shamuddin
323 T.R.V. Prasad
324 A.B. Amber Rao

325 Ramesh Kumar Bhaggal	367 Ashif Ali Beigh	409 Satish Chand
326 A. Sakthivel	368 Rafiq Ahmed Khan	410 Sanjay Kumar Singh
327 Aneesh Philip	369 K.C. Sahoo	411 Vir Singh
328 Ram Bhuwan Yadav	370 K.N. Sheikh	412 K.K. Yadav
329 H.R. Gedam	371 Shivalingayya Mathapati	413 Jagtar Singh
330 Shambhu Prasad Bhagat	372 Shailendra Singh Bhadouriya	414 Santosh Saw
331 Mithai Lal	373 Inderjeet Singh	415 G. Jayachandran
332 Dhananjay Singh	374 Amit Kumar	416 Pramod Kumar
333 Ghanshyam Kumar	375 Bappaditya Ghosh	417 Basappa Bajantri
334 Deepak Sharma	376 Mallikarjun R.	418 Shri Sahab Shukla
335 Rugha Ram	377 R. Raja Shekar	419 Riyaz Ahmad Rather
336 Subhash Chander	378 Desh Raj	420 Jaswant Singh
337 V.P. Chandran	379 D. Pratap Singh	421 Dhanawade Ravindra Baban
338 G.V. Kamat	380 Ramesh Halwa	422 Borase Dinesh Dipak
339 Madan Lal	381 A.K. Upadhyay	423 Mohammad Yaseen Tali
340 Pradeep Sikdar	382 Prabhakar Singh	424 Kuldip Roy
341 Mohammad Avesh	383 Kuldeep Singh	425 Mohammad Tafail
342 Kapil Kumar Yadav	384 Shiv Shankar Das	426 Pradip Kumar Panda
343 Kedar Nath Mishra	385 R. Mohan Lal	427 Sharief-ud-Din Ganaie
344 Akhilesh Kumar	386 Mohar Singh	428 Rajender Kumar Nain
345 Jaswant Singh	387 Basant Kumar Mehdi	429 Mohammad Mujhahid Khan
346 Jitender Singh	388 Balram Tigga	430 Reyaz Ahmad Zarger
347 Rins Thomas	389 Om Prakash	431 Nisar Ahmad Wani
348 Ganesh Kumar	390 Praveen Singh Rajput	432 Mandeep Kumar
349 Srikanta Mishra	391 A.B. Singh	433 Mishri Lal Meena
350 P. Devendran	392 Om Prakash	434 Sandeep Kumar Yadav
351 Brindavan Sharma	393 L.Perumal	435 Shankar Lal Barala
352 Vinod Kumar	394 Subash Sourav	436 Naseer Ahmed Rather
353 Hemant Kumar Sharma	395 Sateesha	437 Chandrika Prasad
354 Rajendra Kumar	396 Raju Ram Samota	438 Mahesh Kumar Meena
355 Nishar Ahmed Lone	397 Mahesh Kumar Barhadiya	439 Guru H.
356 Vaghela Baldev Singh	398 Pradeep Ghana	440 Vasatha Kumar V.V.
357 Ayaz Ahmed Mir	399 Udit Narayan	441 Maneswar Basumatari
358 Sushil Kumar Patra	400 Kirtikar Nishad	442 Sanjay Kumar Sinha
359 Bhagwan Singh	401 Samsher Singh	443 Ratan Kumar Thakur
360 Y. Tejeswar Rao	402 Satish Kumar	444 Tilak Raj
361 I. Jagappa	403 Mohite Suraj Sarje Rao	445 Naseer Ahmed
362 Yumnan Romio Meitei	404 Tilak Raj	446 Vijay Soreng
363 Shishupal Singh	405 Omkar Nath Singh	447 Ashvni Kumar Kaochi
364 Mohammad Rafiq	406 Bhola Singh	448 Sanjay Rajput
365 Manoj Kumar	407 R.K. Rana	449 Rathod Nitin Shivaji
366 Shyam Singh	408 Rajesh Kumar	450 Prasanna Kumar Sahoo

451 Manoj Kumar Behra	472 Shyam Babu	493 Ashwani Kumar Yadav
452 Jaimal Singh	473 Vijay Kumar Mourya	494 Chandrasekar C.
453 Sukhjinder Singh	474 Pankaj Kumar Tripathi	495 Kale Sunil
454 Kulwinder Singh	475 Mahesh Kumar	496 Shyamal Kumar Dey
455 Maninder Singh Attri	476 Ramesh Yadav	497 Deep Chand Verma
456 Hemraj Meena	477 Koushal Kumar Rawat	498 Kuldeep Oraon
457 Narayan Lal Gurjar	478 Amit Kumar	499 Khurshid Khan
458 Jeet Ram	479 Pintu Kumar Singh	500 Sharma Lavkush Sudarshan
459 Bhagirath Singh	480 Vinod Kumar	501 Naresh Umrao Badole
460 Rohitash Lamba	481 Shyam Narain Singh Yadav	502 Dhirendra Tripathi
461 C. Sivachandran	482 Nirod Sharma	503 Shailendra Pratap Singh
462 Subramanian G.	483 Ramesh Kumar	504 Mritunjoy Chutia
463 Mohan Lal	484 Mahesh Kumar Kushwaha	505 Netrapal Singh
464 Virendra Singh	485 Sandeep Yadav	506 Manga Ram Deb Barma
465 Bablu Santra	486 Satendra Kumar	507 Ashok Kumar
466 Sudip Biswas	487 Ramesh Ranjan	508 Jagannath Roy
467 Ram Vakeel	488 Shiv Lal Netam	509 Mukhtar Ahmad Doie
468 Awadhesh Kumar Yadav	489 Chandrakant Bhakre	510 Vishal Kumar
469 Pradeep Singh	490 Parmar Satyapal Sinh	511 Vinod Kumar
470 Pradeep Kumar	491 Rajeev Sharma	
471 Ajit Kumar Azad	492 Santosh Kumar Mishra	

Acknowledgements

Educators say it takes a village to raise a child. I now realize it takes a village to write a book. A book that aims to synthesize my four decades as a police officer within the broader realms of politics history, and society is bound to accumulate a fair amount of intellectual, editorial and motivational debt. I benefited from the curiosity, comments and support of my children, Miti, Gaurav and Kavita, as well as my grandchildren Dhruv, Raghav and Noor. The book became better after comments and discussions with many colleagues and friends: Farooq Khan, Farooq Ahmad, Ashok Bhan, Ashok Suri, Kuldeep Khoda, P.S. Gill, B.B. Vyas, Niaz Mir, Hafeez Akhtar, Kiran Narain, Anil Kumar, Gopal Sharma, K. Rajendra, Javaid Gillani and R.R. Swain. I got valuable professional input from Kaveree Bamzai, Praveen Swami, Manoj Joshi, R.C. Ganjoo, Rivka Israel and my brother-in-law Rajiv Tandon. Inputs from Girish Aivalli, Kiran Narain, Narayan Ramachandran, Sundeep Khanna, Jayakanth Srinivasan helped refine the book. And God bless the next generation – Debashish Ghoshal, Talha Salaria, Amuleek Bijral, Jay Srinivasan, Ashok Reddy and Priya Gopalakrishnan – who improved the draft significantly. I must single out Rasil Kaur Ahuja for her detailed input – writing books for children has honed her demands for precision.

This book required many skills I don't have. I dictated the first draft to Mankirat Kaur, but it suffered from the many flaws civil servant-written books often do: too sequential, too detailed, too many adjectives and too long. The feedback that my first draft read like a police FIR was tough to hear, but accurate. My son Manish helped me transform the structure and content. Pretika Khanna brought her considerable research skills as a former political reporter to bear. We had heard nightmarish stories about publisher torture but could not have found a better partner than Juggernaut with Chiki Sarkar, Parth Mehrotra, Nishtha Kapil, Niyati Dhuldhoya, Padmini Smetacek and Samarth Menon to publish this book.

This book draws upon my memory, conversations and reading. This terrifies me because I am old enough to realize how all three are often selective, biased and wrong. I find solace in great historian Will Durant's end-of-life conclusion that most of history is guesswork and the rest prejudice. This is my first and last book – please give it vast margin for flaws.